# 12th Conference of the European Chapter of the Association for Computational Linguistics 2009 (EACL 2009)



## Student Research Workshop

**Athens, Greece**
**2 April 2009**

ISBN: 978-1-63266-011-4

**Printed from e-media with permission by:**

Curran Associates, Inc.
57 Morehouse Lane
Red Hook, NY 12571

**Some format issues inherent in the e-media version may also appear in this print version.**



Printed by Curran Associates, Inc. (2014)

For permission requests, please contact the Association for Computational Linguistics at the address below.

Association for Computational Linguistics
209 N. Eighth Street
Stroudsburg, Pennsylvania 18360

Phone: 1-570-476-8006
Fax: 1-570-476-0860

acl@aclweb.org

**Additional copies of this publication are available from:**

Curran Associates, Inc.
57 Morehouse Lane
Red Hook, NY 12571 USA
Phone: 845-758-0400
Fax: 845-758-2634
Email: curran@proceedings.com
Web: www.proceedings.com

**EACL 2009**

# Proceedings of the Student Research Workshop

2 April 2009
Megaron Athens International Conference Centre
Athens, Greece

# Preface

On behalf of the Programme Committee, we are pleased to present the proceedings of the Student Research Workshop held at the 12th Conference of the European Chapter of the Association for Computational Linguistics. Following the tradition of providing a forum for student researchers and the success of the previous workshops held in Bergen (1999), Toulouse (2001), Budapest (2003) and Trento (2006), a panel of senior researchers will take part in the presentation of the papers, providing detailed comments on the work of the authors.

The Student Workshop will run as four parallel sessions, during which 11 papers will be presented. These high standard papers were carefully chosen from a total of 38 submissions coming from 18 countries.

We would like to take this opportunity to thank the many people that have contributed in various ways to the success of the Student Workshop: the members of the Programme Committee for their evaluation of the submissions and for taking the time to provide useful detailed comments and suggestions for the improvement of papers; the panelists for providing detailed feedback directly; and the students for their hard work in preparing their submissions.

We are also very grateful to the EACL for providing sponsorship for students who would otherwise be unable to attend the workshop and present their work. And finally, thanks to those who have given us advice and assistance in planning this workshop (especially Nuria Bertomeu, Alex Lascarides, Joakim Nivre, Konstantinos Stamatakis).

We hope you enjoy the Student Research Workshop.

Vera Demberg, University of Edinburgh
Yanjun Ma, Dublin City University
Nils Reiter, Heidelberg University

EACL 2009 Student Research Workshop Chairs

# Program Committee

**Program Chairs:**

Vera Demberg, University of Edinburgh (UK)
Yanjun Ma, Dublin City University (Ireland)
Nils Reiter, Heidelberg University (Germany)

**Program Committee Members:**

Eneko Agirre, Basque Country University (Spain)
Timothy Baldwin, University of Melbourne (Australia)
Srinivas Bangalore, AT&T Research (USA)
Yassine Benajiba, Polytechnic University of Valencia (Spain)
Alexandra Birch, University of Edinburgh (UK)
Tamás Biró, University of Groningen (The Netherlands)
Thorsten Brants, Google Inc. (USA)
João Cabral, University of Edinburgh (UK)
Aoife Cahill, Stuttgart University (Germany)
Marine Carpuat, Hong Kong University of Science & Technology (Hong Kong)
Ben Carterette, University of Delaware (USA)
Pi-Chuan Chang, Stanford University (USA)
Ciprian Chelba, Google Inc. (USA)
Trevor Cohn, University of Edinburgh (UK)
Irene Cramer, Dortmund University (Germany)
Ido Dagan, Bar Ilan University (Israel)
Hal Daumé III, University of Utah (USA)
Güneş Erkan, Google Inc. (USA)
Raquel Fernández, University of Amsterdam (The Netherlands)
Sharon Goldwater, University of Edinburgh (UK)
Hany Hassan, Dublin City University (Ireland)
Julia Hockenmaier, University of Illinois (USA)
Akshay Java, Microsoft Live Labs (USA)
Sittichai Jiampojamarn, University of Alberta (Canada)
Gareth Jones, Dublin City University (Ireland)
Alexander Koller, Saarland University (Germany)
Jochen Leidner, Thomson Reuters (UK)
Vanessa Murdock, Yahoo! Research Barcelona (Spain)
Malvina Nissim, University of Bologna (Italy)
Stefan Oepen, University of Oslo (Norway)
Ulrike Padó, Pearson Knowledge Technologies (USA)
Simone Ponzetto, Heidelberg University (Germany)
David Reitter, Carnegie Mellon University (USA)
Bogdan Sacaleanu, DFKI GmbH (Germany)
Richard Sproat, Oregon Health & Science University (USA)
Mark Stevenson, University of Sheffield (UK)
Simone Teufel, University of Cambridge (UK)
Sebastian Varges, University of Trento (Italy)
Rui Wang, Saarland University (Germany)
Haifeng Wang, Toshiba Research & Development Centre (PRC)
Andy Way, Dublin City University (Ireland)
Nick Webb, University at Albany, State University of New York (USA)
Feiyu Xu, DFKI GmbH (Germany)
Yi Zhang, Saarland University (Germany)
Thomas Fang Zheng, Tsinghua University (PRC)

# Table of Contents

# Modelling Early Language Acquisition Skills: Towards a General Statistical Learning Mechanism

**Guillaume Aimetti**
University of Sheffield
Sheffield, UK
g.aimetti@dcs.shef.ac.uk

## Abstract

This paper reports the on-going research of a thesis project investigating a computational model of early language acquisition. The model discovers word-like units from cross-modal input data and builds continuously evolving internal representations within a cognitive model of memory. Current cognitive theories suggest that young infants employ general statistical mechanisms that exploit the statistical regularities within their environment to acquire language skills. The discovery of lexical units is modelled on this behaviour as the system detects repeating patterns from the speech signal and associates them to discrete abstract semantic tags. In its current state, the algorithm is a novel approach for segmenting speech directly from the acoustic signal in an unsupervised manner, therefore liberating it from a pre-defined lexicon. By the end of the project, it is planned to have an architecture that is capable of acquiring language and communicative skills in an online manner, and carry out robust speech recognition. Preliminary results already show that this method is capable of segmenting and building accurate internal representations of important lexical units as 'emergent' properties from cross-modal data.

## 1 Introduction

Conventional Automatic Speech Recognition (ASR) systems can achieve very accurate recognition results, particularly when used in their optimal acoustic environment on examples within their stored vocabularies. However, when taken out of their comfort zone accuracy significantly deteriorates and does not come anywhere near human speech processing abilities for even the simplest of tasks. This project investigates novel computational language acquisition techniques that attempt to model current cognitive theories in order to achieve a more robust speech recognition system.

Current cognitive theories suggest that our surrounding environment is rich enough to acquire language through the use of simple statistical processes, which can be applied to all our senses. The system under development aims to help clarify this theory, implementing a computational model that is general across multiple modalities and has not been pre-defined with any linguistic knowledge.

In its current form, the system is able to detect words directly from the acoustic signal and incrementally build internal representations within a memory architecture that is motivated by cognitive plausibility. The algorithm proposed can be split into two main processes, automatic segmentation and word discovery. Automatically segmenting speech directly from the acoustic signal is made possible through the use of dynamic programming (DP); we call this method acoustic DP-ngram's. The second stage, key word discovery (KWD), enables the model to hypothesise and build internal representations of word classes that associates the discovered lexical units with discrete abstract semantic tags.

Cross-modal input is fed to the system through the interaction of a carer module as an 'audio' and 'visual' stream. The audio stream consists of an acoustic signal representing an utterance, while the visual stream is a discrete abstract semantic tag referencing the presence of a key word within the utterance.

Initial test results show that there is significant potential with the current algorithm, as it segments in an unsupervised manner and does not rely on a predefined lexicon or acoustic phone models that constrain current ASR methods.

*Proceedings of the EACL 2009 Student Research Workshop*, pages 1–9,
Athens, Greece, 2 April 2009. ©2009 Association for Computational Linguistics

The rest of this paper is organized as follows. Section 2 reviews current developmental theories and computational models of early language acquisition. In section 3, we present the current implementation of the system. Preliminary experiments and results are described in sections 4 and 5 respectively. Conclusions and further work are discussed in sections 6 and 7 respectively.

## 2 Background

### 2.1 Current Developmental Theories

The 'nature' vs. 'nurture' debate has been fought out for many years now; are we born with innate language learning capabilities, or do we solely use the input from the environment to find structure in language?

Nativists believe that infants have an innate capability for acquiring language. It is their view that an infant can acquire linguistic structure with little input and that it plays a minor role in the speed and sequence with which they learn language. Noam Chomsky is one of the most cited language acquisition nativists, claiming children can acquire language "On relatively slight exposure and without specific training" (Chomsky, 1975, p.4).

On the other hand, non-nativists argue that the input contains much more structural information and is not as full of errors as suggested by nativists (Eimas *et al.*, 1971; Best *et al.*, 1988; Jusczyk *et al.*, 1993; Saffran *et al.*, 1996; Christiansen *et al.*, 1998; Saffran *et al.*, 1999; Saffran *et al.*, 2000; Kirkham *et al.*, 2002; Anderson *et al.*, 2003; Seidenberg *et al.*, 2002; Kuhl, 2004; Hannon and Trehub, 2005).

Experiments by Saffran *et al.* (1996, 1999) show that 8-month old infants use the statistical information in speech as an aid for word segmentation with only two minutes of familiarisation.

Inspired by these results, Kirkham *et al.* (2002) suggest that the same statistical processes are also present in the visual domain. Kirkham *et al.* (2002) carried out experiments showing that preverbal infants are able to learn patterns of visual stimuli with very short exposure.

Other theories hypothesise that statistical and grammatical processes are both used when learning language (Seidenberg *et al.*, 2002; Kuhl, 2004). The hypothesis is that newborns begin life using statistical processes for simpler problems, such as learning the sounds of their native language and building a lexicon, whereas grammar is learnt via non-statistical methods later on. Seidenberg *et al.* (2002) believe that learning grammar begins when statistical learning ends. This has proven to be a very difficult boundary to detect.

### 2.2 Current Computational Models

There has been a lot of interest in trying to segment speech in an unsupervised manner, therefore liberating it from the required expert knowledge needed to predefine the lexical units for conventional ASR systems. This has led speech recognition researchers to delve into the cognitive sciences to try and gain an insight into how humans achieve this without much difficulty and model it.

Brent (1999) states that for a computational algorithm to be cognitively plausible it must:

- Start with no prior knowledge of general language structure.
- Learn in a completely unsupervised manner.
- Segment incrementally.

An automatic segmentation method similar to that of the acoustic DP-ngram method is segmental DTW. Park & Glass (2008) have adapted dynamic time warping (DTW) to find matching acoustic patterns between two utterances. The discovered units are then clustered, using an adjacency graph method, to describe the topic of the speech data.

Statistical Word Discovery (SWD) (ten Bosch and Cranen, 2007) and the Cross-channel Early Lexical Learning (CELL) model (Roy and Pentland, 2002), also similar methods to the one described in this paper, discover word-like units and then updating internal representations through clustering processes. The downfall of the CELL approach is that it assumes speech is observed as an array of phone probabilities.

A more radical approach is Non-negative matrix factorization (NMF) (Stouten *et al.*, 2008). NMF detects words from 'raw' cross-modal input without any kind of segmentation during the whole process, coding recurrent speech fragments into to 'word-like' entities. However, the factorisation process removes all temporal information.

## 3 The Proposed System

### 3.1 ACORNS

The computational model reported in this paper is being developed as part of a European project called ACORNS (Acquisition of Communication and Recognition Skills). The ACORNS project intends to design an artificial agent (Little Acorns) that is capable of acquiring human verbal communication skills. The main objective is to develop an end-to-end system that is biologically plausible; restricting the computational and mathematical methods to those that model behavioural data of human speech perception and production within five main areas:

**Front-end Processing:** Research and development of new feature representations guided by phonetic and psycho-linguistic experiments.

**Pattern Discovery:** Little Acorns (LA) will start life without any prior knowledge of basic speech units, discovering them from patterns within the continuous input.

**Memory Organisation and Access:** A memory architecture that approaches cognitive plausibility is employed to store discovered units.

**Information Discovery and Integration:** Efficient and effective techniques for retrieving the patterns stored in memory are being developed.

**Interaction and Communication:** LA is given an innate need to grow his vocabulary and communicate with the environment.

### 3.2 The Computational Model

There are two key processes to the language acquisition model described in this paper; automatic segmentation and word discovery. The automatic segmentation stage allows the system to build a library of similar repeating speech fragments directly from the acoustic signal. The second stage associates these fragments with the observed semantic tags to create distinct key word classes.

#### Automatic Segmentation

The acoustic DP-ngram algorithm reported in this section is a modification of the preceding DP-ngram algorithm (Sankoff and Kruskal, 1983; Nowell and Moore, 1995). The original DP-ngram model was developed by Sankoff and Kruskal (1983) to find two similar portions of gene sequences. Nowell and Moore (1995) then modified this model to find repeated patterns within a single phone transcription sequence through self-similarity. Expanding on these methods, the author has developed a variant that is able to segment speech, directly from the acoustic signal; automatically segmenting important lexical fragments by discovering 'similar' repeating patterns. Speech is never the same twice and therefore impossible to find exact repetitions of importance (e.g. phones, words or sentences).

The use of DP allows this algorithm to accommodate temporal distortion through dynamic time warping (DTW). The algorithm finds partial matches, portions that are similar but not necessarily identical, taking into account noise, speed and different pronunciations of the speech.

Traditional template based speech recognition algorithms using DP would compare two sequences, the input speech vectors and a word template, penalising insertions, deletions and substitutions with negative scores. Instead, this algorithm uses quality scores, positive and negative, to reward matches and prevent anything else; resulting in longer, more meaningful subsequences.

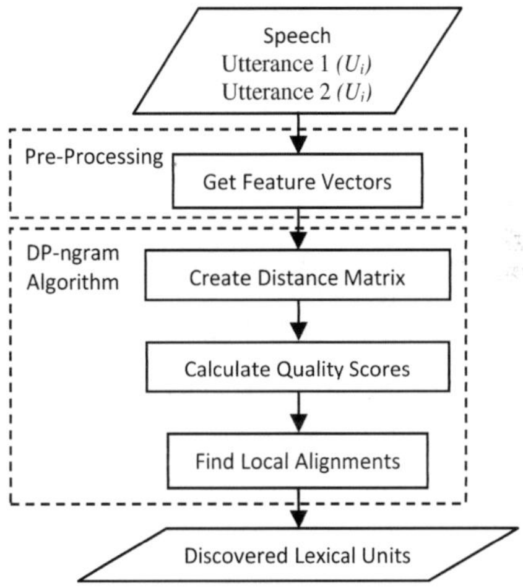


Figure 1: Acoustic DP-ngram Processes.

Figure 1 displays the simplified architecture of the acoustic DP-ngram algorithm. There are four main stages to the process:

**Stage 1:** The ACORNS MFCC front-end is used to parameterise the raw speech signal of the two utterances being fed to the system. The default settings have been used to output a series of 37-element feature vectors. The front-end is based on Mel-Frequency Coefficients (MFCC), which reflects the frequency sensitivity of the auditory system, to give 12 MFCC coefficients. A measure of the raw energy is added along with 12 differential (Δ) and 12 2$^{nd}$ differential (ΔΔ) coefficients. The front-end also allows the option for cepstral mean normalisation (CMN) and cepstral mean and variance normalisation (CMVN).

**Stage 2:** A local-match distance matrix is then calculated by measuring the cosine distance between each pair of frames $(v_1, v_2)$ from the two sequences, which is defined by:

$$d(v_1, v_2) = (v_1^T . v_2) / (\|v_1\|^T . \|v_2\|) \quad (1)$$

**Stage 3:** The distance matrix is then used to calculate accumulative quality scores for successive frame steps. The recurrence defined in equation (2) is used to find all quality scores $q_{i,j}$.

In order to maximize on quality, substitution scores must be positive and both insertion and deletion scores must be negative as initialised in equation (3).

$$q_{i,j} = \max \begin{cases} q_{i-1,j} + \left(s_{a_i,\varphi} \cdot \left|d_{i-1,j} - 1\right| . q_{i-1,j}\right), \\ q_{i,j-1} + \left(s_{\varphi,b_j} \cdot \left|d_{i,j-1} - 1\right| . q_{i,j-1}\right), \\ q_{i-1,j-1} + \left(s_{a_i,b_j} . d_{i-1,j-1} . q_{i-1,j-1}\right), \\ 0, \end{cases} \quad (2)$$

where,

$$\begin{aligned} s_{a_i,\varphi} &= -1.1 \quad \text{(Insertion score)} \\ s_{\varphi,b_j} &= -1.1 \quad \text{(Deletion score)} \\ s_{a_i,b_j} &= +1.1 \quad \text{(Substitution score)} \quad (3) \\ d_{i,j} &= \text{frame-frame distance} \\ q_{i,j} &= \text{Accumulative quality score} \end{aligned}$$

The recurrence in equation (2) stops past dissimilarities causing global effects by setting all negative scores to zero, starting a fresh new homologous relationship between local alignments.

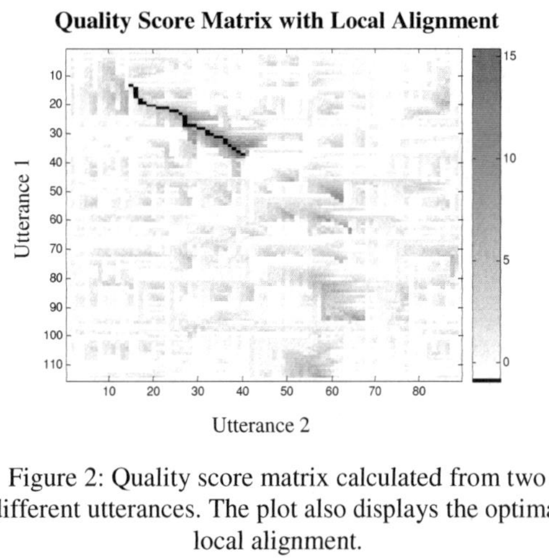


Figure 2: Quality score matrix calculated from two different utterances. The plot also displays the optimal local alignment.

Figure 2 shows the plot of the quality scores calculated from two different utterances. The shaded areas show repeating structure; longer and more accurate fragments attain greater quality scores, indicated by the darker areas within the plot.

Applying a substitution score of 1 will cause the accumulative quality score to grow as a linear function. The current settings defined by equation (3) use a substitution score greater than 1, thus allowing local accumulative quality scores to grow exponentially, giving longer alignments more importance.

By setting insertion and deletion scores to values less than -1, the model will find closer matching acoustic repetitions; whereas a value greater than -1 and less than 0 allows the model to find repeated patterns that are longer and less accurate, therefore allowing control over the tolerance for temporal distortion.

**Stage 4:** The final stage is to discover local alignments from within the quality score matrix. Backtracking pointers $(bt)$ are maintained at each step of the recursion:

$$bt_{i,j} = \begin{cases} (i-1, j), & \text{(Insertion)} \\ (i, j-1), & \text{(Deletion)} \\ (i-1, j-1), & \text{(Substitution)} \\ (0,0) & \text{(Initial pointer)} \end{cases} \quad (4)$$

When the quality scores have been calculated through equation (2), it is possible to backtrack from the highest score to obtain the local alignments in order of importance with equation (4). A threshold is set so that only local alignments above a desired quality score are to be retrieved. Figure 2 presents the optimal local alignment that was discovered by the acoustic DP-ngram algorithm for the utterances "Ewan is shy" and "Ewan sits on the couch".

The discovered repeated pattern (the dark line in figure 2) is [y uw ah n]. Start and stop times are collected which allows the model to retrieve the local alignment from the original audio signal in full fidelity when required.

## Key Word Discovery

The milestone set for all systems developed within the ACORNS project is for LA to learn 10 key words. To carry out this task, the DP-ngram algorithm has been modified with the addition of a key word discovery (KWD) method that continues the theme of a general statistical learning mechanism. The acoustic DP-ngram algorithm exploits the co-occurrence of similar acoustic patterns within different utterances; whereas, the

KWD method exploits the co-occurrence of the associated discrete abstract semantic tags. This allows the system to associate cross-modal repeating patterns and build internal representations of the key words.
KWD is a simple approach that creates a class for each key word (semantic tag) observed, in which all discovered exemplar units representing each key word are stored. With this list of episodic segments we can perform a clustering process to derive an ideal representation of each key word.

For a single iteration of the DP-ngram algorithm, the current utterance $(Utt_{cur})$ is compared with another utterance in memory $(Utt_n)$. KWD hypothesises whether the segments found within the two utterances are potential key words, by simply comparing the associated semantic tags. There are three possible paths for a single iteration:

**1:** If the tag of $Utt_{cur}$ has never been seen then create a new key word class and store the whole utterance as an exemplar of it. Do not carry out the acoustic DP-ngram process and proceed to the next utterance in memory $(Utt_{n+1})$.

**2:** If both utterances share the same tag then proceed with the acoustic DP-ngram process and append discovered local alignments to the key word class representing that tag. Proceed to the next utterance in memory $(Utt_{n+1})$.

**3:** If both utterances contain different tags then do not carry out acoustic DP-ngram's and proceed to the next utterance in memory $(Utt_{n+1})$.

By creating an exemplar list for each key word class we are able to carry out a clustering process that allows us to create a model of the ideal representation. Currently, the clustering process implemented simply calculates the 'centroid' exemplar, finding the local alignment with the shortest distance from all the other local alignments within the same class. The 'centroid' is updated every time a new local alignment is added, therefore the system is creating internal representations that are continuously evolving and becoming more accurate with experience.

For recognition tasks the system can be set to use either the 'centroid' exemplar or all the stored local alignments for each key word class.

### LA Architecture

The algorithm runs within a memory structure (fig. 3) developed with inspiration from current cognitive theories of memory (Jones *et al.*, 2006). The memory architecture works as follows:

**Carer:** The carer interacts with LA to continuously feed the system with cross-modal input (acoustic & semantic).

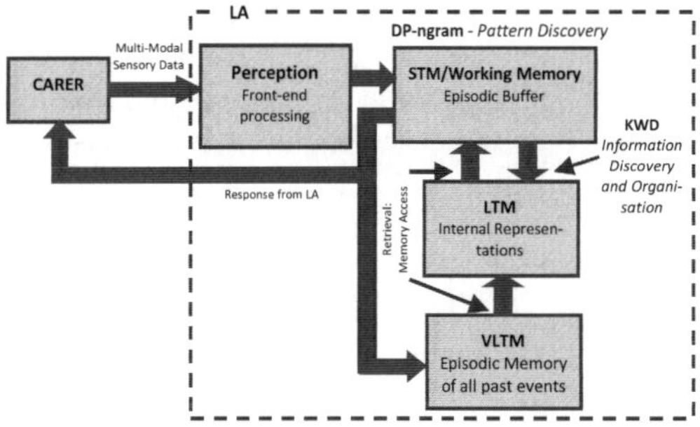


Figure 3: Little Acorns' memory architecture.

**Perception:** The stimulus is processed by the 'perception' module, converting the acoustic signal into a representation similar to the human auditory system.

**Short Term Memory (STM):** The output of the 'perception' module is stored in a limited STM which acts as a circular buffer to store *n* past utterances. The *n* past utterances are compared with the current input to discover repeated patterns in an incremental fashion. As a batch process LA can only run on a limited number of utterances as the search space is unbound. As an incremental process, LA could potentially handle an infinite number of utterances, thus making it a more cognitively plausible system.

**Long Term Memory (LTM):** The ever increasing lists of discovered units for each key word representation are stored in LTM. Clustering processes can then be applied to build and update internal representations. The representations stored within LTM are only pointers to where the segment lies within the very long term memory.

**Very Long Term Memory:** The very long term memory is used to store every observed utterance. It is important to note that unless there is a pointer for a segment of speech within LTM then the data cannot be retrieved. But, future work may be carried out to incorporate additional 'sleeping' processes on the data stored in VLTM to re-organise internal representations or carry out additional analysis.

## 4 Experiments

Accuracy of experiments within the ACORNS project is based on LA's response to its carer. The correct response is for LA to predict the key word tag associated with the current incoming utterance while only observing the speech signal. LA re-uses the acoustic DP-ngram algorithm to solve this task in a similar manner to traditional DP template based speech recognition. The recognition process is carried out by comparing exemplars, of discovered key words, against the current incoming utterance and calculating a quality distance (as described in stage 3 of section 3.2). Thus, the exemplar producing the highest quality score, by finding the longest alignment, is taken to be the match, with which we can predict its associated visual tag.

A number of different experiments have been carried out:

**E1 - Optimal STM Window:** This experiment finds the optimal utterance window length for the system as an incremental process. Varying values of the utterance window length (from 1 to 100) were used to obtain key word recognition accuracy results across the same data set.

**E2 - Batch vs. Incremental:** The optimal window length chosen for the incremental implementation is compared against the batch implementation of the algorithm.

**E3 - Centroid vs. Exemplars:** The KWD process stores a list of exemplars representing each key word class. For the recognition task we can either use all the exemplars in each key word list or a single 'centroid' exemplar that best represents the list. This experiment will compare these two methods for representing internal representations of the key words.

**E4 – Speaker Dependency:** The algorithm is tested on its ability to handle the variation in speech from different speakers with different feature vectors.

$V_1$ = HTK MFCC's (no norm)
$V_2$ = ACORNS MFCC's (no norm)
$V_3$ = ACORNS MFCC's (Cepstral Mean Norm)
$V_4$ = ACORNS MFCC's (Cepstral Mean and Variance Norm)

Using normalisation methods will reduce the information within the feature vectors, removing some of the speaker variation. Therefore, key word detection should be more accurate for a data set of multiple speakers with normalisation.

### 4.1 Test Data

The ACORNS English corpus is used for the above experiments. Sentences were created by combining a carrier sentence with a keyword. A total of 10 different carrier sentences, such as "*Do you see the X*", "*Where is the X*", etc., where *X* is a keyword, were combined with one of ten different keywords, such as "*Bottle*", "*Ball*", etc. This created 100 unique sentences which were repeated 10 times and recorded with 4 different speakers (2 male and 2 female) to produce 4000 utterances.

In addition to the acoustic data, each utterance is associated with an abstract semantic tag. As an example, the utterance *"What matches this **shoe**"* will contain the tag referring to *"**shoe**"*. The tag does not give any location or phonetic information about the key word within the utterance.

**E1** and **E2** use a sub-set of 100 different utterances from a single speaker. **E3** is carried out on a sub-set of 200 utterances from a single speaker and the database used for **E4** is a sub-set of 200 utterances from all four speakers (2 male and 2 female) presented in a random order.

## 5 Results

**E1:** LA was tested on 100 utterances with varying utterance window lengths. The plot in figure 4 shows the total key word detection accuracy for each window length used. The x-axis displays the utterance window lengths (1–100) and the y-axis displays the total accuracy.

The results are as expected. Longer window lengths achieve more accurate results. This is because longer window lengths produce a larger search space and therefore have more chance of capturing repeating events. Shorter window lengths are still able to build internal representations, but over a longer period.

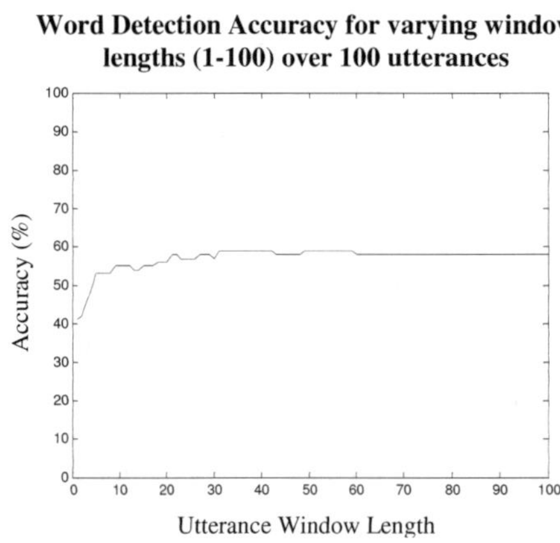


Figure 4: Single speaker key word accuracy using varying utterance window lengths of 1-100.

Accuracy results reach a maximum with an utterance window length of 21 and then stabilize at around 58% (±1%). From this we can conclude that 21 is the minimum window length needed to build accurate internal representations of the words within the test set, and will be used for all subsequent experiments.

**E2:** The plot in figure 4 displays the total key word detection accuracy for the different utterance window lengths and does not show the gradual word acquisition process. Figure 5 compares the word detection accuracy of the system (y-axis) as a function of the number of utterances observed (x-axis). Accuracy is recorded as the percentage of correct replies for the last ten observations. The long discontinuous line in the plot shows the word detections accuracy for randomly guessing the key word.

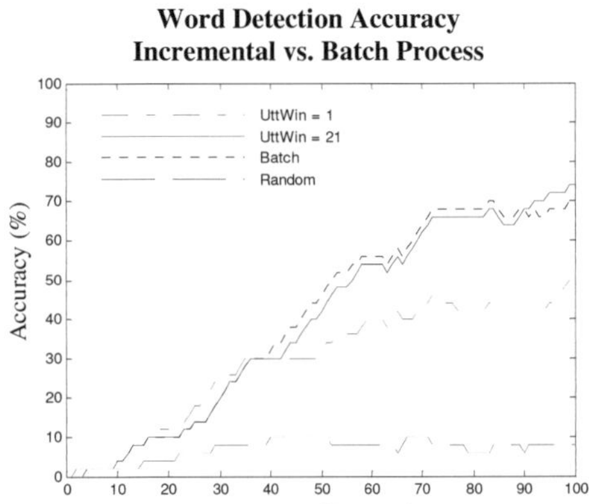


Figure 5: Word detection accuracy LA running as a batch and incremental process. Results are plotted as a function of the past 10 utterances observed.

It can be seen from the plot in figure 5 that the system begins life with no word representations. At the beginning, the system hypothesises new word units from which it can begin to bootstrap its internal representations.

As an incremental process, with the optimal window length, the system is able to capture enough repeating patterns and even begins to outperform the batch process after 90 utterances. This is due to additional alignments discovered by the batch process that are temporarily distorting a word representation, but the batch process would 'catch up' in time.

Another important result to take into account is that only comparing the current incoming utterance with the last observed utterance is enough to build word representations. Although this is very efficient, the problem is that there is a greater possibility that some words will never be discovered if they are not present in adjacent utterances within the data set.

**E3:** Currently the recognition process uses all the discovered exemplars within each key word class. This process causes the computational complexity to increase exponentially. It is also not suitable for an incremental process with the potential of running on an infinite data set.

To tackle this problem, recognition was carried out using the 'centroid' exemplar of each key word class. Figure 6 shows the word detection accuracy as a function of utterances observed for both methods.

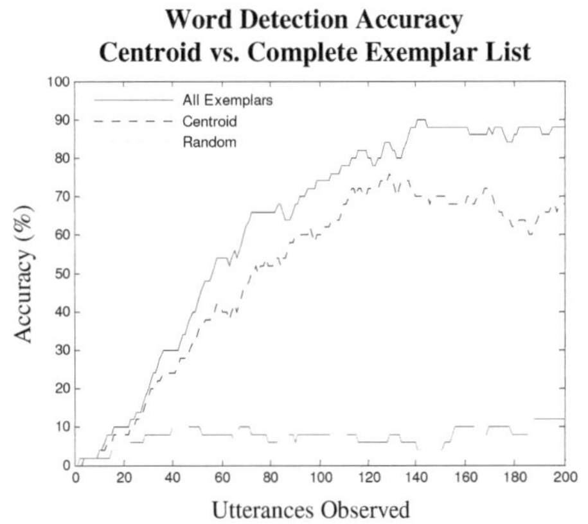


Figure 6: Word detection accuracy using centroids and complete exemplar list for recognition.

The results show that the 'centroid' method is quickly outperformed and that the word detection accuracy difference increases with experience. After 120 utterances performance seems to gradually decline. This is because the 'centroid' method cannot handle the variation in the acoustic speech data. Using all the discovered units for recognition allows the system to reach an accuracy of 90% at around 140 utterances, where it then seems to stabilise at around 88%.

**E4:** The addition of multiple speakers will add greater variation to the acoustic signal, distorting patterns of the same underlying unit. Over the 200 utterances observed, word detection accuracy of the internal representations increases, but at a much slower rate than the single speaker experiments (fig. 7).

The assumption that using normalisation methods would achieve greater word detection accuracy, by reducing speaker variation, does not hold true. On reflection this comes as no surprise, as the system collects exemplar units with a larger relative fidelity for each speaker.

This raises an important issue; the optimal utterance window length for the algorithm as an incremental process was calculated for a single speaker, therefore, increasing the search space will allow the model to find more repeating patterns from the same speaker. Following this logic, it could be hypothesised that the optimal search space should be four times the size used for one speaker and that it will take four times as many observations to achieve the same accuracy.

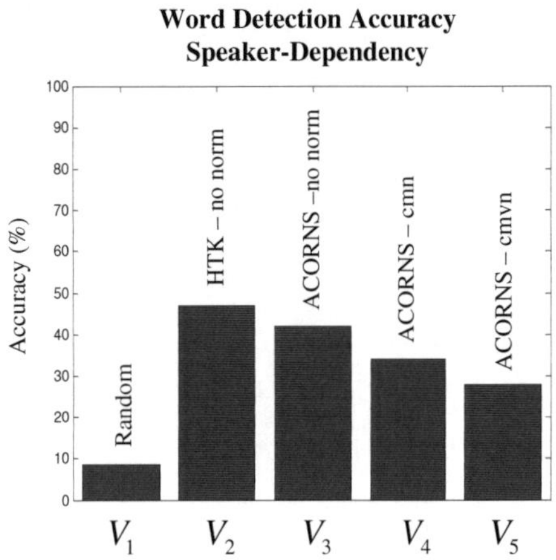


Figure 7: Total accuracy using different feature vectors after 200 observed utterances.

## 6 Conclusions

Preliminary results indicate that the environment is rich enough for word acquisition tasks. The pattern discovery and word learning algorithm implemented within the LA memory architecture has proven to be a successful approach for building stable internal representations of word-like units. The model approaches cognitive plausibility by employing statistical processes that are general across multiple modalities. The incremental approach also shows that the model is still able to learn correct word representations with a very limited working memory model.

Additionally to the acquisition of words and word-like units, the system is able to use the discovered tokens for speech recognition. An important property of this method, that differentiates it from conventional ASR systems, is that it does not rely on a pre-defined vocabulary, therefore reducing language-dependency and out-of-dictionary errors.

Another advantage of this system, compared to systems such as NMF, is that it is able to give temporal information of the whereabouts of important repeating structure which can be used to code the acoustic signal as a lossless compression method.

## 7 Discussion & Future Work

A key question driving this research is whether modelling human language acquisition can help create a more robust speech recognition system. Therefore further development of the proposed architecture will continue to be limited to cognitively plausible approaches and should exhibit similar developmental properties as early human language learners. In its current state, the system is fully operational and intends to be used as a platform for further development and experiments.

The experimental results are promising. However, it is clear to see that the model suffers from speaker-dependency issues. The problem can be split into two areas, front-end processing of the incoming acoustic signal and the representation of discovered lexical units in memory.

Development is being carried out on various clustering techniques that build constantly evolving internal representations of internal lexical classes in an attempt to model speech variation. Additionally, a secondary update process, implemented as a re-occurring 'sleeping phase' is being investigated. This phase is going to allow the memory organisation to re-structure itself by looking at events over a longer history, which could be carried out as a batch process.

The processing of prosodic cues, such as speech rhythm and pitch intonation, will be incorporated within the algorithm to increase the key word detection accuracy and further exploit the richness of the learners surrounding environment. Adults, when speaking to infants, will highlight words of importance through infant directed speech (IDS). During IDS adults place more pitch variance on words that they want the infant to attend to.

Further experiments have been planned to see if the model exhibits similar patterns of learning behaviour as young multiple language learners. Experiments will be carried out with the multiple languages available in the ACORNS database (English, Finnish and Dutch).


## Acknowledgement

This research was funded by the European Commission, under contract number FP6-034362, in the ACORNS project (www.acorns-project.org). The author would also like to thank Prof. Roger K. Moore for helping to shape this work.

## References


A. Park and J. R. Glass. 2008. Unsupervised Pattern Discovery in Speech. *Transactions on Audio, Speech and Language Processing*, 16(1):186-197.

C. T. Best, G. W. McRoberts and N. M. Sithole. 1988. Examination of the perceptual re-organization for speech contrasts: Zulu click discrimination by English-speaking adults and infants. *Journal of Experimental Psychology: Human Perception and Performance*, 14:345-360.

D. M. Jones, R. W. Hughes and W. J. Macken. 2006. Perceptual Organization Masquerading as Phonological Storage: Further Support for a Perceptual-Gestural View of Short-Term Memory. *Journal of Memory and Language,* 54:265-328.

D. Roy and A. Pentland. 2002. Learning Words from Sights and Sounds: A Computational Model. *Cognitive Science*, 26(1):113-146.

D. Sankoff and Kruskal J. B. 1983. *Time Warps, String Edits, and Macromolecules: The Theory and Practice of Sequence Comparison.* Addison-Wesley Publishing Company, Inc.

E. E. Hannon and S. E. Trehub. 2005. Turning in to Musical Rhythms: Infants Learn More readily than Adults. *PNAS*, 102(35):12639-12643.

J. L. Anderson, J. L. Morgan and K. S. White. 2003. A Statistical Basis for Speech Sound Discrimination. *Language and Speech*, 46(43):155-182.

J. R. Saffran, R. N. Aslin and E. L. Newport. 1996. Statistical Learning by 8-Month-Old Infants. *SCIENCE*, 274:1926-1928.

J. R. Saffran, E. K. Johnson, R. N. Aslin and E. L. Newport. 1999. Statistical Learning of Tone Sequences by Human Infants and Adults. *Cognition*, 70(1):27-52.

J. R. Saffran, A. Senghashas and J. C. Trueswell. 2000. The Acquisition of Language by Children. *PNAS*, 98(23):12874-12875.

L. ten Bosch and B. Cranen. 2007. A Computational Model for Unsupervised Word Discovery. *INTERSPEECH 2007*, 1481-1484.

M. H. Christiansen, J. Allen and M. Seidenberg. 1998. Learning to Segment Speech using Multiple Cues. *Language and Cognitive Processes*, 13:221-268.

M. S. Seidenberg, M. C. MacDonald and J. R. Saffran. 2002. Does Grammar Start Where Statistics Stop?. *SCIENCE*, 298:552-554.

M. R. Brent. 1999. Speech Segmentation and Word Discovery: A Computational Perspective. *Trends in Cognitive Sciences*, 3(8):294-301.

N. Chomsky. 1975. *Reflections on Language*. New York: Pantheon Books.

N. Z. Kirkham, A. J. Slemmer and S. P. Johnson. 2002. Visual Statistical Learning in Infancy: Evidence for a Domain General Learning Mechanism. *Cognition*, 83:B35-B42.

P. D. Eimas, E. R. Siqueland, P. Jusczyk and J. Vigorito. 1971. Speech Perception in Infants. *Science*, 171(3968):303-606.

P. K. Kuhl. 2004. Early Language Acquisition: Cracking the Speech Code. *Nature*, 5:831-843.

P. Nowell and R. K. Moore. 1995. The Application of Dynamic Programming Techniques to Non-Word Based Topic Spotting. *EuroSpeech '95*, 1355-1358.

P. W. Jusczyk, A. D. Friederici, J. Wessels, V. Y. Svenkerud and A. M. Jusczyk. 1993. Infants' Sensitivity to the Sound Patterns of Native Language Words. *Journal of Memory & Language*, 32:402-420.

V. Stouten, K. Demuynck and H. Van hamme. 2008. Discovering Phone Patterns in Spoken Utterances by Non-negative Matrix Factorisation. *IEEE Signal Processing Letters*, 131-134.

# A Memory-Based Approach to the Treatment of Serial Verb Construction in Combinatory Categorial Grammar

**Prachya Boonkwan**[†‡]

† School of Informatics
University of Edinburgh
10 Crichton Street
Edinburgh EH8 9AB, UK

‡ National Electronics
and Computer Technology Center
112 Phahon Yothin Rd.
Pathumthani 12120, Thailand

Email: p.boonkwan@sms.ed.ac.uk

## Abstract

CCG, one of the most prominent grammar frameworks, efficiently deals with deletion under coordination in natural languages. However, when we expand our attention to more analytic languages whose degree of pro-dropping is more free, CCG's decomposition rule for dealing with gapping becomes incapable of parsing some patterns of intra-sentential ellipses in serial verb construction. Moreover, the decomposition rule might also lead us to overgeneration problem. In this paper the composition rule is replaced by the use of memory mechanism, called **CCG-MM**. Fillers can be memorized and gaps can be induced from an input sentence in functional application rules, while fillers and gaps are associated in coordination and serialization. Multimodal slashes, which allow or ban memory operations, are utilized for ease of resource management. As a result, CCG-MM is more powerful than canonical CCG, but its generative power can be bounded by partially linear indexed grammar.

## 1 Introduction

Combinatory Categorial Grammar (CCG, Steedman (2000)) is a prominent categorial grammar framework. Having a strong degree of lexicalism (Baldridge and Kruijff, 2003), its grammars are encoded in terms of lexicons; that is, each lexicon is assigned with syntactic categories which dictate the syntactic derivation. One of its striking features is the combinatory operations that allow coordination of incomplete constituents. CCG is *nearly* context-free yet powerful enough for natural languages as it, as well as TAG, LIG, and HG, exhibits the lowest generative power in the mildly context-sensitive grammar class (Vijay-Shanker and Weir, 1994).

CCG accounts for gapping in natural languages as a major issue. Its combinatory operations resolve deletion under coordination, such as right-node raising (SV&SVO) and gapping (SVO&SO). In case of gapping, a specialized rule called *decomposition* is used to handle with forward gapping (Steedman, 1990) by extracting the filler required by a gap from a complete constituent.

However, serial verb construction is a challenging topic in CCG when we expand our attention to more analytic languages, such as Chinese and Thai, whose degree of pro-dropping is more free.

In this paper, I explain how we can deal with serial verb construction with CCG by incorporating memory mechanism and how we can restrict the generative power of the resulted hybrid. The integrated memory mechanism is motivated by anaphoric resolution mechanism in Categorial Type Logic (Hendriks, 1995; Moortgat, 1997), Type Logical Grammar (Morrill, 1994; Jäger, 1997; Jäger, 2001; Oehrle, 2007), and CCG (Jacobson, 1999), and gap resolution in Memory-Inductive Categorial Grammar (Boonkwan and Supnithi, 2008), as it is designed for associating fillers and gaps found in an input sentence. Theoretically, I discuss how this hybrid efficiently helps us deal with serial verb construction and how far the generative power grows after incorporating the memory mechanism.

**Outline:** I introduce CCG in §2, and then motivate the need of memory mechanism in dealing with serial verb construction in CCG in §3. I describe the hybrid model of CCG and the filler-gap memory in §4. I then discuss the margin of generative power introduced by the memory mechanism in §5. Finally, I conclude this paper in §6.

*Proceedings of the EACL 2009 Student Research Workshop*, pages 10–18,
Athens, Greece, 2 April 2009. 

## 2 Combinatory Categorial Grammar

CCG is a lexicalized grammar; i.e. a grammar is encoded in terms of lexicons assigned with one or more syntactic categories. The syntactic categories may be atomic elements or curried functions specifying linear directions in which they seek their arguments. A word is assigned with a syntactic category by the turnstile operator $\vdash$. For example, a simplified English CCG is given below.

(1) John $\vdash$ $\mathtt{np}$ sandwiches $\vdash$ $\mathtt{np}$
eats $\vdash$ $\mathtt{s\backslash np/np}$

The categories $\mathtt{X\backslash Y}$ (and $\mathtt{X/Y}$) denotes that $\mathtt{X}$ seeks the argument $\mathtt{Y}$ from the left (right) side.

Combinatory rules are used to combine words forming a derivation of a sentence. For basic combination, forward (>) and backward (<) functional applications, defined in (2), are used.

(2)
$$\mathtt{X/Y}\ \ \mathtt{Y} \Rightarrow \mathtt{X} \qquad [>]$$
$$\mathtt{Y}\ \ \mathtt{X\backslash Y} \Rightarrow \mathtt{X} \qquad [<]$$

We can derive the sentence *John eats sandwiches* by the rules and the grammar in (1) as illustrated in (3). CCG is semantic-transparent; i.e. a logical form can be built compositionally in parallel with syntactic derivation. However, semantic interpretation is suppressed in this paper.

(3)

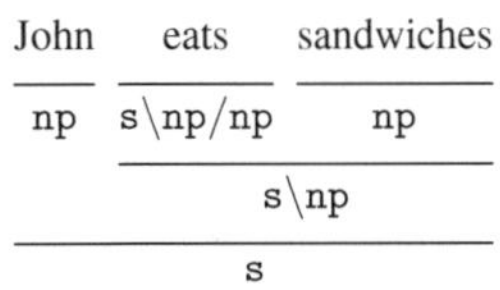


For coordination of two constituents, the coordination rules are used. There are two types of coordination rules regarding their directions: forward coordination (> **&**) and backward coordination (< **&**), defined in (4).

(4)
$$\&\ \ \mathtt{X} \Rightarrow [\mathtt{X}]_{\&} \qquad [>\&]$$
$$\mathtt{X}\ \ [\mathtt{X}]_{\&} \Rightarrow \mathtt{X} \qquad [<\&]$$

By the coordination rules, we can derive the sentence *John eats sandwiches and drinks coke* in (5).

(5)

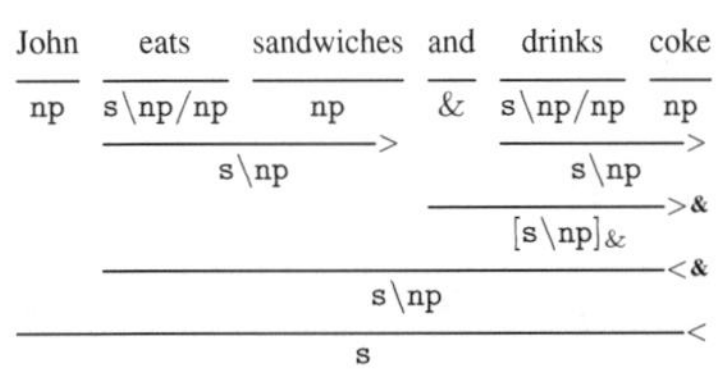


Beyond functional application and coordination, CCG also makes use of rules motivated by combinators in combinatory logics: functional composition (**B**), type raising (**T**), and substitution (**S**), namely. Classified by directions, the functional composition and type raising rules are described in (6) and (7), respectively.

(6)
$$\mathtt{X/Y}\ \ \mathtt{Y/Z} \Rightarrow \mathtt{X/Z} \qquad [>\mathbf{B}]$$
$$\mathtt{Y\backslash Z}\ \ \mathtt{X\backslash Y} \Rightarrow \mathtt{X\backslash Z} \qquad [<\mathbf{B}]$$

(7)
$$\mathtt{X} \Rightarrow \mathtt{Y/(Y\backslash X)} \qquad [>\mathbf{T}]$$
$$\mathtt{X} \Rightarrow \mathtt{Y\backslash(Y/X)} \qquad [<\mathbf{T}]$$

These rules permit associativity in derivation resulting in that coordination of incomplete constituents with similar types is possible. For example, we can derive the sentence *John likes but Mary dislikes sandwiches* in (8).

(8)

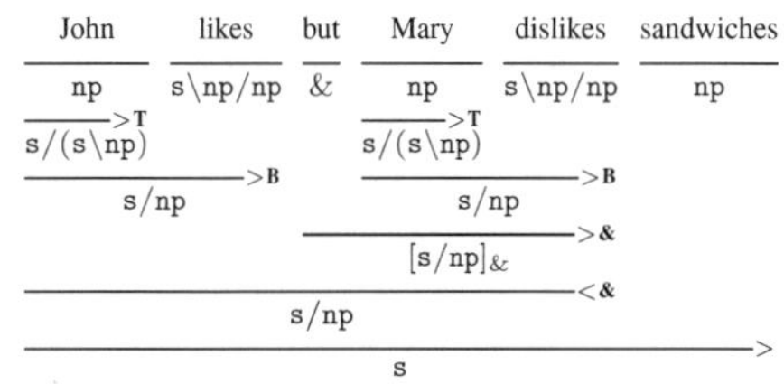


CCG also allows functional composition with permutation called *disharmonic functional composition* to handle constituent movement such as heavy NP shift and dative shift in English. These rules are defined in (9).

(9)
$$\mathtt{X/Y}\ \ \mathtt{Y\backslash Z} \Rightarrow \mathtt{X\backslash Z} \qquad [>\mathbf{B}_{\times}]$$
$$\mathtt{Y/Z}\ \ \mathtt{X\backslash Y} \Rightarrow \mathtt{X/Z} \qquad [<\mathbf{B}_{\times}]$$

By disharmonic functional composition rules, we can derive the sentence *I wrote briefly a long story of Sinbad* as (10).

(10)

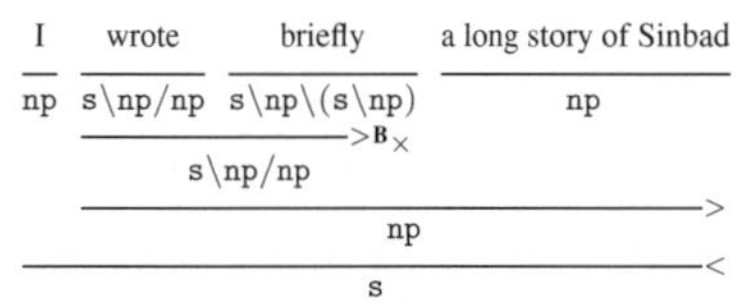


To handle the gapping coordination SVO&SO, the decomposition rule was proposed as a separate mechanism from CCG (Steedman, 1990). It decomposes a complete constituent into two parts for being coordinated with the other incomplete constituent. The decomposition rule is defined as follows.

(11)
$$\mathtt{X} \Rightarrow \mathtt{Y}\ \ \mathtt{X\backslash Y} \qquad [\mathbf{D}]$$

where $\mathtt{Y}$ and $\mathtt{X\backslash Y}$ must be seen earlier in the derivation. The decomposition rule allows us to derive the sentence *John eats sandwiches, and Mary, noodles* as (12). Steedman (1990) stated that English is forward gapping because gapping always takes place at the right conjunct.

(12)

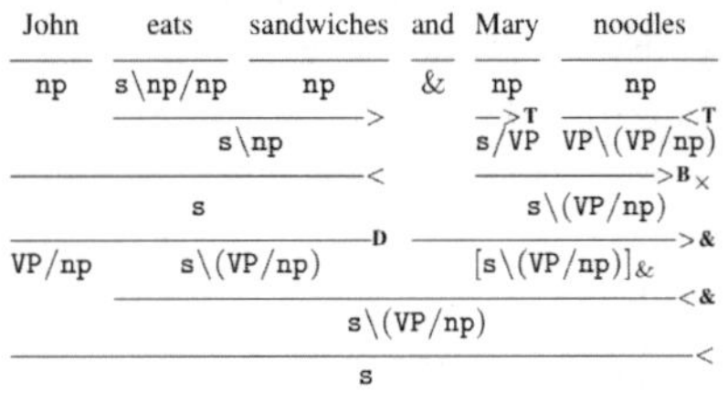


where $\mathtt{VP} = \mathtt{s\backslash np}$.

A multimodal version of CCG (Baldridge, 2002; Baldridge and Kruijff, 2003) restricts generative power for a particular language by annotating modalities to the slashes to allow or ban specific combinatory operations. Due to the page limitation, the multimodal CCG is not discussed here.

## 3 Dealing with Serial Verb Construction

CCG deals with deletion under coordination by several combinatory rules: functional composition, type raising, disharmonic functional composition, and decomposition rule. This enables CCG to handle a number of coordination patterns such as SVO&VO, SV&SVO, and SVO&SO. However, the decomposition rule cannot solve some patterns of SVC in analytic languages such as Chinese and Thai in which pro-dropping is prevalent.

The notion *serial verb construction* (SVC) in this paper means a sequence of verbs or verb phrases concatenated without connectives in a single clause which expresses simultaneous or consecutive events. Each of the verbs is marked or understood to have the same grammatical categories (such as tense, aspect, and modality), and shares at least one argument, i.e. a grammatical subject. As each verb is tensed, SVC is considered as coordination with implicit connective rather than subordination in which either infinitivization or subclause marker is made use. Motivated by Li and Thompson (1981)'s generalized form of Chinese SVC, the form of Chinese and Thai SVC is generalized in (13).

(13) $(\mathsf{Subj})\mathsf{V}_1(\mathsf{Obj}_1)\mathsf{V}_2(\mathsf{Obj}_2)\ldots\mathsf{V}_n(\mathsf{Obj}_n)$

The subject Subj and any objects $\mathrm{Obj}_i$ of the verb $\mathrm{V}_i$ can be dropped. If the subject or one of the objects is not dropped, it will be understood as linearly shared through the sequence. Duplication of objects in SVC is however questionable as it deteriorates the compactness of utterance.

In order to deal with SVC in CCG, I considered it syntactically similar to coordination where the connective is implicit. The serialization rule ($\Sigma$) was initially defined by imitating the forward coordination rule in (14).

(14) $\mathtt{X} \Rightarrow [\mathtt{X}]_{\&} \qquad [\boldsymbol{\Sigma}]$

This rule allows us to derive by CCG some types of SVC in Chinese and Thai as exemplified in (15) and (16), respectively.

(15) wǒ zhé zhǐ zuò yí ge hézi
I fold paper make one CL box
'I fold paper to make a box.'

(16) $\mathrm{k^h}$ǎo rî:p ʋîŋ $\mathrm{k^h}$â:m $\mathrm{t^h}$ànǒn
he hurry run cross road
'He hurriedly runs across the road.'

One can derive the sentence (15) by considering *zhé* 'fold' and *zuò* 'make' as $\mathtt{s\backslash np/np}$ and applying the serialization rule in (14). In (16), the derivation can be done by assigning *rî:p* 'hurry' and *ʋîŋ* 'run' as $\mathtt{s\backslash np}$, and *$k^h$â:m* 'cross' as $\mathtt{s\backslash np/np}$.

Since Chinese and Thai are pro-drop languages, they allow some arguments of the verbs to be prodropped, particularly in SVC. For example, let us consider the following Thai sentence.

(17) klâ: pāj tā:m hǎ: nāj râj·ʔɔ̂i tcɔ̄:
Kla $\mathrm{go_{DIR}}$ $\mathrm{follow_{V1}}$ $\mathrm{seek_{V2}}$ in cane-field $\mathrm{find_{V3}}$
lā:j tcà dɔ̄:n tcà:k pāj
Laay FUT $\mathrm{walk_{V4}}$ $\mathrm{leave_{V5}}$ $\mathrm{go_{DIR}}$
**Lit:** 'Kla goes out, he follows Laay (his cow), he seeks it in the cane field, and he finds that it will walk away.'
**Sem:** 'Kla goes out to seek Laay in the cane field and he finds that it is about to walk away.'

The sentence in (17) are split into two SVCs: the series of $\mathrm{V}_1$ to $\mathrm{V}_3$ and the series of $\mathrm{V}_4$ to $\mathrm{V}_5$, because they do not share their tenses. The directional verb *pāj* 'go' performs as an adverb identifying the outward direction of the action.

Syntactically speaking, there are two possible analyses of this sentence. First, we can consider the SVC $\mathrm{V}_4$ to $\mathrm{V}_5$ as a complement of the SVC $\mathrm{V}_1$ to $\mathrm{V}_3$. Pro-drops occur at the object positions of the verbs $\mathrm{V}_1$, $\mathrm{V}_2$, and $\mathrm{V}_3$. On the other hand, we can also consider the SVC $\mathrm{V}_1$ to $\mathrm{V}_3$ and the SVC $\mathrm{V}_4$ to $\mathrm{V}_5$ as *adjoining construction* (Muansuwan, 2002) which indicates resultative events in Thai (Thepkanjana, 1986) as exemplified in (18).

(18) pìtì tī: ŋū: tòk ná:m
Piti hit snake fall water
'Piti hits a snake and it falls into the water.'

In this case, the pro-drop occurs at the subject position of the SVC $V_4$ to $V_5$, and can therefore be treated as object control (Muansuwan, 2002). However, the sentence in (17) does not show resultative events. I then assume that the first analysis is correct and will follow it throughout this paper.

We have consequently reached the question that the verb *tcɔ̄:* 'find' should exhibit object control by taking two arguments for the object and the VP complementary, or it should take the entire sentence as an argument. To explicate the proliferation of arguments in SVC, we prefer the first choice to the second one; i.e. the verb *tcɔ̄:* 'find' is preferably assigned as $\mathtt{s\backslash np/(s\backslash np)/np}$. In (17), the object *lā:j* 'Laay' is dropped from the verbs $V_1$ and $V_2$ but appears as one of $V_3$'s arguments.

Let us take a closer look on the CCG analysis of (17). It is useful to focus on the SVCs of the verbs $V_1$-$V_2$ and $V_3$. It is shown below that the decomposition rule fails to parse the tested sentence through its application illustrated in (19).

(19)

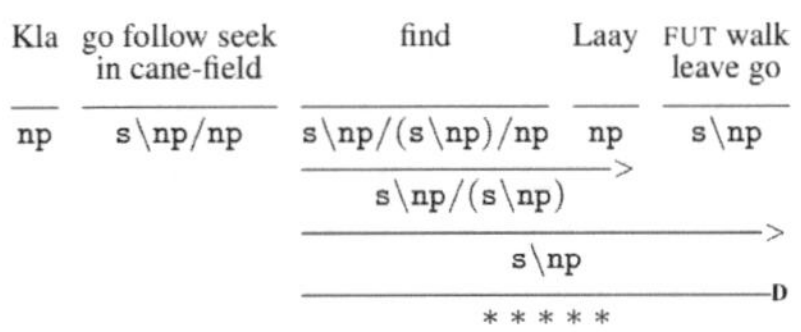


The verbs $V_1$ and $V_2$ are transitive and assigned as $\mathtt{s\backslash np/np}$, while $V_4$ and $V_5$ are intransitive and assigned as $\mathtt{s\backslash np}$. From the case (19), it follows that the decomposition rule cannot capture some patterns of intra-sentential ellipses in languages whose degree of pro-dropping is more free. Both types of intra-sentential ellipses which are prevalent in SVC of analytic languages should be captured for the sake of applicability.

The use of decomposition rule in analytic languages is not appealing for two main reasons. First, the decomposition rule does not support certain patterns of intra-sentential ellipses which are prevalent in analytic languages. As exemplified in (19), the decomposition rule fails to parse the Thai SVC whose object of the left conjunct is pro-dropped, since the right conjunct cannot be decomposed by (11). To tackle a broader coverage of intra-sentential ellipses, the grammar should rely on not only decomposition but also a supplement memory mechanism. Second, the decomposition rule allows arbitrary decomposition which leads to over-generation. From their definitions the variable $\mathtt{Y}$ can be arbitrarily substituted by any syntactic categories resulting in ungrammatical sentences generated. For example we can derive the ungrammatical sentence **Mary eats noodles and quickly* by means of the decomposition rule in (20).

(20)

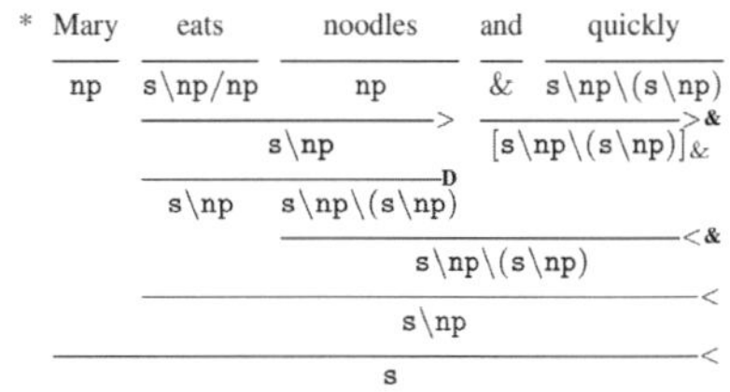


The issues of handling ellipses in SVC and overgeneration of the decomposition rule can be resolved by replacing the decomposition rule with a memory mechanism that associates fillers to their gaps. The memory mechanism also makes grammar rules more manageable because it is more straightforward to identify particular syntactic categories allowed or banned from pro-dropping. I will show how the memory mechanism improves the CCG's coverage of serial verb construction in the next section.

## 4 CCG with Memory Mechanism (CCG-MM)

As I have elaborated in the last section, CCG needs a memory mechanism (1) to resolve intra-sentential ellipses in serial verb construction of analytic languages, and (2) to improve resource management for over-generation avoidance. To do so, such memory mechanism has to extend the generative power of the decomposition rule and improve the ease of resource management in parallel.

The memory mechanism used in this paper is motivated by a wide range of previous work from computer science to symbolic logics. The notion of memory mechanism in natural language parsing can be traced back to HOLD registers in ATN (Woods, 1970) in which fillers (antecedents) are held in registers for being filled to gaps found in the rest of the input sentence. These registers are too powerful since they enable ATN to recognize the full class of context-sensitive grammars. In Type Logical Grammar (TLG) (Morrill, 1994; Jäger, 1997; Jäger, 2001; Oehrle, 2007), Gentzen's sequent calculus was incorporated with variable quantification to resolve pro-forms and VP ellipses to their antecedents. The variable quantification in TLG is comparable to the use of memory in storing antecedents and anaphora.

In Categorial Type Logic (CTL) (Hendriks, 1995; Moortgat, 1997), gap induction was incorporated. Syntactic categories were modified with modalities which permit or prohibit gap induction in derivation. However, logical reasoning obtained from TLG and CTL are an NP-complete problem. In CCG, Jacobson (1999) attempted to explicitly denote non-local anaphoric requirement whereby she introduced the anaphoric slash (|) and the anaphoric connective (**Z**) to connect anaphors to their antecedents. However, this framework does not support anaphora whose argument is not its antecedent, such as possessive adjectives. Recently, a filler-gap memory mechanism was again introduced to Categorial Grammar, called Memory-Inductive Categorial Grammar (MICG) (Boonkwan and Supnithi, 2008). Fillers and gaps, encoded as memory modalities, are modified to syntactic categories, and they are associated by the gap-resolution connective when coordination and serialization take place. Though their framework is successful in resolving a wide variety of gapping, its generative power falls between LIG and Indexed Grammar, theoretically too powerful for natural languages.

The memory mechanism introduced in this paper deals with fillers and gaps in SVC. It is similar to anaphoric resolution in ATN, Jacobson's model, TLG, and CTL. However, it also has prominent distinction from them: The anaphoric mechanisms mentioned earlier are dealing with unbounded dependency or even inter-sentential ellipses, while the memory mechanism in this paper is dealing only with intra-sentential bounded dependency in SVC as generalized in (13). Moreover, choices of filler-gap association can be pruned out by the use of combinatory directionality because the word order of analytic languages is fixed. It is noticeable that we can simply determine the grammatical function (subject or object) of arbitrary np's in (13) from the directionality (the subject on the left and the object on the right). With these reasons, I therefore adapted the notions of MICG's memory modalities and gap-resolution connective (Boonkwan and Supnithi, 2008) for the backbone of the memory mechanism.

In CCG with Memory Mechanism (CCG-MM), syntactic categories are modalized with memory modalities. For each functional application, a syntactic category can be stored, or *memorized*, into the filler storage and the resulted category is modalized with the filler $\Box$. A syntactic category can also be induced as a gap in a unary derivation called *induction* and the resulted category is modalized with the gap $\Diamond$.

There are two constraint parameters in each modality: the combinatory directionality $d \in \{<, >\}$ and the syntactic category $c$, resulting in the filler and the gap denoted in the forms $\Box_c^d$ and $\Diamond_c^d$, respectively. For example, the syntactic category $\Box_{\texttt{np}}^{<}\Diamond_{\texttt{np}}^{>}\texttt{s}$ has a filler of type np on the left side and a gap of type np on the right side.

The filler $\Box_c^d$ and the gap $\Diamond_c^d$ of the same directionality and syntactic categories are said to be *symmetric* under the gap-resolution connective $\oplus$; that is, they are matched and canceled in the gap resolution process. Apart from MICG, I restrict the associative power of $\oplus$ to match only a filler and a gap, not between two gaps, so that the generative power can be preserved linear. This topic will be discussed in §5. Given two strings of modalities $m_1$ and $m_2$, the gap-resolution connective $\oplus$ is defined in (21).

(21)
$$\begin{aligned} \Box_c^d m_1 \oplus \Diamond_c^d m_2 &\equiv m_1 \oplus m_2 \\ \Diamond_c^d m_1 \oplus \Box_c^d m_2 &\equiv m_1 \oplus m_2 \\ \epsilon \oplus \epsilon &\equiv \epsilon \end{aligned}$$

The notation $\epsilon$ denotes an empty string. It means that a syntactic category modalized with an empty modality string is simply *unmodalized*; that is, any modalized syntactic categories $\epsilon\texttt{X}$ are equivalent to the unmodalized ones X.

Since the syntactic categories are modalized by a modality string, all combinatory operations in canonical CCG must preserve the modalities after each derivation step. However, there are two conditions to be satisfied:

**Condition A:** At least one operands of functional application must be unmodalized.

**Condition B:** Both operands of functional composition, disharmonic functional composition, and type raising must be unmodalized.

Both conditions are introduced to preserve the generative power of CCG. This topic will be discussed in §5.

As adopted from MICG, there are two memory operations: memorization and induction.

**Memorization:** a filler modality is pushed to the top of the memory when an functional application rule is applied, where the filler's syntactic category must be unmodalized. Let $m$ be a modality string, the memorization operation is defined in (22).

(22)
$$\begin{array}{llll} \epsilon\mathtt{X}/\mathtt{Y} \ \ m\mathtt{Y} & \Rightarrow & \Box^{<}_{\mathtt{X}/\mathtt{Y}} m\mathtt{X} & [>\mathbf{M}_F] \\ m\mathtt{X}/\mathtt{Y} \ \ \epsilon\mathtt{Y} & \Rightarrow & \Box^{>}_{\mathtt{Y}} m\mathtt{X} & [>\mathbf{M}_A] \\ \epsilon\mathtt{Y} \ \ m\mathtt{X}\backslash\mathtt{Y} & \Rightarrow & \Box^{<}_{\mathtt{Y}} m\mathtt{X} & [<\mathbf{M}_A] \\ m\mathtt{Y} \ \ \epsilon\mathtt{X}\backslash\mathtt{Y} & \Rightarrow & \Box^{>}_{\mathtt{X}\backslash\mathtt{Y}} m\mathtt{X} & [<\mathbf{M}_F] \end{array}$$

**Induction:** a gap modality is pushed to the top of the memory when a gap of such type is induced at either side of the syntactic category. Let $m$ be a modality string, the induction operation is defined in (23).

(23)
$$\begin{array}{llll} m\mathtt{X}/\mathtt{Y} & \Rightarrow & \Diamond^{>}_{\mathtt{Y}} m\mathtt{X} & [>\mathbf{I}_A] \\ m\mathtt{Y} & \Rightarrow & \Diamond^{<}_{\mathtt{X}/\mathtt{Y}} m\mathtt{X} & [>\mathbf{I}_F] \\ m\mathtt{X}\backslash\mathtt{Y} & \Rightarrow & \Diamond^{<}_{\mathtt{Y}} m\mathtt{X} & [<\mathbf{I}_A] \\ m\mathtt{Y} & \Rightarrow & \Diamond^{>}_{\mathtt{X}\backslash\mathtt{Y}} m\mathtt{X} & [<\mathbf{I}_F] \end{array}$$

Because the use of memory mechanism elucidates fillers and gaps hidden in the derivation, we can then replace the decomposition rule of the canonical CCG with the gap resolution process of MICG. Fillers and gaps are associated in the coordination and serialization by the gap-resolution connective $\oplus$. For any given $m_1, m_2$, if $m_1 \oplus m_2$ exists then always $m_1 \oplus m_2 \equiv \epsilon$. Given two modality strings $m_1$ and $m_2$ such that $m_1 \oplus m_2$ exists, the coordination rule ($\Phi$) and serialization rule ($\Sigma$) are redefined on $\oplus$ in (24).

(24)
$$\begin{array}{llll} m_1\mathtt{X} \ \ \& \ \ m_2\mathtt{X} & \Rightarrow & \mathtt{X} & [\mathbf{\Phi}] \\ m_1\mathtt{X} \ \ m_2\mathtt{X} & \Rightarrow & \mathtt{X} & [\mathbf{\Sigma}] \end{array}$$

At present, the memory mechanism was developed in Prolog for the sake of unification mechanism. Each induction rule is nondeterministically applied and variables are sometimes left uninstantiated. For example, the sentence in (12) can be parsed as illustrated in (25).

(25)
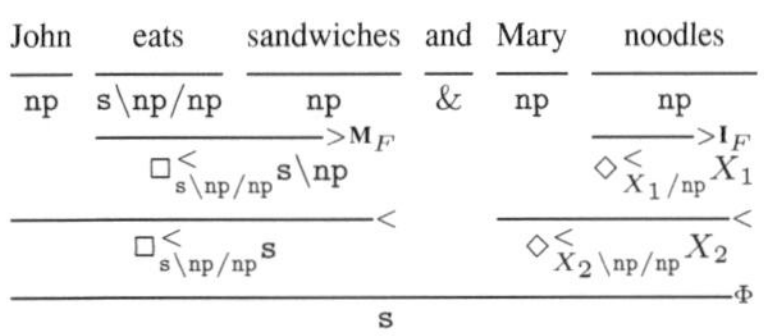


Let us consider the derivation in the right conjunct. The gap induction is first applied on np resulting in $\Diamond^{<}_{X_1/\mathtt{np}} X_1$, where $X_1$ is an uninstantiated variable. Then the backward application is applied, so that $X_1$ is unified with $X_2\backslash\mathtt{np}$. Finally, the left and the right conjuncts are coordinated yielding that $X_2$ is unified with $\mathtt{s}$ and $X_1$ with $\mathtt{s}\backslash\mathtt{np}$. For convenience of type-setting, let us suppose that we can always choose the right type in each induction step and suppress the unification process.

Table 1: Slash modalities for memory operations.

| | - Left | + Left |
|---|---|---|
| - Right | $\star$ | $\triangleleft$ |
| + Right | $\triangleright$ | $\cdot$ |

Once we instantiate $X_1$ and $X_2$, the derivation obtained in (25) is quite more straightforward than the derivation in (12). The filler *eats* is introduced on the left conjunct, while the gap of type $\mathtt{s}\backslash\mathtt{np}/\mathtt{np}$ is induced on the right conjunct. The coordination operation associates the filler and the gap resulting in a complete derivation.

A significant feature of the memory mechanism is that it handles all kinds of intra-sentential ellipses in SVC. This is because the coordination and serialization rules allow pro-dropping in either the left or the right conjunct. For example, the intra-sentential ellipses pattern in Thai SVC illustrated in (19) can be derived as illustrated in (26).

(26)
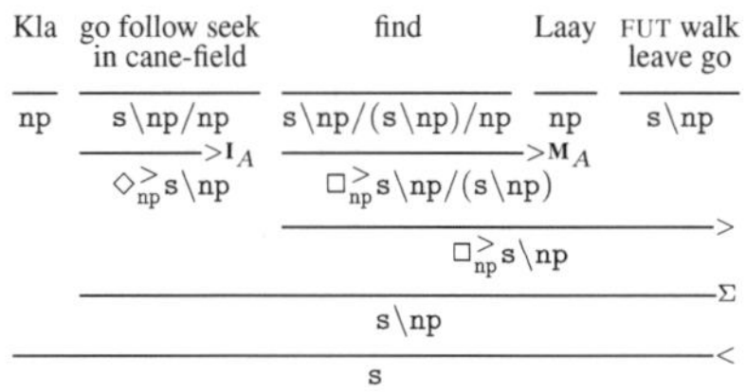


By replacing the decomposition rule with the memory mechanism, CCG accepts all patterns of pro-dropping in SVC. It should also be noted that the derivation in (20) is *per se* prohibited by the coordination rule.

Similar to canonical CCG, CCG-MM is also *resource-sensitive*; that is, each combinatory operation is allowed or prohibited with respect to the resource we have (Baldridge and Kruijff, 2003). Baldridge (2002) showed that we can obtain a cleaner resource management in canonical CCG by the use of modalized slashes to control combinatory behavior. His multimodal schema of slash permissions can also be applied to the memory mechanism in much the same way. I assume that there are four modes of memory operations according to direction and allowance of memory operations as in Table 1.

The modes can be organized into the type hierarchy shown in Figure 1. The slash modality $\star$, the most limited mode, does not allow any memory operations on both sides. The slash modalities $\triangleleft$ and $\triangleright$ allow memorization and induction on the

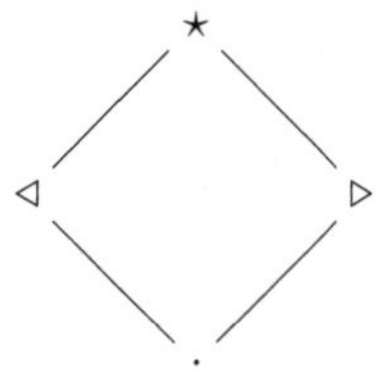


Figure 1: Hierarchy of slash modalities for memory operations.

left and right sides, respectively. Finally, the slash modality $\cdot$ allows memorization and induction on both sides. In order to distinguish the memory operation's slash modalities from Baldridge's slash modalities, I annotate the first as a superscript and the second as a subscript of the slashes. For example, the syntactic category $\mathtt{s}\backslash^{\triangleleft}_{\times}\mathtt{np}$ denotes that $\mathtt{s}\backslash\mathtt{np}$ allows permutation in crossed functional composition ($\times$) and memory operations on the left side ($\triangleleft$). As with Baldridge's multimodal framework, the slash modality $\cdot$ can be omitted from writing. By defining the slash modalities, it follows that the memory operations can be defined in (27).

(27)
$$
\begin{array}{rcll}
m\mathtt{X}/^{\triangleright}\mathtt{Y} \quad \epsilon\mathtt{Y} & \Rightarrow & \Box^{>}_{\mathtt{Y}} m\mathtt{X} & [> \mathbf{M}_F] \\
\epsilon\mathtt{X}/^{\triangleleft}\mathtt{Y} \quad m\mathtt{Y} & \Rightarrow & \Box^{<}_{\mathtt{X}/^{\triangleleft}\mathtt{Y}} m\mathtt{X} & [> \mathbf{M}_A] \\
\epsilon\mathtt{Y} \quad m\mathtt{X}\backslash^{\triangleleft}\mathtt{Y} & \Rightarrow & \Box^{<}_{\mathtt{Y}} m\mathtt{X} & [< \mathbf{M}_A] \\
m\mathtt{Y} \quad \epsilon\mathtt{X}\backslash^{\triangleright}\mathtt{Y} & \Rightarrow & \Box^{>}_{\mathtt{X}\backslash^{\triangleright}\mathtt{Y}} m\mathtt{X} & [< \mathbf{M}_F] \\
m\mathtt{X}/^{\triangleright}\mathtt{Y} & \Rightarrow & \Diamond^{>}_{\mathtt{Y}} m\mathtt{X} & [> \mathbf{I}_A] \\
m\mathtt{Y} & \Rightarrow & \Diamond^{<}_{\mathtt{X}/^{\triangleleft}\mathtt{Y}} m\mathtt{X} & [> \mathbf{I}_F] \\
m\mathtt{X}\backslash^{\triangleleft}\mathtt{Y} & \Rightarrow & \Diamond^{<}_{\mathtt{Y}} m\mathtt{X} & [< \mathbf{I}_A] \\
m\mathtt{Y} & \Rightarrow & \Diamond^{>}_{\mathtt{X}\backslash^{\triangleright}\mathtt{Y}} m\mathtt{X} & [< \mathbf{I}_F]
\end{array}
$$

When incorporating with the memory mechanism and the slash modalities, CCG becomes flexible enough to handle all patterns of intra-sentential ellipses in SVC which are prevalent in analytic languages, and to manage its lexical resource. I will now show that CCG-MM extends the generative power of the canonical CCG.

## 5 Generative Power

In this section, we will informally discuss the margin of generative power introduced by the memory mechanism. Since Vijay-Shanker (1994) showed that CCG and Linear Indexed Grammar (LIG) (Gazdar, 1988) are weakly equivalent; i.e. they generate the same sets of strings, we will first compare the CCG-MM with the LIG. As will be shown, its generative power is beyond LIG; we will find the closest upper bound in order to locate it in the Chomsky's hierarchy.

We will follow the equivalent proof of Vijay-Shanker and Weir (1994) to investigate the generative power of CCG-MM. Let us first assume that we are going to construct an LIG $G = (V_N, V_T, V_S, S, P)$ that subsumes CCG-MM. To construct $G$, let us define each of its component as follows.

> $V_N$ is a finite set of syntactic categories,
> $V_T$ is a finite set of terminals,
> $V_S$ is a finite set of stack symbols having the form $\Box^d_c$, $\Diamond^d_c$, $/c$, or $\backslash c$,
> $S \in V_N$ is the start symbol, and
> $P$ is a finite set of productions, having the form
>
> $$
\begin{array}{rcl}
A[] & \rightarrow & a \\
A[\circ\circ l] & \rightarrow & A_1[] \ldots A_i[\circ\circ l'] \ldots A_n[]
\end{array}
$$
>
> where each $A_k \in V_N$, $d \in \{<, >\}$, $c \in V_N$, $l, l' \in V_S$, and $a \in V_T \cup \{\epsilon\}$.

The notation for stacks uses $[\circ\circ l]$ to denote an arbitrary stack whose top symbol is $l$. The *linearity* of LIG comes from the fact that in each production there is only one daughter that share the stack features with its mother. Let us also define $\Delta(\sigma)$ as the homomorphic function that converts each modality in a modality string $\sigma$ into its symmetric counterpart, i.e. a filler $\Box^d_c$ into a gap $\Diamond^d_c$, and vice versa. The stack in this LIG is used for storing (1) tailing slashes of a syntactic category for harmonic/disharmonic functional composition rules, and (2) modalities of a syntactic category for gap resolution.

We start out by transforming the lexical item. For every lexical item of the form $w \vdash \mathtt{X}$ where $\mathtt{X}$ is a syntactic category, add the following production to $P$:

(28) $$\mathtt{X}[] \quad \rightarrow \quad w$$

We add two unary rules for converting between tailing slashes and stack values. For every syntactic category $\mathtt{X}$ and $\mathtt{Y}_1, \ldots, \mathtt{Y}_n$, the following rules are added.

(29)
$$
\begin{array}{rcl}
\mathtt{X}|_1\mathtt{Y}_1 \ldots |_n\mathtt{Y}_n[\circ\circ] & \rightarrow & \mathtt{X}[\circ\circ\,|_1\mathtt{Y}_1 \ldots |_n\mathtt{Y}_n] \\
\mathtt{X}[\circ\circ\,|_1\mathtt{Y}_1 \ldots |_n\mathtt{Y}_n] & \rightarrow & \mathtt{X}|_1\mathtt{Y}_1 \ldots |_n\mathtt{Y}_n[\circ\circ]
\end{array}
$$

where the top of $\circ\circ$ must be a filler or a gap, or $\circ\circ$ must be empty. This constraint preserves the ordering of combinatory operations.

We then transform the functional application rules into LIG productions. From Condition A, we can generalize the functional application rules in (2) as follows.

(30)
$$\begin{array}{lll} m\mathtt{X/Y}\ \ \mathtt{Y} & \Rightarrow & m\mathtt{X} \\ \mathtt{X/Y}\ \ m\mathtt{Y} & \Rightarrow & m\mathtt{X} \\ m\mathtt{Y}\ \ \mathtt{X\backslash Y} & \Rightarrow & m\mathtt{X} \\ \mathtt{Y}\ \ m\mathtt{X\backslash Y} & \Rightarrow & m\mathtt{X} \end{array}$$

where $m$ is a modality string. Condition A preserves the linearity of the generative power in that it prevents the functional application rules from involving the two stacks of the daughters at once. We can convert the rules in (30) into the following productions.

(31)
$$\begin{array}{lll} \mathtt{X}[\circ\circ] & \rightarrow & \mathtt{X}[\circ\circ/\mathtt{Y}]\ \ \mathtt{Y}[] \\ \mathtt{X}[\circ\circ] & \rightarrow & \mathtt{X}[/\mathtt{Y}]\ \ \mathtt{Y}[\circ\circ] \\ \mathtt{X}[\circ\circ] & \rightarrow & \mathtt{Y}[\circ\circ]\ \ \mathtt{X}[\backslash\mathtt{Y}] \\ \mathtt{X}[\circ\circ] & \rightarrow & \mathtt{Y}[]\ \ \mathtt{X}[\circ\circ\backslash\mathtt{Y}] \end{array}$$

We can generalize the harmonic and disharmonic, forward and backward composition rules in (6) and (9) as follows.

(32)
$$\begin{array}{lll} \mathtt{X/Y}\ \ \mathtt{Y}|_1\mathtt{Z}_1\ldots|_n\mathtt{Z}_n & \Rightarrow & \mathtt{X}|_1\mathtt{Z}_1\ldots|_n\mathtt{Z}_n \\ \mathtt{Y}|_1\mathtt{Z}_1\ldots|_n\mathtt{Z}_n\ \ \mathtt{X\backslash Y} & \Rightarrow & \mathtt{X}|_1\mathtt{Z}_1\ldots|_n\mathtt{Z}_n \end{array}$$

where each $|_i \in \{\backslash, /\}$. By Condition B, we obtain that all operands are unmodalized so that we can treat only tailing slashes. That is, Condition B prevents us from processing both tailing slashes and memory modalities at once where the linearity of the rules is deteriorated. We can therefore convert these rules into the following productions.

(33)
$$\begin{array}{lll} \mathtt{X}[\circ\circ] & \rightarrow & \mathtt{X}[/\mathtt{Y}]\ \ \mathtt{Y}[\circ\circ] \\ \mathtt{X}[\circ\circ] & \rightarrow & \mathtt{Y}[\circ\circ]\ \ \mathtt{X}[\backslash\mathtt{Y}] \end{array}$$

The memorization and induction rules described in (27) are transformed into the following productions.

(34)
$$\begin{array}{rll} \mathtt{X}[\circ\circ\Box^{<}_{\mathtt{X/Y}}] & \rightarrow & \mathtt{X}[/\mathtt{Y}]\ \ \mathtt{Y}[\circ\circ] \\ \mathtt{X}[\circ\circ\Box^{>}_{\mathtt{Y}}] & \rightarrow & \mathtt{X}[\circ\circ/\mathtt{Y}]\ \ \mathtt{Y}[] \\ \mathtt{X}[\circ\circ\Box^{<}_{\mathtt{Y}}] & \rightarrow & \mathtt{Y}[]\ \ \mathtt{X}[\circ\circ\backslash\mathtt{Y}] \\ \mathtt{X}[\circ\circ\Box^{>}_{\mathtt{X\backslash Y}}] & \rightarrow & \mathtt{Y}[\circ\circ]\ \ \mathtt{X}[\backslash\mathtt{Y}] \\ \mathtt{X}[\circ\circ\Diamond^{>}_{\mathtt{Y}}] & \rightarrow & \mathtt{X}[\circ\circ/\mathtt{Y}] \\ \mathtt{X}[\circ\circ\Diamond^{<}_{\mathtt{X/Y}}] & \rightarrow & \mathtt{Y}[\circ\circ] \\ \mathtt{X}[\circ\circ\Diamond^{<}_{\mathtt{Y}}] & \rightarrow & \mathtt{X}[\circ\circ\backslash\mathtt{Y}] \\ \mathtt{X}[\circ\circ\Diamond^{>}_{\mathtt{X\backslash Y}}] & \rightarrow & \mathtt{Y}[\circ\circ] \end{array}$$

However, it is important to take into account the coordination and serialization rules, because they involve two stacks which have similar stack values if we convert one of them into the symmetric form with $\Delta$. Those rules can be transformed as follows.

(35)
$$\begin{array}{lll} \mathtt{X}[] & \rightarrow & \mathtt{X}[\circ\circ]\ \ \&[]\ \ \mathtt{X}[\Delta(\circ\circ)] \\ \mathtt{X}[] & \rightarrow & \mathtt{X}[\circ\circ]\ \ \mathtt{X}[\Delta(\circ\circ)] \end{array}$$

It is obvious that the rules in (35) are not LIG production; that is, CCG-MM cannot be generated by any LIGs; or more precisely, CCG-MM is properly more powerful than CCG. We therefore have to find an upper bound of its generative power.

Though CCG-MM is more powerful than CCG and LIG, the rules in (35) reveal a significant property of Partially Linear Indexed Grammar (PLIG) (Keller and Weir, 1995), an extension of LIG whose productions are allowed to have two or more daughters sharing stack features with each other but these stacks are not shared with their mother as shown in (36).

(36)
$$A[] \rightarrow A_1[]\ldots A_i[\circ\circ]\ldots A_j[\circ\circ]\ldots A_n[]$$

Whereby restricting the power of the gap-resolution connective, the two stacks of the daughters are shared but not with their mother. An interesting trait of PLIG is that it can generate the language $\{w^k | w \text{ is in a regular language and } k \in \mathcal{N}\}$. This is similar to the pattern of SVC in which a series of verb phrase can be reduplicated.

To conclude this section, CCG-MM is more powerful than LIG but less powerful than PLIG. From (Keller and Weir, 1995), we can position the CCG-MM in the Chomsky's hierarchy as follows: CFG $<$ CCG = TAG = HG = LIG $<$ CCG-MM $\leq$ PLIG $\leq$ LCFRS $<$ CSG.

## 6 Conclusion and Future Work

I have presented an approach to treating serial verb construction in analytic languages by incorporating CCG with a memory mechanism. In the memory mechanism, fillers and gaps are stored as modalities that modalize a syntactic category. The fillers and the gaps are then associated in the coordination and the serialization rules. This results in a more flexible way of dealing with intra-sentential ellipses in SVC than the decomposition rule in canonical CCG. Theoretically speaking, the proposed memory mechanism increases the generative power of CCG into the class of partially linear indexed grammars.

Future research remains as follows. First, I will investigate constraints that reduce the search space of parsing caused by gap induction. Second, I will apply the memory mechanism in solving discontinuous gaps. Third, I will then extend this framework to free word-ordered languages. Fourth and finally, the future direction of this research is to develop a wide-coverage parser in which statistics is also made use to predict memory operations occuring in derivation.

## References


Jason Baldridge and Geert-Jan M. Kruijff. 2003. Multimodal combinatory categorial grammar. In *Proceedings of the 10th Conference of the European Chapter of the ACL 2003*, pages 211–218, Budapest, Hungary.

Jason Baldridge. 2002. *Lexically Specified Derivational Control in Combinatory Categorial Grammar*. Ph.D. thesis, University of Edinburgh.

Prachya Boonkwan and Thepchai Supnithi. 2008. Memory-inductive categorial grammar: An approach to gap resolution in analytic-language translation. In *Proceedings of The Third International Joint Conference on Natural Language Processing*, volume 1, pages 80–87, Hyderabad, India, January.

Gerald Gazdar. 1988. Applicability of indexed grammars to natural languages. In U. Reyle and C. Rohrer, editors, *Natural Language Parsing and Linguistic Theories*, pages 69–94. Reidel, Dordrecht.

Petra Hendriks. 1995. Ellipsis and multimodal categorial type logic. In *Proceedings of Formal Grammar Conference*, pages 107–122. Barcelona, Spain.

Pauline Jacobson. 1999. Towards a variable-free semantics. *Linguistics and Philosophy*, 22:117–184, October.

Gerhard Jäger. 1997. Anaphora and ellipsis in type-logical grammar. In *Proceedings of the 11th Amsterdam Colloquium*, pages 175–180, Amsterdam, the Netherland. ILLC, Universiteit van Amsterdam.

Gerhard Jäger. 2001. Anaphora and quantification in categorial grammar. In *Lecture Notes in Computer Science; Selected papers from the 3rd International Conference, on logical aspects of Computational Linguistics*, volume 2014/2001, pages 70–89.

Bill Keller and David Weir. 1995. A tractable extension of linear indexed grammars. In *In Proceedings of the 7th European Chapter of ACL Conference*.

Charles N. Li and Sandra A. Thompson. 1981. *Mandarin Chinese: A Functional Reference Grammar*. Berkeley: University of California Press.

Michael Moortgat. 1997. Categorial type logics. In van Benthem and ter Meulen, editors, *Handbook of Logic and Language*, chapter 2, pages 163–170. Elsevier/MIT Press.

Glyn Morrill. 1994. Type logical grammar. In *Categorial Logic of Signs*. Kluwer, Dordrecht.

Nuttanart Muansuwan. 2002. *Verb Complexes in Thai*. Ph.D. thesis, University at Buffalo, The State University of New York.

Richard T. Oehrle, 2007. *Non-Transformational Syntax: A Guide to Current Models*, chapter Multimodal Type Logical Grammar. Oxford: Blackwell.

Mark Steedman. 1990. Gapping as constituent coordination. *Linguistics and Philosophy*, 13:207–263.

Mark Steedman. 2000. *The Syntactic Process*. The MIT Press, Cambridge, Massachusetts.

Kingkarn Thepkanjana. 1986. *Serial Verb Constructions in Thai*. Ph.D. thesis, University of Michigan.

K. Vijay-Shanker and David J. Weir. 1994. The equivalence of four extensions of context-free grammars. *Mathematical Systems Theory*, 27(6):511–546.

William A. Woods. 1970. Transition network grammars for natural language analysis. *Communications of the ACM*, 13(10):591–606, October.

# Combining a Statistical Language Model with Logistic Regression to Predict the Lexical and Syntactic Difficulty of Texts for FFL

**Thomas L. François**
Aspirant FNRS
CENTAL (Center for Natural Language Processing)
Université catholique de Louvain
1348 Louvain-la-Neuve, Belgium
thomas.francois@uclouvain.be

## Abstract

Reading is known to be an essential task in language learning, but finding the appropriate text for every learner is far from easy. In this context, automatic procedures can support the teacher's work. Some tools exist for English, but at present there are none for French as a foreign language (FFL). In this paper, we present an original approach to assessing the readability of FFL texts using NLP techniques and extracts from FFL textbooks as our corpus. Two logistic regression models based on lexical and grammatical features are explored and give quite good predictions on new texts. The results shows a slight superiority for multinomial logistic regression over the proportional odds model.

## 1 Introduction

The current massive mobility of people has put increasing pressure on the language teaching sector, in terms of the availability of instructors and suitable teaching materials. The development of Intelligent Computer Aided Language Learning (ICALL) has helped both these needs, while the Internet has increasingly been used as a source of exercises. Indeed, it allows immediate access to a huge number of texts which can be used for educational purposes, either for classical reading comprehension tasks, or as a corpus for the creation of various automatically generated exercises.

However, the strength of the Internet is also its main flaw : there are so many texts available to the teacher that he or she can get lost. Having gathered some documents suitable in terms of subject matter, teachers still have to check if their readability levels are suitable for their students : a highly time-consuming task. This is where NLP applications able to classify documents according to their reading difficulty level can be invaluable.

Related research will be discussed in Section 2. In Section 3, the distinctive features of the corpus used in this study and a difficulty scale suitable for FFL text classification are described. Section 4 focuses on the independent linguistic variables considered in this research, while the statistical techniques used for predictions are covered in Section 5. Section 6 gives some details of the implementations, and Section 7 presents the first results of our models. Finally, Section 8 sums up the contribution of this article before providing a programme for future work and improvement of the results.

## 2 Related research

The measurement of the reading difficulty of texts has been a major concern in the English-speaking literature since the 1920s and the first formula developed by Lively and Pressey (1923). The field of readability has since produced many formulae based on simple lexical and syntactic measures such as the average number of syllables per word, the average length of sentences in a piece of text (Flesch, 1948; Kincaid et al., 1975), or the percentage of words not on a list combined with the average sentence length (Chall and Dale, 1995).

French-speaking researchers discovered the field of readability in 1956 through the work of André Conquet, *La lisibilité* (1971), and the first two formulae for French were adapted from Flesch (1948) by Kandel and Moles (1958) and de Landsheere (1963). Both of these researchers stayed quite close to the Flesch formula, and in so doing they failed to take into account some specificities of the French language.

Henry (1975) was the first to introduce specific formulae for French. He used a larger set of variables to design three formulae : a complete, an automatic and a short one, each of which

*Proceedings of the EACL 2009 Student Research Workshop*, pages 19–27,
Athens, Greece, 2 April 2009. ©2009 Association for Computational Linguistics

was adapted for three different educational levels. His formulae are by far the best and most frequently used in the French-speaking world. Later, Richaudeau (1979) suggested a criteria of "linguistic efficiency" based on experiments on short-term memory, while Mesnager (1989) coined what is still, to the best of our knowledge, the most recent specific formula for French, with children as its target.

Compared to the mass of studies in English, readability in French has never enthused the research community. The cultural reasons for this are analysed by Bossé-Andrieu (1993) (who basically argues that the idea of measuring text difficulty objectively seems far too pragmatic for the French spirit). It follows that there is little current research in this field: in Belgium, the Flesch formula is still used to assess the readability of articles in journalism studies. This example also shows that the French-specific formulae are not much used, probably because of their complexity (Bossé-Andrieu, 1993).

Of course, if there is little work on French readability, there is even less on French as a foreign language. We only know the study of Cornaire (1988), which tested the adaptation of Henry's short formula to French as a foreign language, and that of Uitdenbogerd (2005), which developed a new measure for English-speaking learners of French, stressing the importance of cognates when developing a new formula for a related language.

Therefore, we had to draw our inspiration from the English-speaking world, which has recently experienced a revival of interest in research on readability. Taking advantage of the increasing power of computers and the development of NLP techniques, researchers have been able to experiment with more complex variables. Collins-Thompson et al. (2005) presented a variation of a multinomial naive Bayesian classifier they called the "Smoothed Unigram" model. We retained from their work the use of language models instead of word lists to measure lexical complexity. Schwarm and Ostendorf (2005) developed a SVM categoriser combining a classifier based on trigram language models (one for each level of difficulty), some parsing features such as average tree height, and variables traditionally used in readability. Heilman et al. (2007) extended the "Smoothed Unigram" model by the recognition of syntactic structures, in order to assess L2 English texts. Later, they improved the combination of their various lexical and grammatical features using regression methods (Heilman et al., 2008). We also found regression methods to be the most efficient of the statistical models with which we experimented. In this article, we consider some ways to adapt these various ideas to the specific case of FFL readability.

## 3 Corpus description

In the development of a new readability formula, the first step is to collect a corpus labelled by reading-difficulty level, a task that implies agreement on the difficulty scale. In the US, a common choice is the 12 American grade levels corresponding to primary and secondary school. However, this scale is less relevant for FFL education in Europe. So, we looked for another scale.

Given that we are looking for an automatic way of measuring text complexity for FFL learners participating in an educational programme, an obvious choice was the difficulty scale used for assessing students' levels in Europe, that is the *Common European Framework of Reference for Languages* (CEFR) (Council of Europe, 2001) . The CEFR has six levels: A1 (Breakthrough); A2 (Waystage); B1 (Threshold); B2 (Vantage); C1 (Effective Operational Proficiency) and C2 (Mastery). However differences in learners' skills can be quite substantial at lower levels, so we divided each of the A1, A2 and B1 grades in two, thus obtaining a total of nine levels.

We still needed to find a corpus labelled according to these nine classes. Unlike traditional approaches, based on a limited set of texts usually standardised by applying a closure test to a target population, our NLP-oriented approach required a large number of texts on which the statistical models could be trained. For that reason we opted for FFL textbooks as a corpus. With the appearance of the CEFR, FFL textbooks have undergone a kind of standardisation and their levels have been clarified. It is thus feasible to gather a large number of documents already labelled in terms of the CEFR scale by experts with an educational background.

However, not every textbook can be used as a document source. Likewise, not all the material from FFL textbooks is appropriate. We established the following criteria for selecting textbooks and texts:

- The CEFR was published in 2001, so only

textbooks published since then were considered. This restriction also ensures that the language resembles present-day spoken French.

- The target population for our formula is young people and adults. Therefore, only textbooks intended for this public were used.
- We retained only those texts made up of complete sentences, linked to a reading comprehension task. So, all the transcriptions of listening comprehension tasks were ignored. Similarly, all instructions to the students were excluded, because there is no guarantee the language employed there is the same as the rest of the textbook material (metalinguistic terms and so on can be found there).

Up to now, using these criteria, we have gathered more than 1,500 documents containing about 440,000 tokens. Texts cover a wide variety of subjects ranging from French literature to newspaper articles, as well as numerous dialogues, extracts from plays, cooking recipes, etc. The goal is to have as wide a coverage as possible, to achieve maximum generalisability of the formula, and also to check what sort of texts it does not fit (e.g. statistical descriptive analyses have considered songs and poems as outliers).

## 4 Selection of lexical and syntactic variables

Any text classification tasks require an object (here a text) to be parameterised into variables, whether qualitative or quantitative. These independent variables must correlate as strongly as possible with the dependent variable representing difficulty in order to explain the text's complexity, and they should also account for the various dimensions of the readability phenomenon. Traditional approaches to readability have been sharply criticised with respect to this second requirement by Kintsch and Vipond (1979) and Kemper (1983), who both insist on the importance of including the conceptual properties of texts (such as the relations between propositions and the "inference load"). However, these new approaches have not resulted in any easily reproducible computational models, leading current researchers to continue to use the classic semantic and grammatical variables, enhancing them with NLP techniques.

Because this research only spans the last year, attempts to discover interesting variables are still at an early stage. We explored the efficiency of some traditional features such as the type-token ratio, the number of letters per word, and the average sentence length, and found that, on our corpus, only the word length and sentence length correlated significantly with difficulty. Then, we add two NLP-oriented features, as described below: a statistical language model and a measure of tense difficulty.

### 4.1 The language model

The lexical difficulty of a text is quite an elaborate phenomenon to parameterise. The logistic regression models we used in this study require us to reduce this complex reality to just one number, the challenge being to achieve the most informative number. Some psychological work (Howes and Solomon, 1951; Gerhand and Barry, 1998; Brysbaert et al., 2000) suggests that there is a strong relationship between the frequency of words and the speed with which they are recognised. We therefore opted to model the lexical difficulty for reading as the global probability of a text T (with N tokens) occurring:

$$P(T) = P(t_1)P(t_2 \mid t_1) \cdots P(t_n \mid t_1, t_2, \ldots, t_{n-1}) \quad (1)$$

This equation raises two issues :

1. Estimating the conditional probabilities. It is well-known that it is impossible to train such a model on a corpus, even the largest one, because some sequences in this equation are unlikely to be encountered more than once. However, following Collins-Thompson and Callan (2005), we found that a simple smoothed unigram model could give good results for readability. Thus, we assumed that the global probability of a text T could be reduced to:

$$P(T) = \prod_{i=1}^{n} p(t_i) \quad (2)$$

where $p(t_i)$ is the probability of meeting the token $t_i$ in French; and $n$ is the number of tokens in a text.

2. Deciding what is the best linguistic unit to consider. The equations introduced above use

tokens, as is traditional in readability formulae, but the inflected nature of French suggests that lemmas may be a better alternative. Using tokens means that words taking numerous inflected forms (such as verbs), have their overall probability split between these different forms. Consequently, compared to seldom – or never – inflected words (such as adverbs, prepositions, conjunctions), they seem less frequent than they really are. Second, using tokens presupposes a theoretical position according to which learners are not able to link an inflected form with its lemma. Such a view seems highly questionable for the majority of regular forms.

In order to settle this issue, we trained three language models: one with lemmas (LM1), another with inflected forms disambiguated according to their tags (LM2), and a third one with inflected forms (LM3). The experiment was not very conclusive, since the models all correlated with the dependent variable to a similar extent, having Pearson's $r$ coefficients of $-0.58$, $-0.58$, and $-0.59$ respectively. However, three factors militate in favour of the lemma model: as well as theoretical likelihood, it is the model which is most sensitive to outliers and most prone to measurement error. This suggests that, if we can reduce this error, the lemma model may prove to be the best predictor of the three.

As a consequence of these considerations, we decided to compute the difficulty of the text by using Equation 2 adapted for lemmas and, for computational reasons, the logarithm of the probabilities:

$$P(T) = exp(\sum_{i=1}^{n} \log[p(lem_i)]) \quad (3)$$

The resulting value is still correlated with the length of the text, so it has to be normalised by dividing it by N (the number of words in the text). These operations give in a final value suitable for the logistic regression model. More information about the origin and smoothing of the probabilities is given in Section 6.

### 4.2 Measuring the tense difficulty

Having considered the complexity of a text's syntactic structures through the traditional factor of the "mean number of words per sentence", we decided to also take into account the difficulty of the conjugation of the verbs in the text. For this purpose, we created 11 variables, each representing one tense or class of tenses: conditional, future, imperative, imperfect, infinitive, past participle, present participle, present, simple past, subjunctive present and subjunctive imperfect.

The question then arose as to whether it would be better to treat these variables as binary or continuous. Theoretical justifications for a binary parameterisation lie in the fact that a text becomes more complex for a L2 language learner when there is a large variety of tenses, especially difficult ones. The proportion of each tense seems less significant. For this reason, we opted for binary variables. The other way of parameterising the data should nevertheless be tested in further research.

## 5 The regression models

By the end of the parameterisation stage, each text of the corpus has been reduced to a vector comprising the 14 following predictive variables : the result of the language model, the average number of letters per word[1], the average number of words per sentence and the 11 binary variables for tense complexity.

Each vector also has a label representing the level of the text, which is the dependent variable in our classification problem. From a statistical perspective, this variable may be considered as a nominal, ordinal, or interval variable, each level of measurement being linked to a particular regression technique: multiple linear regression for interval data; a popular cumulative logit model called proportional odds for ordinal data; and multinomial logistic regression for nominal variables. Therefore, identifying the best scale of measurement is an important issue for readability.

From a theoretical perspective, viewing the levels of difficulty as an interval scale would imply that they are ordered and evenly spaced. However, most FFL teachers would disagree with this assumption: it is well known that the higher levels take longer to complete than the earlier ones. So, a more realistic position is to consider text difficulty as an ordinal variable (since the CEFR levels are

[1]Pearson's $r$ coefficient between the language model and the average number of letters in the words was $-0.68$. This suggests that there is some independent information in the length of the words that can be used for prediction.

ordered). The third alternative, treating the levels as a nominal scale, is not intuitively obvious to a language teacher, because it suggests that there is no particular order to the CEFR levels.

From a practical perspective, things are not so clear. Traditional approaches have usually viewed difficulty as an interval scale and applied multiple linear regression. Recent NLP perspective have either considered difficulty as an ordinal variable (Heilman et al., 2008), making use of logistic regression, or as a nominal one, implementing classifiers such as the naive Bayes, SVM or decision tree. Such a variety of practices convinced us that we should experiment with all three scales of measurement.

In an exploratory phase, we compared regression methods and decision tree classifiers on the same corpus. We found that regression was more precise and more robust, due to the current limited size of the corpus. Linear regression was discarded because it gave poor results during the test phase. So we retained two logistic regression models, the PO model and the MLR model, which are presented in the next section.

### 5.1 Proportional odds (PO) model

Logistic regression is a statistical technique first developed for binary data. It generally describes the probability of a 0 or 1 outcome with an S-shaped logistic function (see Hosmer and Lemeshow (1989) for details). Adaptation of the logistic regression for $J$ ordinal classes involves a model with $J - 1$ response curves of the same shape. For a fixed class $j$, each of these response functions is comparable to a logistic regression curve for a binary response with outcomes $Y \leq j$ and $Y > j$ (Agresti, 2002), where Y is the dependent variable.

The PO model can be expressed as:

$$\text{logit}[P(Y \leq j \mid \mathbf{x})] = \alpha_j + \boldsymbol{\beta}'\mathbf{x} \qquad (4)$$

In Equation 4, $\mathbf{x}$ is the vector containing the independent variables, $\alpha_j$ is the intercept parameter for the $j_{th}$ level and $\boldsymbol{\beta}$ is the vector of regression coefficients. From this formula, the particularity of the PO model can be observed: it has the same set, $\boldsymbol{\beta}$, of parameters for each level. So, the response functions only differ in their intercepts, $\alpha_j$. This simplification is only possible under the assumption of ordinality.

Using this cumulative model, when $2 \leq j \leq J$, the estimated probability of a text $Y$ belonging to the class $j$ can be computed as:

$$\begin{aligned} P(Y = j \mid \mathbf{x}) = {} & \text{logit}[P(Y \leq j \mid \mathbf{x})] \\ & -\text{logit}[P(Y \leq j-1 \mid \mathbf{x})] \quad (5) \end{aligned}$$

When j = 1, $P(Y = 1 \mid \mathbf{x})$ is equal to $P(Y \leq j \mid \mathbf{x})$.

We said above that this model involves a simplification, based on the proportional odds assumption. This assumption needs to be tested with the chi-squared form of the score test (Agresti, 2002). The lower the chi-squared value, the better the PO model fits the data.

### 5.2 Multinomial logistic regression

Multinomial logistic regression is also called "baseline category", because it compares each class Y with a reference category, often the first one ($Y_1$), in order to regress to the binary case. Each pair of classes ($Y_j$, $Y_1$) can then be described by the ratio (Agresti, 2002, p. 268):

$$log\frac{P(Y = j \mid \mathbf{x})}{P(Y = 1 \mid \mathbf{x})} = \alpha_j + \boldsymbol{\beta}_j{}'\mathbf{x} \qquad (6)$$

where the notation is as given above. On the basis of these J-1 regression equations, it is possible to compute the probability of a text belonging to difficulty level $j$ using the values of its features contained in the vector $\boldsymbol{x}$. This may be calculated using the equation (Agresti, 2002, p. 271):

$$P(Y = j \mid \mathbf{x}) = \frac{\exp(\alpha_j + \boldsymbol{\beta}_j{}'\mathbf{x})}{1 + \sum_{h=2}^{J} \exp(\alpha_h + \boldsymbol{\beta}_j{}'\mathbf{x})} \qquad (7)$$

Notice that for the baseline category (here, $j = 1$), $\alpha_1$ and $\boldsymbol{\beta_1} = 0$. Thus, when looking for the probability of a text belonging to the baseline level, it is easy to compute the numerator, since $\exp(0) = 1$. The value of the denominator is the same for each $j$.

Heilman et al. (2008) drew attention to the fact that the MLR model multiplies the number of parameters by $J - 1$ compared to the PO model. Because of this, they recommend using the PO model.

## 6 Implementation of the models

Having covered the theoretical aspects of our model, we will now describe some of the particularities of our implementation.

### 6.1 The language model: probabilities and smoothing

For our language model, we need a list of French lemmas with their frequencies of occurrence. Getting robust estimates for a large number of lemmas requires a very large corpus and is a time-consuming process. We used *Lexique3*, a lexicon provided by New et al. (2001) and developed from two corpora: the literary corpus *Frantext* containing about 15 million of words; and a corpus of film subtitles (New et al., 2007), with about 50 million words. The authors drew up a list of more than 50,000 tagged lemmas, each of which is associated with two frequency estimates, one from each corpus.

We decided to use the frequencies from the subtitle corpus, because we think it gives a more accurate image of everyday language, which is the language FFL teaching is mainly concerned with. The frequencies were changed into probabilities, and smoothed with the Simple Good-Turing algorithm described by Gale and Sampson (1995). This step is necessary to solve another well-known problem in language models: the appearance in a new text of previously unseen lemmas. In this case, since the logarithm of probabilities is used, an unseen lemma would result in a infinite value. In order to prevent this, a smoothing process is used to shift some of the model's probability mass from seen lemmas to unseen ones.

Once we had obtained a good estimate of the probabilities, we could analyse the texts in the corpus. Each of them was lemmatised and tagged using the TreeTagger (Schmid, 1994). This NLP tool allows us to distinguish between homographs that can represent different levels of difficulty. For instance, the word *actif* is quite common as an adjective, but the noun is infrequent and is only used in the business lexicon. This distinction is possible because *Lexique3* provides tagged lemmas.

### 6.2 Variable selection

Having gathered the values for the 14 dependent variables, it was possible to train the two statistical models.[2] However, an essential requirement prior to training is feature selection. This procedure, described by Hosmer and Lemeshow (1989), consists of examining models with one, two, three, etc., variables and comparing them to the full model according to some specified criteria so as to select one that is both efficient and parsimonious. For logistic regression, the criterion selected is the AIC (Akaike's Information Criterion) of the model. This can be obtained from:

$$\text{AIC} = -2\text{log-likelihood} + 2k \qquad (8)$$

where $k$ is the number of parameters in the model, and the log-likelihood value is the result of a calculation detailed by Hosmer and Lemeshow (1989).

We applied the stepwise algorithm to our data, trying both a backward and a forward procedure. They converged to a simpler model containing only 10 variables: the value obtained from our language model, the number of letters per word, the number of words per sentence, the past participle, the present participle, and the imperfect, infinitive, conditional, future and present subjunctive tenses. Presumable the imperative and present tenses are so common that they do not have much discriminative power. On the other hand, the imperfect subjunctive is so unusual that it is not useful for a classification task. However, the non-appearance of the simple past is surprising, since it is a narrative tense which is not usually introduced until an advanced stage in the learning of French. This phenomenon deserves further investigation in the future.

## 7 First results

To the best of our knowledge, no one has previously applied NLP technologies to the specific issue of the readability of texts for FFL learners. So, any comparisons with previous studies are somewhat flawed by the fact that neither the target population nor the scale of difficulty is the same. However, our results can be roughly compared to some of the numerous studies on L1 English readability presented in Section 2. Before making this comparison, we will analyse the predictive ability of the two models.

### 7.1 Models evaluation

The evaluation measures most commonly employed in the literature are Pearson's product-moment correlation coefficient, prediction accuracy as defined by Tan et al. (2005), and adjacent accuracy. Adjacent accuracy is defined by Heilman et al. (2008) as "the proportion of predictions that were within one level of the human-assigned

[2]All statistical computations were performed with the MASS package (Venables and Ripley, 2002) of the R software.

| Measure | PO model | MLR model |
|---|---|---|
| **Results on training folds** | | |
| Correl. | 0.786 | 0.777 |
| Exact Acc. | 32.5% | 38% |
| Adj. Acc. | 70% | 71.3% |
| **Results on test folds** | | |
| Correl. | 0.783 | 0.772 |
| Exact Acc. | 32.4% | 38% |
| Adj. Acc. | 70% | 71.2% |

Table 1: Mean Pearson's $r$ coefficient, exact and adjacent accuracies for both models with the ten-fold cross-validation evaluation.

label for the given text". They defended this measure by arguing that even human-assigned reading levels are not always consistent. Nevertheless, it should not be forgotten that it can give optimistic values when the number of classes is small.

Exploratory analysis of the corpus highlighted the importance of having a similar number of texts per class. This requirement made it impossible to use all the texts from the corpus. Some 465 texts were selected, distributed across the 9 levels in such a way that each level contained about 50 texts. Within each class, an automatic procedure discarded outliers located more than $3\sigma$ from the mean, leaving 440 texts. Both models were trained on these texts.

The results on the training corpus were promising, but might be biased. So, we turned to a ten-fold cross-validation process which guarantees more reliable values for the three evaluation measures we had chosen, as well as a better insight into the generalisability of the two models. The resulting evaluation measures for training and test folds are shown in Table 1. The similarity between them clearly shows that, with 440 observations, both the models were quite robust. On this corpus, multinomial logistic regression was significantly more accurate (with 38% of texts correctly classified against 32.4% for the PO model), while Pearson's R was slightly higher for the PO model.

These results suggest that the exact accuracy may be a better indicator of performance than the correlation coefficient. However they conflict with Heilman et al.'s (2008) conclusion that the PO model performed better than the MLR one. This discrepancy might arise because the PO model was less accurate for exact predictions, but better when the adjacent accuracy by level was taken into account. However, the data in Table 2 do not support this hypothesis; rather they confirm the superiority of the MLR model when adjacent accuracy is considered. In fact, PO model's lower performance seems to be due to a lack of fit to the data, as revealed by the result of the score test for the proportional-odds assumption. This yielded a p-value below 0.0001, clearly showing that the PO model was not a good fit to the corpus.

There remains one last issue to be discussed before comparing our results to those of other studies: the empirical evidence for tense being a good predictor of reading difficulty. We selected tenses because of our experience as FLE teacher rather than on theoretical or empirical grounds. However we found that exact accuracy decreased by 10% when the tense variables were omitted from the models. Further analysis showed that the tense contributed significantly to the adjacent accuracy of classifying the C1 and C2 texts.

### 7.2 Comparison with other studies

As stated above, it is not easy to compare our results with those of previous studies, since the scale, population of interest and often the language are different. Furthermore, up till now, we have not been able to run the classical formulae for French (such as de Landsheere (1963) or Henry (1975)) on our corpus. So we are limited to comparing our evaluation measures with those in the published literature.

With multinomial logistic regression, we obtained a mean adjacent accuracy of 71% for 9 classes. This result seems quite good compared to similar research on L1 English by Heilman et al. (2008). Using more complex syntactic features, they obtained an adjacent accuracy of 52% with a PO model, and 45% with a MLR model. However, they worked with 12 levels, which may explain their lower percentage.

For French, Collins-Thompson and Callan (2005) reported a Pearson's R coefficient of 0.64 for a 5-classes naive Bayes classifier while we obtained 0.77 for 9 levels with MLR. This difference might be explained by the tagging or the use of better-estimated probabilities for the language model. Further research on this point to determine the specificities of an efficient approach to French readability appears very promising.

| Level | A1 | A1+ | A2 | A2+ | B1 | B1+ | B2 | C1 | C2 | Mean |
|---|---|---|---|---|---|---|---|---|---|---|
| **PO model** | 91% | 91% | 67% | 68% | 53% | 55% | 56% | 86% | 68% | 70% |
| **MLR model** | 93% | 90% | 69% | 51% | 59% | 56% | 64% | 88% | 73% | 71% |

Table 2: Mean adjacent accuracy per level for PO model and MLR model (on the test folds).

## 8 Discussion and future research

This paper has proposed the first readability "formula" for French as a foreign language using NLP and statistical models. It takes into account some particularities of French such as its inflected nature. A new scale to assess FFL texts within the CECR framework, and a new criteria for the corpus involving the use of textbooks, have also been proposed. The two logistic models applied to a 440-text corpus gave results consistent with the literature. They also showed the superiority of the MLR model over the PO model. Since Heilman et al. (2008) found the opposite, and the intuitive view is that levels should be described by an ordinal scale of measurement, this issue clearly needs further investigation.

This research is still in progress, and further analyses are planned. The predictive capacity of some other lexical and grammatical features will be explored. At the lexical level, statistical language models seems to be best, and tagging the texts to work with lemmas turned out to be efficient for French, although it has not been shown to be superior to disambiguated inflected forms. Moreover, due to their higher sensibility to context, smoothed n-grams might represent an alternative to lemmas.

Once the best unit has been selected, some other issues remain: it is not clear whether a model using the probabilities of this unit in the whole language or probabilities per level (Collins-Thompson and Callan, 2005) would be more efficient. We also wonder whether the L1 frequencies of words are similar to those in L2 ? FFL textbooks use a controlled vocabulary, linked to specific situational tasks, which suggests that it is highly possible that the frequencies of words in FFL differ from those in mother-tongue French.

Grammatical features have been taken into account through simple parameterisation. More complex measures (such as the presence of some syntactic structures (Heilman et al., 2007) or the characteristics of a syntactic-parsing tree) have been explored in the literature. We hope that including such factors may result in improved accuracy for our model. However, these techniques are probably dependent on the quality of the parser's results. Parsers for French are less accurate than those for English, which may generate some noise in the analysis.

Finally, we intend to explore the performance of other classification techniques. Logistic regression was the most efficient of the statistical models we tested, but as our corpus grows, more and more data is becoming available, and data mining approaches may become applicable to the text-categorization problem for FFL readability. Support vector machines have already been shown to be useful for readability purposes (Schwarm and Ostendorf, 2005). We also want to try aggregating approaches such as boosting, bagging, and random forests (Breiman, 2001), since they claim to be effective when the sample is not perfectly representative of the population (which could be true for our data). These analyses would aim to illuminate some of the assets and flaws of each of the statistical models considered.

## Acknowledgments

Thomas L. François is supported by the Belgian Fund for Scientific Research (FNRS), as is the research programme from which this material comes.

I would like to thank my directors, Prof. Cédrick Fairon and Prof. Anne-Catherine Simon, my colleagues, Laure Cuignet and the anonymous reviewers for their valuable comments.

## References

Alan Agresti. 2002. *Categorical Data Analysis. 2nd edition.* Wiley-Interscience, New York.

J. Bossé-Andrieu. 1993. La question de la lisibilité dans les pays anglophones et les pays francophones. *Technostyle, Association canadienne des professeurs de rédaction technique et scientifique*, 11(2):73–85.

L. Breiman. 2001. Random forests. *Machine Learning*, 45(1):5–32.

M. Brysbaert, M. Lange, and I. Van Wijnendaele. 2000. The effects of age-of-acquisition and frequency-of-occurrence in visual word recognition: Further evidence from the Dutch language. *European Journal of Cognitive Psychology*, 12(1):65–85.

J.S. Chall and E. Dale. 1995. *Readability Revisited: The New Dale-Chall Readability Formula*. Brookline Books, Cambridge.

K. Collins-Thompson and J. Callan. 2005. Predicting reading difficulty with statistical language models. *Journal of the American Society for Information Science and Technology*, 56(13):1448–1462.

A. Conquet. 1971. *La lisibilité*. Assemblée Permanente des CCI de Paris, Paris.

C.M. Cornaire. 1988. La lisibilité : essai d'application de la formule courte d'Henry au français langue étrangère. *Canadian Modern Language Review*, 44(2):261–273.

Council of Europe and Education Committee and Council for Cultural Co-operation. 2001. *Common European Framework of Reference for Languages: Learning, Teaching, Assessment*. Press Syndicate of the University of Cambridge.

G. De Landsheere. 1963. Pour une application des tests de lisibilité de Flesch à la langue française. *Le Travail Humain*, 26:141–154.

R. Flesch. 1948. A new readability yardstick. *Journal of Applied Psychology*, 32(3):221–233.

W.A. Gale and G. Sampson. 1995. Good-Turing frequency estimation without tears. *Journal of Quantitative Linguistics*, 2(3):217–237.

S. Gerhand and C. Barry. 1998. Word frequency effects in oral reading are not merely age-of-acquisition effects in disguise. *Journal of Experimental Psychology. Learning, Memory, and Cognition*, 24(2):267–283.

M. Heilman, K. Collins-Thompson, J. Callan, and M. Eskenazi. 2007. Combining lexical and grammatical features to improve readability measures for first and second language texts. In *Proceedings of NAACL HLT*, pages 460–467.

M. Heilman, K. Collins-Thompson, and M. Eskenazi. 2008. An analysis of statistical models and features for reading difficulty prediction. *Association for Computational Linguistics*, The 3rd Workshop on Innovative Use of NLP for Building Educational Applications:1–8.

G. Henry. 1975. *Comment mesurer la lisibilité*. Labor.

D.W. Hosmer and S. Lemeshow. 1989. *Applied Logistic Regression*. Wiley, New York.

D.H. Howes and R.L. Solomon. 1951. Visual duration threshold as a function of word probability. *Journal of Experimental Psychology*, 41(40):1–4.

L. Kandel and A. Moles. 1958. Application de l'indice de Flesch à la langue française. *Cahiers Études de Radio-Télévision*, 19:253–274.

S. Kemper. 1983. Measuring the inference load of a text. *Journal of Educational Psychology*, 75(3):391–401.

J. Kincaid, R.P. Fishburne, R. Rodgers, and B. Chissom. 1975. Derivation of new readability formulas for navy enlisted personnel. *Research Branch Report*, 85.

W. Kintsch and D. Vipond. 1979. Reading comprehension and readability in educational practice and psychological theory. *Perspectives on Memory Research*, pages 329–366.

B.A. Lively and S.L. Pressey. 1923. A method for measuring the vocabulary burden of textbooks. *Educational Administration and Supervision*, 9:389–398.

J. Mesnager. 1989. Lisibilité des textes pour enfants: un nouvel outil? *Communication et Langages*, 79:18–38.

B. New, C. Pallier, L. Ferrand, and R. Matos. 2001. Une base de données lexicales du français contemporain sur internet: LEXIQUE. *LAnnée Psychologique*, 101:447–462.

B. New, M. Brysbaert, J. Veronis, and C. Pallier. 2007. The use of film subtitles to estimate word frequencies. *Applied Psycholinguistics*, 28(04):661–677.

F. Richaudeau. 1979. Une nouvelle formule de lisibilité. *Communication et Langages*, 44:5–26.

H. Schmid. 1994. Probabilistic part-of-speech tagging using decision trees. In *Proceedings of International Conference on New Methods in Language Processing*, volume 12. Manchester, UK.

S.E. Schwarm and M. Ostendorf. 2005. Reading level assessment using support vector machines and statistical language models. *Proceedings of the 43rd Annual Meeting on Association for Computational Linguistics*, pages 523–530.

P.-N. Tan, M. Steinbach, and V. Kumar. 2005. *Introduction to Data Mining*. Addison-Wesley, Boston.

S. Uitdenbogerd. 2005. Readability of French as a foreign language and its uses. In *Proceedings of the Australian Document Computing Symposium*, pages 19–25.

W.N. Venables and B.D. Ripley. 2002. *Modern Applied Statistics with S*. Springer, New York.

# Finding Word Substitutions Using a Distributional Similarity Baseline and Immediate Context Overlap

**Aurelie Herbelot**
University of Cambridge
Computer Laboratory
J.J. Thompson Avenue
Cambridge
ah433@cam.ac.uk

## Abstract

This paper deals with the task of finding generally applicable substitutions for a given input term. We show that the output of a distributional similarity system baseline can be filtered to obtain terms that are not simply similar but frequently substitutable. Our filter relies on the fact that when two terms are in a common entailment relation, it should be possible to substitute one for the other in their most frequent surface contexts. Using the Google 5-gram corpus to find such characteristic contexts, we show that for the given task, our filter improves the precision of a distributional similarity system from 41% to 56% on a test set comprising common transitive verbs.

## 1 Introduction

This paper looks at the task of finding word substitutions for simple statements in the context of KB querying. Let us assume that we have a knowledge base made of statements of the type 'subject – verb – object':

1. Bank of America – acquire – Merrill Lynch
2. Lloyd's – buy – HBOS
3. Iceland – nationalise – Kaupthing

Let us also assume a simple querying facility, where the user can enter a word and be presented with all statements containing that word, in a typical search engine fashion. If we want to return all acquisition events present in the knowledge base above (as opposed to nationalisation events), we might search for 'acquire'. This will return the first statement (about the acquisition of Merrill Lynch) but not the second statement about HBOS. Ideally, we would like a system able to generate words similar to our query, so that a statement containing the verb 'buy' gets returned when we search for 'acquire'.

This problem is closely related to the clustering of semantically similar terms, which has received much attention in the literature. Systems that perform such clustering usually do so under the assumption of *distributional similarity* (Harris, 1954) which state that two words appearing in similar contexts will be close in meaning. This observation is statistically useful and has contributed to successful systems within two approaches: the pattern-based approach and the feature vector approach (we describe those two approaches in the next section). The definition of similarity used by those systems is fairly wide, however. Typically, a query on the verb 'produce' will return verbs such as 'export', 'import' or 'sell', for instance (see DIRT demo from `http://demo.patrickpantel.com/Content/LexSem/paraphrase.htm`, Lin and Pantel, 2001.)

This fairly wide notion of similarity is not fully appropriate for our word substitutions task: although cats and dogs are similar types of entities, querying a knowledge base for 'cat' shouldn't return statements about dogs; statements about Siamese, however, should be acceptable. So, following Dagan and Glickman (2004), we refine our concept of similarity as that of *entailment*, defined here as the relation whereby the meaning of a word $w_1$ is 'included' in the meaning of word $w_2$ (practically speaking, we assume that the 'meaning' of a word is represented by the contexts in which it appears and require that if $w_1$ entails $w_2$, the contexts of $w_2$ should be a subset of the contexts of $w_1$). Given an input term $w$, we therefore attempt to extract words which either entail or are entailed by $w$. (We do not extract directionality at this stage.)

*Proceedings of the EACL 2009 Student Research Workshop*, pages 28–36,
Athens, Greece, 2 April 2009. 

The definition of entailment usually implies that an entailing word must be *substitutable* for the entailed one, in *some* contexts at least. Here, we consider word substitution queries in cases where no additional contextual information is given, so we cannot assume that possible, but rare, substitutions will fit the query intended by the user ('believe' correctly entails 'buy' in some cases but we can be reasonably sure that the query 'buy' is meant in the 'purchase' sense.) We thus require that our output will fit the *most* common contexts. For instance, given the query 'kill', we want to return 'murder' but not 'stop'. Given 'produce', we want to return both 'release' and 'generate' but not 'fabricate' or 'hatch'.[1] Taking this into account, we generally define *substitutability* as the ability of a word to replace another one in a given sentence without changing the meaning or acceptability of the sentence, and this *in the most frequent cases*. (By *acceptability*, we mean whether the sentence is likely to be uttered by a native speaker of the language under consideration.)

In order to achieve both entailment and general substitutability, we propose to filter the output of a conventional distributional similarity system using a check for lexical substitutability in frequent contexts. The idea of the filter relies on the observation that entailing words tend to share more frequent immediate contexts than just related ones. For instance, when looking at the top 200 most frequent Google 3-gram contexts (Brants and Franz, 2006) appearing after the terms 'kill', 'murder' and 'abduct', we find that 'kill' and 'murder' share 54 while 'kill' and 'abduct' only share 2, giving us the indication that as far as usage is concerned, 'murder' is closer to 'kill' than 'abduct'. Additionally, context frequency provides a way to identify substitutability for the most common uses of the word, as required.

In what follows, we briefly present related work, and introduce our corpus and algorithm, including a discussion of our 'immediate context overlap' filter. We then review the results of an experiment on the extraction of entailment pairs for 30 input verbs.

[1]In fact, we argue that even in systems where context is available, searching for all entailing words is not necessary an advantage: consider the query 'What does Dole produce?' to a search engine. The verb 'fabricate' entails 'produce' in the correct sense of the word, but because of its own polysemy, and unless an expensive layer of WSD is added to the system, it will return sentences such as 'Dole fabricated stories about her opponent', which is clearly not the information that the user was looking for.

## 2 Previous Work

### 2.1 Distributional Similarity

#### 2.1.1 Principles

Systems using distributional similarity usually fall under two approaches:

1. The pattern-based approach (e.g. Ravichadran and Hovy, 2002). The most significant contexts for an input seed are extracted as features and those features used to discover words related to the input (under the assumption that words appearing in *at least one* significant context are similar to the seed word). There is also a non-distributional strand of this approach: it uses Hearst-like patterns (Hearst, 1992) which are supposed to indicate the presence of two terms in a certain relation - most often hyponymy or meronymy (see Chklovski and Pantel, 2004).

2. The feature vector approach (e.g. Lin and Pantel, 2001). This method fully embraces the definition of distributional similarity by making the assumption that two words appearing in similar *sets* of features must be related.

#### 2.1.2 Limitations

The problems of the distributional similarity assumption are well-known: the facts that 'a bank lends money' and 'Smith's brother lent him money' do not imply that banks and brothers are similar entities. This effect becomes particularly evident in cases where antonyms are returned by the system; in those cases, a very high distributional similarity actually corresponds to opposite meanings. Producing an output ranked according to distributional similarity scores (weeding out anything under a certain threshold) is therefore not sufficient to retain good precisions for many tasks. Some work has thus focused on a re-ranking strategies (see Geffet and Dagan, 2004 and Geffet and Dagan, 2005, who improve the output of a distributional similarity system for an entailment task using a web-based feature inclusion check, and comment that their filtering produces better outputs than cutting off the similarity pairs with the lowest ranking.)

### 2.2 Extraction Systems

Prominent entailment rule acquisition systems include DIRT (Lin and Pantel, 2001), which uses distributional similarity on a 1 GB corpus to identify semantically similar words and expressions, and TEASE (Szpektor *et al.*, 2004), which extracts entailment relations from the web for a given word by computing characteristic contexts for that word.

Recently, systems that combine both pattern-based and feature vector approaches have also been presented. Lin *et al.* (2003) and Pantel and Ravichandran (2004) have proposed to classify the output of systems based on feature vectors using lexico-syntactic patterns, respectively in order to remove antonyms from a related words list and to name clusters of related terms.

Even more related to our work, Mirkin *et al.* (2006) integrate both approaches by constructing features for the output of both a pattern-based and a vector-based systems, and by filtering incorrect entries with a supervised SVM classifier. (The pattern-based approach uses a set of manually-constructed patterns applied to a web search.)

In the same vein, Geffet and Dagan (2005) filter the result of a pattern-based system using feature vectors. They get their features out of an 18 million word corpus augmented by a web search. Their idea is that for any pair of potentially similar words, the features of the entailed one should comprise all the features of the entailing one.

The main difference between our work and the last two quoted papers is that we add a new layer of verification: we extract pairs of verbs using automatically derived semantic patterns, perform a first stage of filtering using the semantic signatures of each word and apply a final stage of filtering relying on surface substitutability, which we name 'immediate context overlap' method. We also experiment with a smaller size corpus to produce our distributional similarity baseline (a subset of Wikipedia) in an attempt to show that a good semantic parse and adequate filtering can provide reasonable performance even on domains where data is sparse. Our method does not need manually constructed patterns or supervised classifier training.

### 2.3 Evaluation

The evaluation of KB or ontology extraction systems is typically done by presenting human judges with a subset of extracted data and asking them to annotate it according to certain correctness criteria. For entailment systems, the annotation usually relies on two tests: whether the meaning of one word entails the other one in some senses of those words, and whether the judges can come up with contexts in which the words are directly substitutable. Szpektor *et al.* (2007) point out the difficulties in applying those criteria. They note the low inter-annotator agreements obtained in previous studies and propose a new evaluation method based on precise judgement questions applied to a set of relevant contexts. Using their methods, they evaluate the DIRT (Lin and Pantel, 2001) and TEASE (Szpektor *et al.*, 2004) algorithms and obtain upper bound precisions of 44% and 38% respectively on 646 entailment rules for 30 transitive verbs. We follow here their methodology to check the results obtained via the traditional annotation.

## 3 The Data

The corpus used for our distributional similarity baseline consists of a subset of Wikipedia totalling 500 MB in size, parsed first with RASP2 (Briscoe *et al.*, 2006) and then into a Robust Minimal Recursion Semantics form (RMRS, Copestake, 2004) using a RASP-to-RMRS converter. The RMRS representation consists of trees (or tree fragments when a complete parse is not possible) which comprise, for each phrase in the sentence, a semantic head and its arguments. For instance, in the sentence 'Lloyd's rescues failing bank', three subtrees can be extracted:

`lemma:rescue arg:ARG1 var:Lloyd's`

which indicates that 'Lloyd's' is subject of the head 'rescue',

`lemma:rescue arg:ARG2 var:bank`

which indicates that 'bank' is object of the head 'rescue', and

`lemma:failing arg:ARG1 var:bank`

which indicates that the argument of 'failing' is 'bank'.

Note that any tree can be transformed into a feature for a particular lexical item by replacing the slot containing the word with a hole: `lemma:rescue arg:ARG2 var:bank` becomes `lemma:hole_ arg:ARG2 var:bank`, a potentially characteristic context for 'rescue'.

All the experiments reported in this paper concern transitive verbs. In order to speed up processing, we reduced the RMRS corpus to a list of relations with a verbal head and at least two arguments: `lemma:verb-query arg:ARG1 var:subject arg:ARG2 var:object`. Note that we did not force noun phrases in the second argument of the relations and for instance, the verb 'say' was both considered as taking a noun or a clause as second argument ('to say a word', 'to say that the word is...').

## 4 A Baseline

We describe here our baseline, a system based on distributional similarity.

### 4.1 Step 1 - Pattern-Based Pair Extraction

The first step of our algorithm uses a pattern-based approach to get a list of potential entailing pairs. For each word $w$ presented to the system, we extract all semantic patterns containing $w$. Those semantic patterns are RMRS subtrees consisting of a semantic head and its children (see Section 3). We then calculate the Pointwise Mutual Information between each pattern $p$ and $w$:

$$pmi(p, w) = \log \left( \frac{P(p, w)}{P(p)\, P(w)} \right) \qquad (1)$$

where $P(p)$ and $P(w)$ are the probabilities of occurrence of the pattern and the instance respectively and $P(p, w)$ is the probability that they appear together.

PMI is known to have a bias towards less frequent events. In order to counterbalance that bias, we apply a simple logarithm function to the results as a discount:

$$d = \log (c_{wp} + 1) \qquad (2)$$

where $c_{wp}$ is the cooccurrence count of an instance and a pattern.

We multiply the original PMI value by this discount to find the final PMI. We then select the $n$ patterns with highest PMIs and use them as relevant semantic contexts to find all terms $t$ that also appear in those contexts. The result of this step is a list of potential entailment relations, $w - t_1$ ... $w - t_x$ (we do not know the direction of the entailment).

### 4.2 Step 2 - Feature vector Comparison

This step takes the output of the pattern-based extraction and applies a first filter to the potential entailment pairs. The filter relies on the idea that two words that are similar will have similar feature vectors (see Geffet and Dagan, 2005). We define here the feature vector of word $w$ as the list of semantic features containing $w$, together with the PMI of each feature in relation to $w$ as a weight. For each pair of words $(w1, w2)$ we extract the feature vectors of both $w1$ and $w2$ and calculate their similarity using the measure of Lin (1998). Pairs with a similarity under a certain threshold are weeded out. (We use 0.007 in our experiments – the value was found by comparing precisions for various thresholds in a set of initial experiments.)

As a check of how the Lin measure performed on our Wikipedia subset using RMRS features, we reproduced the Miller and Charles experiment (1991) which consists in asking humans to rate the similarity of 30 noun pairs. The experiment is a standard test for semantic similarity systems (see Jarmasz and Szpakowicz, 2003; Lin, 1998; Resnik, 1995 and Hirst and St Onge, 1998 amongst others). The correlations obtained by previous systems range between the high 0.6 and the high 0.8. Those systems rely on edge counting using manually-created resources such as WordNet and the Roget's Thesaurus. We are not actually aware of results obtained on totally automated systems (apart from a baseline computed by Strube and Ponzetto, 2006, using Google hits, which return a correlation of 0.26.)

Applying our feature vector step to the Miller and Charles pairs, we get a correlation of 0.38, way below the edge-counting systems. It turns out, however, that this low result is at least partially due to data sparsity: when ignoring the pairs containing at least one word with frequency under 200 (8 of them, which means ending up with 22 pairs left out of the initial 30), the correlation goes up to 0.69. This is in line with the edge-counting systems and shows that our baseline system produces a decent approximation of human performance, as long as enough data is supplied. [2]

Two issues remain, though. First, fine-grained results cannot be obtained over a general corpus: we note that the pairs 'coast-forest' and 'coast-hill' get very similar scores using distributional similarity while the latter is ranked twice as high as the former by humans. Secondly, distribu-

[2] It seems then that in order to maintain precision to a higher level on our corpus, we could simply disregard pairs with low-frequency words. (We decided here, however, that this would be unacceptable from the point of view of recall and did not attempt to do so.)

tional methods promise to identify 'semantically similar' words, as do the Miller and Charles experiment and edge-counting systems. However, as pointed out in the introduction, there is still a gap between general similarity and entailment: 'coast' and 'hill' are indeed similar in some way but never substitutable. Our baseline is therefore constrained by a theoretical problem that further modules must solve.

## 5 Immediate Context Overlap

Our immediate context overlap module acts as a filter for the system described as our baseline. The idea is that, out of all pairs of 'similar' words, we want to find those that express entailment in at least one direction. So for instance, given the pairs 'kill – murder' and 'kill – abduct', we would like to keep the former and filter the latter out. We can roughly explain why the second pair is not acceptable by saying that, although the semantics of the two words are close (they are both about an act of violence conducted against somebody), they are not substitutable in a given sentence.

To satisfy substitutability, we generally specify that if $w1$ entails $w2$, then there should be surface contexts where $w2$ can replace $w1$, with the substitution still producing an acceptable utterance (see our definition of *acceptability* in the introduction). We further suggest that if one word can substitute the other in frequent immediate contexts, we have the basis to believe that entailment is possible in at least one common sense of the words – while if substitution is impossible or rare, we can doubt the presence of an entailment relation, at least in common senses of the terms. This can be made clearer with an example. We show in Table 1 some of the most frequent trigrams to appear after the verbs 'to kill', 'to murder' and 'to abduct' (those trigrams were collected from the Google 5-gram corpus.) It is immediately noticeable that some contexts are not transferable from one term to the other: phrases such as 'to murder and forcibly recruit someone', or 'to abduct cancer cells' are impossible – or at least unconventional. We also show in italic some common immediate contexts between the three words. As pointed out in the introduction, when looking at the top 200 most frequent contexts for each term, we find that 'kill' and 'murder' share 54 while 'kill' and 'abduct' only share 2, giving us the indication that as far as usage is concerned, 'murder' is closer to 'kill' than 'abduct'. Furthermore, by looking at frequency of occurrence, we partly answer our need to find substitutions that work in very frequent sentences of the language.

The Google 5-gram corpus gives the frequency of each of its n-grams, allowing us to check substitutability on the 5-grams with highest occurrence counts for each potential entailment pair returned by our baseline. For each pair $(w1, w2)$ we select the $m$ most frequent contexts for both $w1$ and $w2$ and simply count the overlap between both lists. If there is any overlap, we keep the pair; if the overlap is 0, we weed it out (the low threshold helps our recall to remain acceptable). We experiment with left and right contexts, i.e. with the query term at the beginning and the end of the n-gram, and with various combinations (see Section 6).

## 6 Results

The results in this section are produced by randomly selecting 30 transitive verbs out of the 500 most frequent in our Wikipedia corpus and using our system to extract non-directional entailment pairs for those verbs, following a similar experiment by Szpektor *et al.* (2007). We use a list of $n = 30$ features in Step 1 of the baseline. We evaluate the results by first annotating them according to a broad definition of entailment: if the annotator can think of any context where one word of the pair could replace the other, preserving surface form and semantics, then the two words are in an entailment relation. (Note again that we do not consider the directionality of entailment at this stage.) We then re-evaluate our best score using the Szpektor *et al.* method (2007), which we think is more suited for checking true substitutability. [3]

The baseline described in Section 4 produces 301 unique pairs, 124 of which we judge correct using our broad entailment definition, yielding a precision of 41%. The average number of relations extracted for each input term is thus 4.1.

Tables 2 and 3 show our results at the end of the immediate context overlap step. Table 2 report results using the $m = 50$ most frequent contexts for each word in the pair while Table 3 uses an expanded list of 200 contexts. Precision is the

[3] Although no direct comparison with the works of Szpektor *et al.* or Lin and Pantel is provided in this paper, we are in the process of evaluating our results against the TEASE output (available at `http://www.cs.biu.ac.il/~szpekti/TEASE_collection.zip`) through a web-based annotation task.

Table 1: Immediate Contexts for 'kill', 'murder' and 'abduct'

| kill | murder | abduct |
|---|---|---|
| two birds with | babies that life | her and make |
| cancer cells and | *his wife and* | an innocent man |
| a mocking bird | thousands of innocent | unsuspecting people and |
| or die for | *women and children* | suspects in foreign |
| or be killed | her husband and | a young girl |
| *another human being* | *in the name* | and forcibly recruit |
| thousands of people | in connection with | a teenage girl |
| *in the name* | *another human being* | and kill her |
| *his wife and* | tens of thousands | a child from |
| members of the | the royal family | *women and children* |

number of correct relations amongst all those returned. Recall is calculated with regard to the 124 pairs judged correct at the end of the previous step (i.e., this is not true recall but recall relative to the baseline results.)

We experimented with six different set-ups:

**1- right context:** the four words following the query term are used as context

**2- left context:** the four words preceding the query term are used as context

**3- right and left contexts:** the best contexts (those with highest frequencies) are selected out of the concatenation of both right and left context lists

**4- concatenation:** the concatenation of the results obtained from 1 and 2

**5- inclusion:** the inclusion set of the results from 1 and 2, that is, the pairs judged correct by *both* the right context and left context methods.

**6- right context with 'to':** identical to 1 but the 5-gram is required to start with 'to'. This ensures that only the verb form of the query term is considered but has the disadvantage of effectively transforming 5-grams into 4-grams.

Our best overall results comes from using 50 immediate contexts starting with 'to', right context only: we obtain 56% precision on a recall of 85% calculated on the results of the previous step.

Table 2: Results using 50 immediate contexts

| Context Used | Precision | Recall | F | Returned | Correct |
|---|---|---|---|---|---|
| Left | 48% | 63% | 54% | 164 | 78 |
| Right | 62% | 26% | 36% | 52 | 32 |
| Left and Right | 53% | 52% | 52% | 122 | 65 |
| Concatenation | 48% | 70% | 57% | 181 | 87 |
| Inclusion | 67% | 19% | 30% | 36 | 24 |
| Right + 'to' | 56% | 85% | 68% | 187 | 105 |

Table 3: Results using 200 immediate contexts

| Context Used | Precision | Recall | F | Returned | Correct |
|---|---|---|---|---|---|
| Left | 44% | 86% | 58% | 244 | 107 |
| Right | 54% | 60% | 57% | 137 | 74 |
| Left and Right | 46% | 85% | 60% | 228 | 105 |
| Concatenation | 44% | 92% | 60% | 260 | 114 |
| Inclusion | 55% | 53% | 54% | 121 | 66 |
| Right + 'to' | 48% | 97% | 64% | 248 | 120 |

### 6.1 Instance-Based Evaluation

We then recalculate our best precision following the method introduced in Szpektor *et al.* (2007). This approach consists in extracting, for each potential entailment relation X-$verb_1$-Y $\Rightarrow$ X-$verb_2$-Y, 15 sentences in which $verb1$ appears and ask annotators to provide answers to three questions:

1. Is the left-hand side of the relation entailed by the sentence? If so...

2. When replacing $verb_1$ with $verb_2$, is the sentence still likely in English? If so...

3. Does the sentence with $verb_1$ entail the sentence with $verb_2$?

We show in Table 4 some potential annotations at various stages of the process.

For each pair, Szpektor *et al.* then calculate a lower-bound precision as

$$P_{lb} = \frac{n_{Entailed}}{n_{LeftHandEntailed}} \quad (3)$$

where $n_{Entailed}$ is the number of entailed sentence pairs (the annotator has answered 'yes' to the third question) and $n_{LeftHandEntailed}$ is the number of sentences where the left-hand relation is entailed (the annotator has answered 'yes' to the first question). They also calculate an upper-bound precision as

$$P_{ub} = \frac{n_{Entailed}}{n_{Acceptable}} \quad (4)$$

where $n_{Acceptable}$ is the number of acceptable $verb_2$ sentences (the annotator has answered 'yes' to the second question). A pair is deemed to contain an entailment relation if the precision for that particular pair is over 80%.

The authors comment that a large proportion of extracted sentences lead to a 'left-hand side not entailed' answer. In order to counteract that effect, we only extract sentences without modals or negation from our Wikipedia corpus and consequently only require 10 sentences per relation (only 11% of our sentences have a 'non-entailed' left-hand side relation against 43% for Szpektor *et al.*).

We obtain an upper bound precision of 52%, which is slightly lower than the one initially calculated using our broad definition of entailment, showing that the more stringent evaluation is useful when checking for general substitutability in the returned pairs. When we calculate the lower bound precision, however, we obtain a low 10% precision due to the large number of sentences judged as 'unlikely English sentences' after substitution (they amount to 33% of all examples with a left-hand side judged 'entailed'). This result illustrates the need for a module able to check sentence acceptability when applying the system to true substitution tasks. Fortunately, as we explain in the next section, it also takes into account requirements that are only necessary for generation tasks, and are therefore irrelevant to our querying task.

## 7 Discussion

Our main result is that the immediate context overlap step dramatically increases our precision (from 41% to 56%), showing that a more stringent notion of similarity can be achieved when adequately filtering the output of a distributional similarity system. However, it also turns out that looking at the most frequent contexts of the word to substitute does not fully solve the issue of surface *acceptability* (leading to a high number of 'right-hand side not entailed' annotations). We argue, though, that the issue of producing an acceptable English sentence is a generation problem separate from the extraction task. Some systems, in fact, are dedicated to related problems, such as identifying whether the senses of two synonyms are the same in a particular lexical context (see Dagan *et al.*, 2006). As far as our needs are concerned in the task of KB querying, we only require accurate searching capabilities as opposed to generational capabilities: the expansion of search terms to include impossible strings is not a problem in terms of result.

Looking at the immediate context overlaps returned for each pair by the system, we find that the overlap (the similarity) can be situated at various linguistic layers:

- in the semantics of the verb's object: 'a new album' is something that one would frequently 'record' or 'release'. The phrase boosts the similarity score between 'record' and 'release' in their music sense.
- in the clausal information of the right context: a context starting with a clause introduced by 'that' is likely to be preceded by a verb expressing cognition or discourse. The tri-gram 'that there is' increases the similarity of pairs such as 'say - argue'.
- in the prepositional information of the right context: 'about' is the preposition of choice after cognition verbs such as 'think' or 'wonder'. The context 'about the future' helps the score of the pair 'think - speculate' in the cognitive sense (note that 'speculate' in a financial sense would take the preposition 'on'.)

Some examples of overlaps are shown in Table 5.

We also note that the system returns a fair proportion of vacuous contexts such as 'one of the' or

Table 4: Annotation Examples Following the Szpektor *et al.* Method

| Word Pair | Sentence | Question 1 | Question 2 | Question 3 |
|---|---|---|---|---|
| acquire – buy | Lloyds acquires HBOS | yes | yes (Lloyds buys HBOS) | yes |
| acquire – praise | Lloyds acquires HBOS | yes | yes (Lloyds praises HBOS) | no |
| acquire – spend | Lloyds acquires HBOS | yes | no (*Lloyds spends HBOS) | – |
| acquire – buy | Lloyds may acquire HBOS | no | – | – |

Table 5: Sample of Immediate Context Overlaps

| think – speculate | say – claim | describe – characterise |
|---|---|---|
| about the future | that it is | the nature of |
| about what the | that there is | the effects of |
| about how the | that it was | it as a |
| | that they were | the effect of |
| | that they have | the role of |
| | that it has | the quality of |
| | | the impact of |
| | | the dynamics of |

Table 6: Sample of Extracted Pairs

| | |
|---|---|
| bring – attract | make - earn |
| *call – form | *name - delegate |
| change – alter | offer - provide |
| create – generate | *perform - discharge |
| describe – characterise | produce – release |
| develop – generate | record – count |
| *do – behave | *release – announce |
| feature – boast | *remain – comprise |
| *find – indicate | require – demand |
| follow – adopt | say – claim |
| *grow – contract | tell – assure |
| *increase - decline | think – believe |
| leave - abandon | *use – abandon |

'part of the' which contribute to the score of many pairs. Our precision would probably benefit from excluding such contexts.

We note that as expected, using a larger set of contexts leads to better recall and decreased precision. The best precision is obtained by returning the inclusion set of both left and right contexts results, but at a high cost in recall. Interestingly, we find that the right context of the verb is far more telling than the left one (potentially, objects are more important than subjects). This is in line with results reported by Alfonseca and Manandhar (2002).

Our best results yield an average of 3.4 relations for each input term. It is in the range reported by the authors of the TEASE system (Szpektor *et al.*, 2004) but well below the extrapolated figures of over 20 relations in Szpektor *et al.*, 2007. We point out, however, that we only search for single word substitutions, as opposed to single and multi-word substitutions for Szpektor *et al.*. Furthermore, our experiments are performed on 500 MB of text only, against 1 GB of news data for the DIRT system and the web for the TEASE algorithm. More data may help our recall, as well as bootstrapping over our best precision system.

We show a sample of our results in Table 6. The pairs with an asterisk were considered incorrect at human evaluation stage.

## 8 Conclusion

We have presented here a system for the extraction of word substitutions in the context of KB querying. We have shown that the output of a distributional similarity baseline can be improved by filtering it using the idea that two words in an entailment relation are substitutable in immediate surface contexts. We obtained a precision of 56% (52% using our most stringent evaluation) on a test set of 30 transitive verbs, and a yield of 3.4 relations per verb.

We also point out that relatively good precisions can be obtained on a parsed medium-sized corpus of 500 MB, although recall is certainly affected.

We note that our current implementation does not always satisfy the requirement for substitutability for generation tasks and point out that the system is therefore limited to our intended use, which involves search capabilities only.

We would like to concentrate in the future on providing a direction for the entailment pairs extracted by the system. We also hope that recall could possibly improve using a larger set of features in the pattern-based step (this is suggested also by Szpektor *et al.*, 2004), together with appropriate bootstrapping.

## Acknowledgements

This work was supported by the UK Engineering and Physical Sciences Research Council (EPSRC: EP/P502365/1). I would also like to thank my supervisor, Dr Ann Copestake, for her support throughout this project, as well as the anonymous reviewers who commented on this paper.

## References

Enrique Alfonseca and Suresh Manandhar. 2002. *Extending a Lexical Ontology by a Combination of Distributional Semantics Signatures.* In Proceedings of EKAW 2002, pp. 1–7, 2002.

Thorsten Brants and Alex Franz. 2006. *Web 1T 5-gram Version 1.* Linguistic Data Consortium, Philadelphia, 2006.

Edward Briscoe, John Carroll and Rebecca Watson. 2006. *The Second Release of the RASP System.* In Proceedings of the COLING/ACL 2006 Interactive Presentation Sessions, Sydney, Australia, 2006.

Timothy Chklovski and Patrick Pantel. 2004. *VerbOcean: Mining The Web for Fine-Grained Semantic Verb Relations.* Proceedings of EMNLP-04, Barcelona, Spain, 2004.

Ann Copestake. 2004. Robust Minimal Recursion Semantics. `www.cl.cam.ac.uk/~aac10/papers/rmrsdraft.pdf`.

Ido Dagan and Oren Glickman. 2004. *Probabilistic Textual Entailment: Generic Applied Modelling of Language Variability.* Proceedings of The PASCAL Workshop on Learning Methods for Text Understanding and Mining, Grenoble, France, 2004.

Ido Dagan, Oren Glickman, Alfio Gliozzo, Efrat Marmorshtein and Carlo Strapparava. 2006. *Direct Word Sense Matching for Lexical Substitution.* Proceedings of COLING-ACL 2006, 17-21 Jul 2006, Sydney, Australia.

Maayan Geffet and Ido Dagan. 2004. *Feature Vector Quality and Distributional Similarity.* Proceedings Of the 20th International Conference on Computational Linguistics, 2004.

Maayan Geffet and Ido Dagan. 2005. *The Distributional Inclusion Hypothesises and Lexical Entailment.* In Proceedings Of the 43rd Annual Meeting of the Association for Computational Linguistics, pp. 107–114, 2005.

Mario Jarmasz and Stan Szpakowicz. 2003. *Roget's Thesaurus and Semantic Similarity.* In Proceedings of International Conference RANLP–03, pp. 212–219, 2003.

Zelig Harris. *Distributional Structure.* In Word, 10, No. 2–3, pp. 146–162, 1954.

Marti Hearst. 1992. *Automatic Acquisition of Hyponyms from Large Text Corpora.* Proceedings of COLING-92, pp.539–545, 1992.

Graeme Hirst and David St-Onge. 1998. *Lexical Chains As Representations of Context for the Detection and Correction of Malapropisms.* In 'WordNet', Ed. Christiane Fellbaum, Cambridge, MA: The MIT Press, 1998.

Dekang Lin. 2003. *An Information-Theoretic Definition of Similarity.* In Proceedings of the 15th International Conference on Machine Learning, pp. 296–304, 1998.

Dekang Lin, Shaojun Zhao, Lijuan Qin and Ming Zhou. 2003. *Identifying Synonyms among Distributionally Similar Words.* In Proceedings of IJCAI-03, Acapulco, Mexico, 2003.

Dekang Lin and Patrick Pantel. 2001. *DIRT – Discovery of Inference Rules from Text.* In Proceedings of ACM 2001, 2001.

George Miller and Walter Charles. 2001. *Contextual Correlates of Semantic Similarity.* In Language and Cognitive Processes, 6(1), pp. 1–28, 1991.

Shachar Mirkin, Ido Dagan and Maayan Geffet. 2004. *Integrating Pattern-Based and Distributional Similarity Methods for Lexical Entailment Acquisition.* In Proceedings of COLING/ACL, Sydney, Australia, pp.579–586, 2006.

Patrick Pantel and Deepak Ravichandran. 2004. *Automatically Labelling Semantic Classes.* In Proceedings of HLT/NAACL04, Boston, MA, pp 321328, 2004.

Deepak Ravichandran and Eduard Hovy. 2002. *Learning Surface Text Patterns for a Question Answering System.* Proceedings of ACL, 2002.

Philip Resnik. 1995. *Using Information Content to Evaluate Semantic Similarity in a Taxonomy.* In Proceedings of IJCAI–95, 1995.

Idan Szpektor, Hristo Tanev, Ido Dagan and Bonaventura Coppola. 2004. *Scaling Web-Based Acquisition of Entailment Relations.* In Proceedings of EMNLP–2004, pp. 41–48, 2004.

Idan Szpektor, Eyal Shnarch and Ido Dagan. 2007. *Instance-Based Evaluation of Entailment Rule Acquisition.* In Proceedings of ACL–07, 2007.

Michael Strube and Simone Ponzetto. 2006. *WikiRelate! Computing Semantic Relatedness Using Wikipedia.* In Proceedings of AAAI–06, pp. 1219–1224, 2006.

# Structural Correspondence Learning for Parse Disambiguation

**Barbara Plank**
Alfa-informatica
University of Groningen, The Netherlands
b.plank@rug.nl

## Abstract

The paper presents an application of Structural Correspondence Learning (SCL) (Blitzer et al., 2006) for domain adaptation of a stochastic attribute-value grammar (SAVG). So far, SCL has been applied successfully in NLP for Part-of-Speech tagging and Sentiment Analysis (Blitzer et al., 2006; Blitzer et al., 2007). An attempt was made in the CoNLL 2007 shared task to apply SCL to non-projective dependency parsing (Shimizu and Nakagawa, 2007), however, without any clear conclusions. We report on our exploration of applying SCL to adapt a syntactic disambiguation model and show promising initial results on Wikipedia domains.

## 1 Introduction

Many current, effective natural language processing systems are based on supervised Machine Learning techniques. The parameters of such systems are estimated to best reflect the characteristics of the training data, at the cost of portability: a system will be successful only as long as the training material resembles the input that the model gets. Therefore, whenever we have access to a large amount of labeled data from some "source" (out-of-domain), but we would like a model that performs well on some new "target" domain (Gildea, 2001; Daumé III, 2007), we face the problem of *domain adaptation*.

The need for domain adaptation arises in many NLP tasks: Part-of-Speech tagging, Sentiment Analysis, Semantic Role Labeling or Statistical Parsing, to name but a few. For example, the performance of a statistical parsing system drops in an appalling way when a model trained on the Wall Street Journal is applied to the more varied Brown corpus (Gildea, 2001).

The problem itself has started to get attention only recently (Roark and Bacchiani, 2003; Hara et al., 2005; Daumé III and Marcu, 2006; Daumé III, 2007; Blitzer et al., 2006; McClosky et al., 2006; Dredze et al., 2007). We distinguish two main approaches to domain adaptation that have been addressed in the literature (Daumé III, 2007): *supervised* and *semi-supervised*.

In *supervised domain adaptation* (Gildea, 2001; Roark and Bacchiani, 2003; Hara et al., 2005; Daumé III, 2007), besides the labeled source data, we have access to a comparably small, but labeled amount of target data. In contrast, *semi-supervised domain adaptation* (Blitzer et al., 2006; McClosky et al., 2006; Dredze et al., 2007) is the scenario in which, in addition to the labeled source data, we only have *unlabeled* and no labeled target domain data. Semi-supervised adaptation is a much more realistic situation, while at the same time also considerably more difficult.

Studies on the supervised task have shown that straightforward baselines (e.g. models based on source only, target only, or the union of the data) achieve a relatively high performance level and are "surprisingly difficult to beat" (Daumé III, 2007). Thus, one conclusion from that line of work is that as soon as there is a reasonable (often even small) amount of labeled target data, it is often more fruitful to either just use that, or to apply simple adaptation techniques (Daumé III, 2007; Plank and van Noord, 2008).

## 2 Motivation and Prior Work

While several authors have looked at the supervised adaptation case, there are less (and especially less successful) studies on semi-supervised domain adaptation (McClosky et al., 2006; Blitzer et al., 2006; Dredze et al., 2007). Of these, McClosky et al. (2006) deal specifically with self-training for data-driven statistical parsing. They show that together with a re-ranker, improvements

*Proceedings of the EACL 2009 Student Research Workshop*, pages 37–45,
Athens, Greece, 2 April 2009. 

are obtained. Similarly, Structural Correspondence Learning (Blitzer et al., 2006; Blitzer et al., 2007; Blitzer, 2008) has proven to be successful for the two tasks examined, PoS tagging and Sentiment Classification. In contrast, Dredze et al. (2007) report on "frustrating" results on the CoNLL 2007 semi-supervised adaptation task for dependency parsing, i.e. "no team was able to improve target domain performance substantially over a state of the art baseline". In the same shared task, an attempt was made to apply SCL to domain adaptation for data-driven dependency parsing (Shimizu and Nakagawa, 2007). The system just ended up at rank 7 out of 8 teams. However, based on annotation differences in the datasets (Dredze et al., 2007) and a bug in their system (Shimizu and Nakagawa, 2007), their results are inconclusive.[1] Thus, the effectiveness of SCL is rather unexplored for parsing.

So far, most previous work on domain adaptation for parsing has focused on *data-driven* systems (Gildea, 2001; Roark and Bacchiani, 2003; McClosky et al., 2006; Shimizu and Nakagawa, 2007), i.e. systems employing (constituent or dependency based) *treebank grammars* (Charniak, 1996). Parse selection constitutes an important part of many parsing systems (Johnson et al., 1999; Hara et al., 2005; van Noord and Malouf, 2005; McClosky et al., 2006). Yet, the adaptation of parse selection models to novel domains is a far less studied area. This may be motivated by the fact that potential gains for this task are inherently bounded by the underlying grammar. The few studies on adapting disambiguation models (Hara et al., 2005; Plank and van Noord, 2008) have focused exclusively on the supervised scenario.

Therefore, the direction we explore in this study is semi-supervised domain adaptation for parse disambiguation. We examine the effectiveness of *Structural Correspondence Learning* (SCL) (Blitzer et al., 2006) for this task, a recently proposed adaptation technique shown to be effective for PoS tagging and Sentiment Analysis. The system used in this study is Alpino, a wide-coverage Stochastic Attribute Value Grammar (SAVG) for Dutch (van Noord and Malouf, 2005; van Noord, 2006). For our empirical evaluation we explore Wikipedia as primary test and training collection.

In the sequel, we first introduce the parsing system. Section 4 reviews Structural Correspondence Learning and shows our application of SCL to parse selection, including all our design choices. In Section 5 we present the datasets, introduce the process of constructing target domain data from Wikipedia, and discuss interesting initial empirical results of this ongoing study.

## 3 Background: Alpino parser

Alpino (van Noord and Malouf, 2005; van Noord, 2006) is a robust computational analyzer for Dutch that implements the conceptual two-stage parsing approach. The system consists of approximately 800 grammar rules in the tradition of HPSG, and a large hand-crafted lexicon, that together with a left-corner parser constitutes the generation component. For parse selection, Alpino employs a discriminative approach based on Maximum Entropy (MaxEnt). The output of the parser is dependency structure based on the guidelines of CGN (Oostdijk, 2000).

The Maximum Entropy model (Berger et al., 1996; Ratnaparkhi, 1997; Abney, 1997) is a conditional model that assigns a probability to every possible parse $\omega$ for a given sentence $s$. The model consists of a set of $m$ feature functions $f_j(\omega)$ that describe properties of parses, together with their associated weights $\theta_j$. The denominator is a normalization term where $Y(s)$ is the set of parses with yield $s$:

$$p_\theta(\omega|s;\theta) = \frac{\exp(\sum_{j=1}^{m} \theta_j f_j(\omega))}{\sum_{y \in Y(s)} \exp(\sum_{j=1}^{m} \theta_j f_j(y)))} \quad (1)$$

The parameters (weights) $\theta_j$ can be estimated efficiently by maximizing the regularized conditional likelihood of a training corpus (Johnson et al., 1999; van Noord and Malouf, 2005):

$$\hat{\theta} = \arg\max_{\theta} \log L(\theta) - \frac{\sum_{j=1}^{m} \theta_j^2}{2\sigma^2} \quad (2)$$

where $L(\theta)$ is the likelihood of the training data. The second term is a regularization term (Gaussian prior on the feature weights with mean zero and variance $\sigma$). The estimated weights determine the contribution of each feature. Features appearing in correct parses are given increasing (positive) weight, while features in incorrect parses are

[1] As shown in Dredze et al. (2007), the biggest problem for the shared task was that the provided datasets were annotated with different annotation guidelines, thus the general conclusion was that the task was ill-defined (Nobuyuki Shimizu, personal communication).

given decreasing (negative) weight. Once a model is trained, it can be applied to choose the parse with the highest sum of feature weights.

The MaxEnt model consists of a large set of features, corresponding to instantiations of feature templates that model various properties of parses. For instance, Part-of-Speech tags, dependency relations, grammar rule applications, etc. The current standard model uses about 11,000 features. We will refer to this set of features as original features. They are used to train the baseline model on the given labeled source data.

## 4 Structural Correspondence Learning

SCL (Structural Correspondence Learning) (Blitzer et al., 2006; Blitzer et al., 2007; Blitzer, 2008) is a recently proposed domain adaptation technique which uses unlabeled data from *both* source and target domain to learn correspondences between features from different domains.

Before describing the algorithm in detail, let us illustrate the intuition behind SCL with an example, borrowed from Blitzer et al. (2007). Suppose we have a Sentiment Analysis system trained on book reviews (domain A), and we would like to adapt it to kitchen appliances (domain B). Features such as "boring" and "repetitive" are common ways to express negative sentiment in A, while "not working" or "defective" are specific to B. If there are features across the domains, e.g. "don't buy", with which the domain specific features are highly correlated with, then we might tentatively align those features.

Therefore, the key idea of SCL is to identify automatically correspondences among features from different domains by modeling their correlations with *pivot features*. Pivots are features occurring frequently and behaving similarly in both domains (Blitzer et al., 2006). They are inspired by auxiliary problems from Ando and Zhang (2005). Non-pivot features that correspond with many of the same pivot-features are assumed to correspond. Intuitively, if we are able to find good correspondences among features, then the augmented labeled source domain data should transfer better to a target domain (where no labeled data is available) (Blitzer et al., 2006).

The outline of the algorithm is given in Figure 1. The first step is to identify $m$ pivot features occurring frequently in the unlabeled data of both domains. Then, a binary classifier is trained for each pivot feature (pivot predictor) of the form: "Does pivot feature $l$ occur in this instance?". The pivots are masked in the unlabeled data and the aim is to predict them using non-pivot features. In this way, we obtain a weight vector $w$ for each pivot predictor. Positive entries in the weight vector indicate that a non-pivot is highly correlated with the respective pivot feature. Step 3 is to arrange the $m$ weight vectors in a matrix $W$, where a column corresponds to a pivot predictor weight vector. Applying the projection $W^T x$ (where $x$ is a training instance) would give us $m$ new features, however, for "both computational and statistical reasons" (Blitzer et al., 2006; Ando and Zhang, 2005) a low-dimensional approximation of the original feature space is computed by applying Singular Value Decomposition (SVD) on $W$ (step 4). Let $\theta = U^T_{h \times n}$ be the top $h$ left singular vectors of $W$ (with $h$ a dimension parameter and $n$ the number of non-pivot features). The resulting $\theta$ is a projection onto a lower dimensional space $\mathbb{R}^h$, parameterized by $h$.

The final step of SCL is to train a linear predictor on the augmented labeled source data $\langle x, \theta x \rangle$. In more detail, the original feature space $x$ is augmented with $h$ new features obtained by applying the projection $\theta x$. In this way, we can learn weights for domain-specific features, which otherwise would not have been observed. If $\theta$ contains meaningful correspondences, then the pre-

*Input:* - labeled source data $\{(x_s, y_s)_{s=1}^{N_s}\}$
- unlabeled data from both source and target domain $x_{ul} = x_s, x_t$

1. Select $m$ pivot features
2. Train $m$ binary classifiers (pivot predictors)
3. Create matrix $W_{n \times m}$ of binary predictor weight vectors $W = [w_1, .., w_m]$, where $n$ is the number of nonpivot features in $x_{ul}$
4. Apply SVD to $W$: $W_{n \times m} = U_{n \times n} D_{n \times m} V^T_{m \times m}$ where $\theta = U^T_{[1:h,:]}$ are the $h$ top left singular vectors of $W$.
5. Apply projection $x_s \theta$ and train a predictor on the original and new features obtained through the projection.

Figure 1: SCL algorithm (Blitzer et al., 2006).

dictor trained on the augmented data should transfer well to the new domain.

### 4.1 SCL for Parse Disambiguation

A property of the pivot predictors is that they can be trained from unlabeled data, as they represent properties of the input. So far, pivot features on the *word level* were used (Blitzer et al., 2006; Blitzer et al., 2007; Blitzer, 2008), e.g. "Does the bigram *not buy* occur in this document?" (Blitzer, 2008).

Pivot features are the key ingredient for SCL, and they should align well with the NLP task. For PoS tagging and Sentiment Analysis, features on the word level are intuitively well-related to the problem at hand. For the task of parse disambiguation based on a conditional model this is not the case.

Hence, we actually introduce an additional and new layer of abstraction, which, we hypothesize, aligns well with the task of parse disambiguation: we first *parse* the unlabeled data. In this way we obtain full parses for given sentences as produced by the grammar, allowing access to more abstract representations of the underlying pivot predictor training data (for reasons of efficiency, we here use only the first generated parse as training data for the pivot predictors, rather than n-best).

Thus, instead of using word-level features, our features correspond to properties of the generated parses: application of grammar rules (*r1,r2* features), dependency relations (*dep*), PoS tags (*f1,f2*), syntactic features (*s1*), precedence (*mf*), bilexical preferences (*z*), apposition (*appos*) and further features for unknown words, temporal phrases, coordination (*h,in_year* and *p1*, respectively). This allows us to get a possibly noisy, but more abstract representation of the underlying data. The set of features used in Alpino is further described in van Noord and Malouf (2005).

**Selection of pivot features** As pivot features should be common across domains, here we restrict our pivots to be of the type *r1,p1,s1* (the most frequently occurring feature types). In more detail, *r1* indicates which grammar rule applied, *p1* whether coordination conjuncts are parallel, and *s1* whether topicalization or long-distance dependencies occurred. We count how often each feature appears in the parsed source and target domain data, and select those *r1,p1,s1* features as *pivot features*, whose count is $> t$, where $t$ is a specified threshold. In all our experiments, we set $t = 5000$. In this way we obtained on average 360 pivot features, on the datasets described in Section 5.

**Predictive features** As pointed out by Blitzer et al. (2006), each instance will actually contain features which are totally predictive of the pivot features (i.e. the pivot itself). In our case, we additionally have to pay attention to 'more specific' features, e.g. *r2* is a feature that extends *r1*, in the sense that it incorporates more information than its parent (i.e. which grammar rules applied in the construction of daughter nodes). It is crucial to remove these predictive features when creating the training data for the pivot predictors.

**Matrix and SVD** Following Blitzer et al. (2006) (which follow Ando and Zhang (2005)), we only use positive entries in the pivot predictors weight vectors to compute the SVD. Thus, when constructing the matrix $W$, we disregard all negative entries in $W$ and compute the SVD ($W = UDV^T$) on the resulting non-negative sparse matrix. This sparse representation saves both time and space.

### 4.2 Further practical issues of SCL

In practice, there are more free parameters and model choices (Ando and Zhang, 2005; Ando, 2006; Blitzer et al., 2006; Blitzer, 2008) besides the ones discussed above.

*Feature normalization and feature scaling.* Blitzer et al. (2006) found it necessary to normalize and scale the new features obtained by the projection $\theta$, in order to "allow them to receive more weight from a regularized discriminative learner". For each of the features, they centered them by subtracting out the mean and normalized them to unit variance (i.e. $x - mean/sd$). They then rescaled the features by a factor $\alpha$ found on held-out data: $\alpha\theta x$.

*Restricted Regularization.* When training the supervised model on the augmented feature space $\langle x, \theta x \rangle$, Blitzer et al. (2006) only regularize the weight vector of the original features, but not the one for the new low-dimensional features. This was done to encourage the model to use the new low-dimensional representation rather than the higher-dimensional original representation (Blitzer, 2008).

*Dimensionality reduction by feature type.* An extension suggested in Ando and Zhang (2005) is to compute separate SVDs for blocks of the matrix $W$ corresponding to feature types (as illustrated in Figure 2), and then to apply separate projection for every type. Due to the positive results in Ando (2006), Blitzer et al. (2006) include this in their standard setting of SCL and report results using block SVDs only.

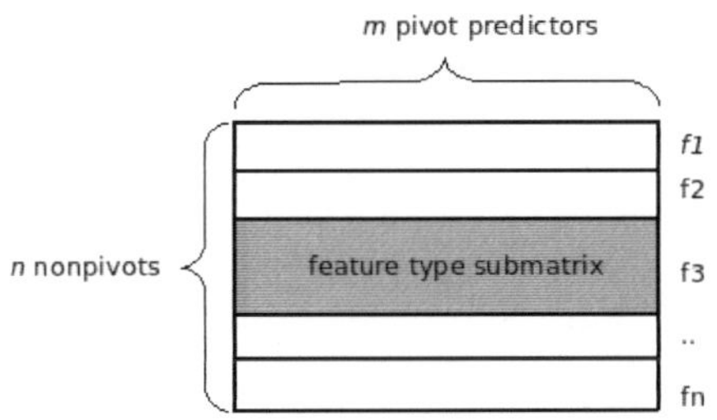


Figure 2: Illustration of dimensionality reduction by feature type (Ando and Zhang, 2005). The grey area corresponds to a feature type (submatrix of $W$) on which the SVD is computed (block SVD); the white area is regarded as fixed to zero matrices.

## 5 Experiments and Results

### 5.1 Experimental design

The base (source domain) disambiguation model is trained on the Alpino Treebank (van Noord, 2006) (newspaper text), which consists of approximately 7,000 sentences and 145,000 tokens. For parameter estimation of the disambiguation model, in all reported experiments we use the TADM[2] toolkit (toolkit for advanced discriminative training), with a Gaussian prior ($\sigma^2$=1000) and the (default) limited memory variable metric estimation technique (Malouf, 2002).

For training the binary pivot predictors, we use the MegaM[3] Optimization Package with the so-called "bernoulli implicit" input format. To compute the SVD, we use SVDLIBC.[4]

The output of the parser is dependency structure. A standard evaluation metric is to measure the amount of generated dependencies that are identical to the stored dependencies (correct labeled dependencies), expressed as f-score. An alternative measure is concept accuracy (CA), which is similar to f-score, but allows possible discrepancy between the number of returned dependencies (van Noord, 2006; Plank and van Noord, 2008). CA is usually slightly lower than f-score. Let $D_p^i$ be the number of dependencies produced by the parser for sentence $i$. $D_g^i$ is the number of dependencies in the treebank parse, and $D_o^i$ is the number of correct dependencies produced by the parser. Then,

$$\text{CA} = \frac{D_o}{\sum_i \max(D_g^i, D_p^i)}$$

If we want to compare the performance of disambiguation models, we can employ the $\phi$ measure (van Noord and Malouf, 2005; van Noord, 2007). Intuitively, it tells us how much of the disambiguation problem has been solved.

$$\phi = \frac{CA - base}{oracle - base} \times 100$$

In more detail, the $\phi$ measure incorporates an upper and lower bound: *base* measures the accuracy of a model that simply selects the first parse for each sentence; *oracle* represents the accuracy achieved by a model that always selects the best parse from the set of potential parses (within the coverage of the parser). In addition, we also report *relative error reduction* (rel.er), which is the relative difference in $\phi$ scores for two models.

As target domain, we consider the Dutch part of Wikipedia as data collection, described in the following.

### 5.2 Wikipedia as resource

In our experiments, we exploit Wikipedia both as testset and as unlabeled data source. We assume that in order to parse data from a very specific domain, say about the artist Prince, then data related to that domain, like information about the New Power Generation, the Purple rain movie, or other American singers and artists, should be of help. Thus, we exploit Wikipedia and its category system to gather domain-specific target data.

**Construction of target domain data** In more detail, we use the Dutch part of Wikipedia provided by WikiXML,[5] a collection of Wikipedia articles converted to XML format. As the corpus is encoded in XML, we can exploit general purpose XML Query Languages, such as XQuery, Xslt and XPath, to extract relevant information from the Wikipedia corpus.

Given a wikipage $p$, with $c \in categories(p)$, we can identify pages related to $p$ of various

[2] http://tadm.sourceforge.net/
[3] http://www.cs.utah.edu/~hal/megam/
[4] http://tedlab.mit.edu/~dr/svdlibc/
[5] http://ilps.science.uva.nl/WikiXML/

types of 'relatedness': directly related pages (those that share a category, i.e. all $p'$ where $\exists c' \in categories(p')$ such that $c = c'$), or alternatively, pages that share a sub- or supercategory of $p$, i.e. $p'$ where $c' \in categories(p')$ and $c' \in sub\_categories(p)$ or $c' \in super\_categories(p)$. For example, Figure 3 shows the categories extracted for the Wikipedia article about pope Johannes Paulus II.

```
<wikipage id="6677">
 <cat t="direct" n="Categorie:Paus"/>
 <cat t="direct" n="Categorie:Pools_theoloog"/>
 <cat t="super" n="Categorie:Religieus leider"/>
 <cat t="super" n="Categorie:Rooms-katholiek persoon"/>
 <cat t="super" n="Categorie:Vaticaanstad"/>
 <cat t="super" n="Categorie:Bisschop"/>
 <cat t="super" n="Categorie:Kerkgeschiedenis"/>
 <cat t="sub" n="Categorie:Tegenpaus"/>
 <cat t="super" n="Categorie:Pools persoon"/>
</wikipage>
```

Figure 3: Example of extracted Wikipedia categories for a given article (direct, sup- and subcats).

To create the set of related pages for a given article $p$, we proceed as follows:

1. Find sub- and supercategories of $p$
2. Extract all pages that are related to $p$ (through sharing a direct, sub or super category)
3. Optionally, filter out certain pages

In our empirical setup, we followed Blitzer et al. (2006) and tried to balance the size of source and target data. Thus, depending on the size of the resulting target domain dataset, and the "broadness" of the categories involved in creating it, we might wish to filter out certain pages. We implemented a filter mechanism that excludes pages of a certain category (e.g. a supercategory that is hypothesized to be "too broad"). Alternatively, we might have used a filter mechanism that excludes certain pages directly.

In our experiments, we always included pages that are directly related to a page of interest, and those that shared a subcategory. Of course, the page itself is not included in that dataset. With regard to supercategories, we usually included all pages having a category $c \in super\_categories(p)$, unless stated otherwise.

**Test collection** Our testset consists of a selection of Wikipedia articles that have been manually corrected in the course of the D-Coi/LASSY project.[6]

[6]Ongoing project, see `http://www.let.rug.nl/~vannoord/Lassy/`

An overview of the testset including size indications is given in Table 1. Table 2 provides information on the target domain datasets constructed from Wikipedia.

| Wiki/DCOI ID | Title | Sents |
|---|---|---|
| 6677/026563 | Prince (musician) | 358 |
| 6729/036834 | Paus Johannes Paulus II | 232 |
| 182654/041235 | Augustus De Morgan | 259 |

Table 1: Size of test datasets.

| Related to | Articles | Sents | Tokens | Relationship |
|---|---|---|---|---|
| Prince | 290 | 9,772 | 145,504 | filtered super |
| Paus | 445 | 8,832 | 134,451 | all |
| De Morgan | 394 | 8,466 | 132,948 | all |

Table 2: Size of related unlabeled data; relationship indicates whether all related pages are used or some are filtered out (see section 5.2).

### 5.3 Empirical Results

For all reported results, we randomly select $n = 200$ maximum number of parses per sentence for evaluation.

**Baseline accuracies** Table 3 shows the baseline performance (of the standard Alpino model) on the various Wikipedia testsets (CA, f-score). The third and fourth column indicate the upper- and lower bound measures (defined in section 5.1).

| Title | CA | f-score | base | oracle |
|---|---|---|---|---|
| Prince (musician) | 85.03 | 85.38 | 71.95 | 88.70 |
| Paus Johannes Paulus II | 85.72 | 86.32 | 74.30 | 89.09 |
| Augustus De Morgan | 80.09 | 80.61 | 70.08 | 83.52 |

Table 3: Baseline results.

While the parser normally operates on an accuracy level of roughly 88-89% (van Noord, 2007) on its own domain (newspaper text), the accuracy on these subdomains drops to around 85%. The biggest performance decrease (to 80%) was on the article about the British logician and mathematician De Morgan. This confirms the intuition that this specific subdomain is the "hardest", given that mathematical expressions might emerge in the data (e.g. "Wet der distributiviteit : a(b+c) = ab+ac" - distributivity law).

**SCL results** Table 4 shows the results of our instantiation of SCL for parse disambiguation, with varying $h$ parameter (dimensionality parameter;

$h = 25$ means that applying the projection $x\theta$ resulted in adding 25 new features to every source domain instance).

| | CA | f-score | $\phi$ | rel.er. |
|---|---|---|---|---|
| baseline Prince | 85.03 | 85.38 | 78.06 | 0.00 |
| SCL[+/-], $h = 25$ | 85.12 | 85.46 | 78.64 | 2.64 |
| SCL[+/-], $h = 50$ | 85.29 | 85.63 | 79.66 | 7.29 |
| SCL[+/-], $h = 100$ | 85.19 | 85.53 | 79.04 | 4.47 |
| SCL[+/-], $h = 200$ | 85.21 | 85.54 | 79.18 | 5.10 |
| baseline Paus | 85.72 | 86.32 | 77.23 | 0.00 |
| SCL[+/-], $h = 25$ | 85.87 | 86.48 | 78.26 | 4.52 |
| SCL[+/-], $h = 50$ | 85.82 | 86.43 | 77.87 | 2.81 |
| SCL[+/-], $h = 100$ | 85.87 | 86.49 | 78.26 | 4.52 |
| SCL[+/-], $h = 200$ | 85.87 | 86.48 | 78.26 | 4.52 |
| baseline DeMorgan | 80.09 | 80.61 | 74.44 | 0.00 |
| SCL[+/-], $h = 25$ | 80.15 | 80.67 | 74.92 | 1.88 |
| SCL[+/-], $h = 50$ | 80.12 | 80.64 | 74.68 | 0.94 |
| SCL[+/-], $h = 100$ | 80.12 | 80.64 | 74.68 | 0.94 |
| SCL[+/-], $h = 200$ | 80.15 | 80.67 | 74.91 | 1.88 |

Table 4: Results of our instantiation of SCL (with varying $h$ parameter and no feature normalization).

The results show a (sometimes) small but consistent increase in absolute performance on all testsets over the baseline system (up to $+0.26$ absolute CA score), as well as an increase in $\phi$ measure (absolute error reduction). This corresponds to a relative error reduction of up to 7.29%. Thus, our first instantiation of SCL for parse disambiguation indeed shows promising results.

We can confirm that changing the dimensionality parameter $h$ has rather little effect (Table 4), which is in line with previous findings (Ando and Zhang, 2005; Blitzer et al., 2006). Thus we might fix the parameter and prefer smaller dimensionalities, which saves space and time.

Note that these results were obtained *without* any of the additional normalization, rescaling, feature-specific regularization, or block SVD issues, etc. (discussed in section 4.2). We used the same Gaussian regularization term ($\sigma^2$=1000) for all features (original and new features), and did not perform any feature normalization or rescaling. This means our current instantiation of SCL is an actually *simplified* version of the original SCL algorithm, applied to parse disambiguation. Of course, our results are preliminary and, rather than warranting many definite conclusions, encourage further exploration of SCL and related semi-supervised adaptation techniques.

### 5.4 Additional Empirical Results

In the following, we describe additional results obtained by extensions and/or refinements of our current SCL instantiation.

**Feature normalization.** We also tested feature normalization (as described in Section 4.2). While Blitzer et al. (2006) found it necessary to normalize (and scale) the projection features, we did not observe any improvement by normalizing them (actually, it slightly degraded performance in our case). Thus, we found this step unnecessary, and currently did not look at this issue any further.

**A look at $\theta$** To gain some insight of which kind of correspondences SCL learned in our case, we started to examine the rows of $\theta$. Recall that applying a row of the projection matrix $\theta_i$ to a training instance $x$ gives us a new real-valued feature. If features from different domains have similar entries (scores) in the projection row, they are assumed to correspond (Blitzer, 2008). Figure 4 shows example of correspondences that SCL found in the Prince dataset. The first column represents the score of a feature. The labels `wiki` and `alp` indicate the domain of the features, respectively. For readability, we here grouped the features obtaining similar scores.

```
0.00010248|dep35('Chaka Khan',name('PER'),hd/su,verb,ben)|wiki
0.00010248|dep35(de,det,hd/det,adj,'Afro-Amerikaanse')|wiki
0.00010248|dep35('Yvette Marie Stevens',name('PER'),hd/app,
                noun,zangeres)|wiki
0.000102772|dep34(leraar,noun,hd/su,verb)|alp

0.000161095|dep34(commissie,noun,hd/obj1,prep)|16|alp
0.00016113|dep34('Confessions Tour',name,hd/obj1,prep)|2|wiki
0.000161241|dep34(orgel,noun,hd/obj1,prep)|1|wiki

0.000217698|dep34(tournee,noun,hd/su,verb)|1|wiki
0.000223301|dep34(regisseur,noun,hd/su,verb)|15|wiki
0.000224517|dep34(voorsprong,noun,hd/su,verb)|2|alp
0.000224684|dep34(wetenschap,noun,hd/su,verb)|2|alp
0.000226617|dep34(pop_rock,noun,hd/su,verb)|1|wiki
0.000228918|dep34(plan,noun,hd/su,verb)|9|alp
```

Figure 4: Example projection from $\theta$ (row 2).

SCL clustered information about 'Chaka Khan', an 'Afro-Amerikaanse' 'zangeres' (afro-american singer) whose real name is 'Yvette Marie Stevens'. She had close connections to Prince, who even wrote one of her singles. These features got aligned to the Alpino feature 'leraar' (teacher). Moreover, SCL finds that 'tournee', 'regisseur' and 'pop_rock' in the Prince domain behave like 'voorsprong' (advance), 'wetenschap' (research) and 'plan' as possible heads in a subject relation in the newspaper domain. Similarly, correspondences between the direct object features 'Confessions Tour' and 'orgel' (pipe organ) to 'commissie' (commission) are discovered.

**More unlabeled data** In the experiments so far, we balanced the amount of source and target data. We started to examine the effect of more unlabeled target domain data. For the Prince dataset, we included all supercategories in constructing the related target domain data. The so obtained dataset contains: 859 articles, 29,186 sentences and 385,289 tokens; hence, the size approximately tripled (w.r.t. Table 2). Table 5 shows the effect of using this larger dataset for SCL with $h = 25$. The accuracy increases (from 85.12 to 85.25). Thus, there seems to be a positive effect (to be investigated further).

| | CA | f-score | $\phi$ | rel.er. |
|---|---|---|---|---|
| baseline Prince | 85.03 | 85.38 | 78.06 | 0.00 |
| SCL[+/-], $h = 25$, all | 85.25 | 85.58 | 79.42 | 6.20 |

Table 5: First result on increasing unlabeled data.

**Dimensionality reduction by feature type** We have started to implement the extension discussed in section 4.2, i.e. perform separate dimensionality reductions based on blocks of nonpivot features. We clustered nonpivots (see section 4.1 for a description) into 9 types (ordered in terms of decreasing cluster size): *dep*, *f1/f2* (pos), *r1/r2* (rules), *appos_person*, *mf*, *z*, *h1*, *in_year*, *dist*. For each type, a separate SVD was computed on submatrix $W_t$ (illustrated in Figure 2). Then, separate projections were applied to every training instance.

The results of these experiments on the Prince dataset are shown in Figure 5. Applying SCL with dimensionality reduction by feature type (SCL block) results in a model that performs better (CA 85.27, $\phi$ 79.52, rel.er. 6.65%) than the model with no feature split (no block SVDs), thus obtaining a relative error reduction of 6.65% over the baseline. The same figure also shows what happens if we remove a specific feature type at a time; the apposition features contribute the most on this Prince domain. As a fact, one third of the sentences in the Prince testset contain constructions with appositions (e.g. about film-, album- and song titles).

## 6 Conclusions and Future Work

The paper presents an application of Structural Correspondence Learning (SCL) to parse disambiguation.

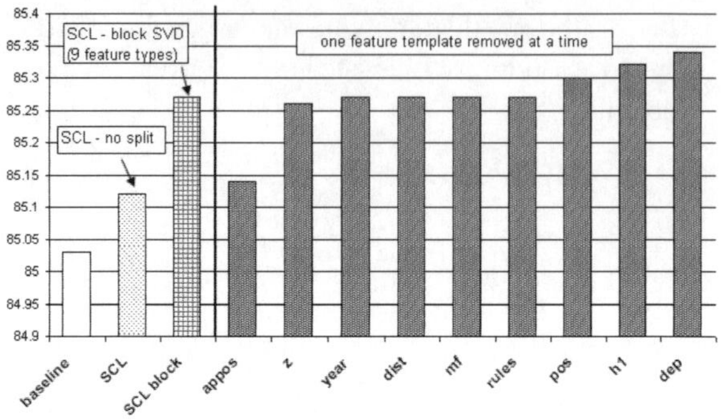


Figure 5: Results of dimensionality reduction by feature type, $h = 25$; block SVD included all 9 feature types; the right part shows the accuracy when one feature type was removed.

While SCL has been successfully applied to PoS tagging and Sentiment Analysis (Blitzer et al., 2006; Blitzer et al., 2007), its effectiveness for parsing was rather unexplored.

The empirical results show that our instantiation of SCL to parse disambiguation gives promising initial results, even without the many additional extensions on the feature level as done in Blitzer et al. (2006). We exploited Wikipedia as primary resource, both for collecting unlabeled target domain data, as well as test suite for empirical evaluation. On the three examined datasets, SCL slightly but constantly outperformed the baseline. Applying SCL involves many design choices and practical issues, which we tried to depict here in detail. A novelty in our application is that we first actually parse the unlabeled data from both domains. This allows us to get a possibly noisy, but more abstract representation of the underlying data on which the pivot predictors are trained.

In the near future, we plan to extend the work on semi-supervised domain adaptation for parse disambiguation, viz. (1) further explore/refine SCL (block SVDs, varying amount of target domain data, other testsets, etc.), and (2) examine self-training. Studies on the latter have focused mainly on generative, constituent based, i.e. data-driven parsing systems. Furthermore, from a machine learning point of view, it would be interesting to know a measure of corpus similarity to estimate the success of porting an NLP system from one domain to another. This relates to the general question of what is meant by domain.

## References


Steven P. Abney. 1997. Stochastic attribute-value grammars. *Computational Linguistics*, 23:597–618.

Rie Kubota Ando and Tong Zhang. 2005. A framework for learning predictive structures from multiple tasks and unlabeled data. *Journal of Machine Learning Research*, 6:1817–1853.

Rie Kubota Ando. 2006. Applying alternating structure optimization to word sense disambiguation. In *Proceedings of the 10th Conference on Computational Natural Language Learning (CoNLL)*.

Adam Berger, Stephen Della Pietra, and Vincent Della Pietra. 1996. A maximum entropy approach to natural language processing. *Computational Linguistics*, 22(1):39–72.

John Blitzer, Ryan McDonald, and Fernando Pereira. 2006. Domain adaptation with structural correspondence learning. In *Conference on Empirical Methods in Natural Language Processing*, Sydney, Australia.

John Blitzer, Mark Dredze, and Fernando Pereira. 2007. Biographies, bollywood, boom-boxes and blenders: Domain adaptation for sentiment classification. In *Association for Computational Linguistics*, Prague, Czech Republic.

John Blitzer. 2008. *Domain Adaptation of Natural Language Processing Systems*. Ph.D. thesis, University of Pennsylvania.

Eugene Charniak. 1996. Tree-bank grammars. In *In Proceedings of the Thirteenth National Conference on Artificial Intelligence*, pages 1031–1036.

Hal Daumé III and Daniel Marcu. 2006. Domain adaptation for statistical classifiers. *Journal of Artificial Intelligence Research*, 26:101–126.

Hal Daumé III. 2007. Frustratingly easy domain adaptation. In *Conference of the Association for Computational Linguistics (ACL)*, Prague, Czech Republic.

Mark Dredze, John Blitzer, Pratha Pratim Talukdar, Kuzman Ganchev, Joao Graca, and Fernando Pereira. 2007. Frustratingly hard domain adaptation for parsing. In *Proceedings of the CoNLL Shared Task Session - Conference on Natural Language Learning*, Prague, Czech Republic.

Daniel Gildea. 2001. Corpus variation and parser performance. In *Proceedings of the 2001 Conference on Empirical Methods in Natural Language Processing (EMNLP)*.

Tadayoshi Hara, Miyao Yusuke, and Jun'ichi Tsujii. 2005. Adapting a probabilistic disambiguation model of an hpsg parser to a new domain. In *Proceedings of the International Joint Conference on Natural Language Processing*.

Mark Johnson, Stuart Geman, Stephen Canon, Zhiyi Chi, and Stefan Riezler. 1999. Estimators for stochastic "unification-based" grammars. In *Proceedings of the 37th Annual Meeting of the ACL*.

Robert Malouf. 2002. A comparison of algorithms for maximum entropy parameter estimation. In *Proceedings of the Sixth Conference on Natural Language Learning (CoNLL-2002)*, Taipei.

David McClosky, Eugene Charniak, and Mark Johnson. 2006. Effective self-training for parsing. In *Proceedings of the Human Language Technology Conference of the NAACL, Main Conference*, pages 152–159, New York City, USA, June. Association for Computational Linguistics.

Nelleke Oostdijk. 2000. The Spoken Dutch Corpus: Overview and first evaluation. In *Proceedings of Second International Conference on Language Resources and Evaluation (LREC)*, pages 887–894.

Barbara Plank and Gertjan van Noord. 2008. Exploring an auxiliary distribution based approach to domain adaptation of a syntactic disambiguation model. In *Proceedings of the Workshop on Cross-Framework and Cross-Domain Parser Evaluation (PE)*, Manchester, August.

A. Ratnaparkhi. 1997. A simple introduction to maximum entropy models for natural language processing. Technical report, Institute for Research in Cognitive Science, University of Pennsylvania.

Brian Roark and Michiel Bacchiani. 2003. Supervised and unsupervised pcfg adaptation to novel domains. In *In Proceedings of the Human Language Technology Conference and Meeting of the North American Chapter of the Association for Computational Linguistics (HLT-NAACL)*.

Nobuyuki Shimizu and Hiroshi Nakagawa. 2007. Structural correspondence learning for dependency parsing. In *Proceedings of the CoNLL Shared Task Session of EMNLP-CoNLL 2007*.

Gertjan van Noord and Robert Malouf. 2005. Wide coverage parsing with stochastic attribute value grammars. Draft available from http://www.let.rug.nl/˜vannoord. A preliminary version of this paper was published in the Proceedings of the IJCNLP workshop Beyond Shallow Analyses, Hainan China, 2004.

Gertjan van Noord. 2006. **At Last Parsing Is Now Operational**. In *TALN 2006 Verbum Ex Machina, Actes De La 13e Conference sur Le Traitement Automatique des Langues naturelles*, pages 20–42, Leuven.

Gertjan van Noord. 2007. Using self-trained bilexical preferences to improve disambiguation accuracy. In *Proceedings of the Tenth International Conference on Parsing Technologies. IWPT 2007, Prague.*, pages 1–10, Prague.

# A Chain-starting Classifier of Definite NPs in Spanish

**Marta Recasens**
CLiC - Centre de Llenguatge i Computació
Department of Linguistics
University of Barcelona
08007 Barcelona, Spain
mrecasens@ub.edu

## Abstract

Given the great amount of definite noun phrases that introduce an entity into the text for the first time, this paper presents a set of linguistic features that can be used to detect this type of definites in Spanish. The efficiency of the different features is tested by building a rule-based and a learning-based *chain-starting* classifier. Results suggest that the classifier, which achieves high precision at the cost of recall, can be incorporated as either a filter or an additional feature within a coreference resolution system to boost its performance.

## 1 Introduction

Although often treated together, anaphoric pronoun resolution differs from coreference resolution (van Deemter and Kibble, 2000). Whereas the former attempts to find an antecedent for each anaphoric pronoun in a discourse, the latter aims to build full coreference chains, namely linking all noun phrases (NPs) – whether pronominal or with a nominal head – that point to the same entity. The output of anaphora resolution[1] are noun-pronoun pairs (or pairs of a discourse segment and a pronoun in some cases), whereas the output of coreference resolution are chains containing a variety of items: pronouns, full NPs, discourse segments... Thus, coreference resolution requires a wider range of strategies in order to build the full chains of coreferent mentions.[2]

One of the problems specific to coreference resolution is determining, once a mention is encountered by the system, whether it refers to an entity previously mentioned or it introduces a new entity into the text. Many algorithms (Aone and Bennett, 1996; Soon et al., 2001; Yang et al., 2003) do not address this issue specifically, but implicitly assume all mentions to be potentially coreferent and examine all possible combinations; only if the system fails to link a mention with an already existing entity, it is considered to be *chain starting*.[3] However, such an approach is computationally expensive and prone to errors, since natural language is populated with a huge number of entities that appear just once in the text. Even definite NPs, which are traditionally believed to refer to old entities, have been demonstrated to start a coreference chain over 50% of the times (Fraurud, 1990; Poesio and Vieira, 1998).

An alternative line of research has considered applying a filter prior to coreference resolution that classifies mentions as either chain starting or coreferent. Ng and Cardie (2002) and Poesio et al. (2005) have tested the impact of such a detector on the overall coreference resolution performance with encouraging results. Our chain-starting classifier is comparable – despite some differences[4] – to the detectors suggested by Ng and Cardie (2002), Uryupina (2003), and Poesio et al. (2005) for English, but not identical to strictly anaphoric ones[5] (Bean and Riloff, 1999; Uryupina, 2003), since a non-anaphoric NP can corefer with a previous mention.

This paper presents a corpus-based study of def-

[1] A different matter is the resolution of anaphoric full NPs, i.e. those semantically dependent on a previous mention.

[2] We follow the ACE terminology (NIST, 2003) but instead of talking of objects in the world we talk of objects in the discourse model: we use *entity* for an object or set of objects in the discourse model, and *mention* for a reference to an entity.

[3] By *chain starting* we refer to those mentions that are the first element – and might be the only one – in a coreference chain.

[4] Ng and Cardie (2002) and Uryupina (2003) do not limit to definite NPs but deal with all types of NPs.

[5] Notice the confusing use of the term *anaphoric* in (Ng and Cardie, 2002) for describing their chain-starting filtering module.

*Proceedings of the EACL 2009 Student Research Workshop*, pages 46–53,
Athens, Greece, 2 April 2009. 

inite NPs in Spanish that results in a set of eight features that can be used to identify chain-starting definite NPs. The heuristics are tested by building two different chain-starting classifiers for Spanish, a rule-based and a learning-based one. The evaluation gives priority to precision over recall in view of the classifier's efficiency as a filtering module.

The paper proceeds as follows. Section 2 provides a qualitative comparison with related work. The corpus study and the empirically driven set of heuristics for recognizing chain-starting definites are described in Section 3. The chain-starting classifiers are built in Section 4. Section 5 reports on the evaluation and discusses its implications. Finally, Section 6 summarizes the conclusions and outlines future work.

## 2 Related Work

Some of the corpus-driven features here presented have a precedent in earlier classifiers of this kind for English while others are our own contribution. In any case, they have been adapted and tested for Spanish for the first time.

We build a list of storage units, which is inspired by research in the field of cognitive linguistics. Bean and Riloff (1999) and Uryupina (2003) have already employed a definite probability measure in a similar way, although the way the ratio is computed is slightly different. The former use it to make a "definite-only list" by ranking those definites extracted from a corpus that were observed at least five times and never in an indefinite construction. In contrast, the latter computes four definite probabilities – which are included as features within a machine-learning classifier – from the Web in an attempt to overcome Bean and Riloff's (1999) data sparseness problem. The definite probabilities in our approach are checked with confidence intervals in order to guarantee the reliability of the results, avoiding to draw any generalization when the corpus does not contain a large enough sample.

The heuristics concerning named entities and storage-unit variants find an equivalent in the features used in Ng and Cardie's (2002) supervised classifier that represent whether the mention is a proper name (determined based on capitalization, whereas our corpus includes both weak and strong named entities) and whether a previous NP is an alias of the current mention (on the basis of a rule-based alias module that tries out different transformations). Uryupina (2003) and Vieira and Poesio (2000) also take capital and low case letters into account.

All four approaches exploit syntactic structural cues of pre- and post- modification to detect complex NPs, as they are considered to be unlikely to have been previously mentioned in the discourse. A more fine-grained distinction is made by Bean and Riloff (1999) and Vieira and Poesio (2000) to distinguish restrictive from non-restrictive post-modification by ommitting those modifiers that occur between commas, which should not be classified as chain starting. The latter also list a series of "special predicates" including nouns like *fact* or *result*, and adjectives such as *first, best, only*, etc. A subset of the feature vectors used by Ng and Cardie (2002) and Uryupina (2003) is meant to code whether the NP is or not modified. In this respect, our contribution lies in adapting these ideas for the way modification occurs in Spanish – where premodifiers are rare – and in introducing a distinction between PP and AP modifiers, which we correlate in turn with the heads of simple definites.

We borrow the idea of classifying definites occurring in the first sentence as chain starting from Bean and Riloff (1999).

The precision and recall results obtained by these classifiers – tested on MUC corpora – are around the eighties, and around the seventies in the case of Vieira and Poesio (2000), who use the Penn Treebank.

Luo et al. (2004) make use of both a linking and a starting probability in their Bell tree algorithm for coreference resolution, but the starting probability happens to be the complementary of the linking one. The chain-starting classifier we build can be used to fine-tune the starting probability used in the construction of coreference chains in Luo et al.'s (2004) style.

## 3 Corpus-based Study

As fully documented by Lyons (1999), definiteness varies cross-linguistically. In contrast with English, for instance, Spanish adds the article before generic NPs (1), within some fixed phrases (2), and in postmodifiers where English makes use of bare nominal premodification (3). Altogether results in a larger number of definite NPs in Spanish and, by extension, a larger number of chain-starting definites (Recasens et al., 2009).

(1) *Tardía incorporación de la mujer al trabajo.*
Late incorporation of the woman to the work.
'Late incorporation of ⊘ women into ⊘ work.'

(2) *Villalobos dio las gracias a los militantes.*
Villalobos gave the thanks to the militants.
'Villalobos gave ⊘ thanks to the militants.'

(3) *El mercado internacional del café.*
The market international of the coffee.
'The international ⊘ coffee market.'

Long-held claims that equate the definite article with a specific category of meaning cannot be hold. The present-day definite article is a category that, although it did originally have a semantic meaning of "identifiability", has increased its range of contexts so that it is often a grammatical rather than a semantic category (Lyons, 1999). Definite NPs cannot be considered anaphoric by default, but strategies need to be introduced in order to classify a definite as either a chain-starting or a coreferent mention. Given that the extent of grammaticization[6] varies from language to language, we considered it appropriate to conduct a corpus study oriented to Spanish: (i) to check the extent to which strategies used in previous work can be extended to Spanish, and (ii) to explore additional linguistic cues.

### 3.1 The corpus

The empirical data used in our corpus study come from AnCora-Es, the Spanish corpus of AnCora – Annotated Corpora for Spanish and Catalan (Taule et al., 2008), developed at the University of Barcelona and freely available from `http://clic.ub.edu/ancora`. AnCora-Es is a half-million-word multilevel corpus consisting of newspaper articles and annotated, among other levels of information, with PoS tags, syntactic constituents and functions, and named entities. A subset of 320 000 tokens (72 500 full NPs[7]) was used to draw linguistic features about definiteness.

### 3.2 Features

As quantitatively supported by the figures in Table 1, the split between simple (i.e. non-modified) and complex NPs seems to be linguistically relevant. We assume that the referential properties of simple NPs differ from complex ones, and this distinction is kept when designing the eight heuristics for recognizing chain-starting definites that we introduce in this section.

1. **Head match.** Ruling out those definites that match an earlier noun in the text has proved to be able to filter out a considerable number of coreferent mentions (Ng and Cardie, 2002; Poesio et al., 2005). We considered both total and partial head match, but stuck to the first as the second brought much noise. On its own, namely if definite NPs are all classified as chain starting only if no mention has previously appeared with the same lexical head, we obtain a precision (P) not less than 84.95% together with 89.68% recall (R). Our purpose was to increase P as much as possible with the minimum loss in R: it is preferred not to classify a chain-starting instance – which can still be detected by the coreference resolution module at a later stage – since a wrong label might result in a missed coreference link.

2. **Storage units.** A very grammaticized definite article accounts for the large number of definite NPs attested in Spanish (column 2 in Table 1): 46% of the total. In the light of Bybee and Hopper's (2001) claim that language structure dynamically results from frequency and repetition, we hypothesized that specific simple definite NPs in which the article has fully grammaticized constitute what Bybee and Hopper (2001) call *storage units*: the more a specific chunk is used, the more stored and automatized it becomes. These article-noun storage units might well head a coreference chain.

   With a view to providing the chain-starting classifier with a list of these article-noun storage units, we extracted from AnCora-Es all simple NPs preceded by a determiner[8] (columns 2 and 3 in the second row of Table 1) and ranked them by their *definite probability*, which we define as the number of simple definite NPs with respect to the number of simple determined NPs. Secondly, we set a threshold of 0.7, considering as storage units

[6] *Grammaticization*, or *grammaticalization*, is a process of linguistic change by which a content word becomes part of the grammar by losing its lexical and phonological load.

[7] By *full* NPs we mean NPs with a nominal head, thus omitting pronouns, NPs with an elliptical head as well as coordinated NPs.

[8] Only noun types occurring a minimum of ten times were included in this study. Singular and plural forms as well as masculine and feminine were kept as distinct types.

| | Definite NPs | Other det. NPs | Bare NPs | Total |
|---|---|---|---|---|
| Simple NPs | 12 739 | 6 642 | 15 183 | 34 564 (48%) |
| Complex NPs | 20 447 | 9 545 | 8 068 | 38 060 (52%) |
| Total | 33 186 (46%) | 16 187 (22%) | 23 251 (32%) | 72 624 (100%) |

Table 1: Overall distribution of full NPs in AnCora-Es (subset).

those definites above the threshold. In order to avoid biased probabilities due to a small number of observed examples in the corpus, a 95 percent confidence interval was computed. The final list includes 191 storage units, such as *la UE* 'the EU', *el euro* 'the euro', *los consumidores* 'the consumers', etc.

3. **Named entities (NEs).** A closer look at the list of storage units revealed that the higher the definite probability, the more NE-like a noun is. This led us to extrapolate that the definite article has completely grammaticized (i.e. lost its semantic load) before simple definites which are NEs (e.g. *los setenta* 'the seventies', *el Congreso_de_Estados_Unidos* 'the_U.S._Congress'[9]), and so they are likely to be chain-starting.

4. **Storage-unit variants.** The fact that some of the extracted storage units were variants of a same entity gave us an additional cue: complementing the plain head_match feature by adding a gazetteer with variants (e.g. *la Unión Europea* 'the European Union' and *la UE* 'the EU') stops the storage_unit heuristic from classifying a simple definite as chain starting if a previous equivalent unit has appeared.

5. **First sentence.** Given that the probability for any definite NP occurring in the first sentence of a text to be chain starting is very high, since there has not been time to introduce many entities, all definites appearing in the first sentence can be classified as chain starting.

6. **AP-preference nouns.** Complex definites represent 62% out of all definite NPs (Table 1). In order to assess to what extent the referential properties of a noun on its own depend on its combinatorial potential to occur with either a prepositional phrase (PP) or an adjectival phrase (AP), complex definites were grouped into those containing a PP (49%) and those containing an AP[10] (27%). Next, the probability for each noun to be modified by a PP or an AP was computed. The results made it possible to draw a distinction – and two respective lists – between PP-preference nouns (e.g. *el inicio* 'the beginning') and nouns that prefer an AP modifier (e.g. *las autoridades* 'the authorities'). Given that APs are not as informative as PPs, they are more likely to modify storage units than PPs. Nouns with a preference for APs turned out to be storage units or behave similarly. Thus, simple definites headed by such nouns are unlikely to be coreferent.

7. **PP-preference nouns.** Nouns that prefer to combine with a PP are those that depend on an extra argument to become referential. This argument, however, might not appear as a nominal modifier but be recoverable from the discourse context, either explicitly or implicitly. Therefore, a simple definite headed by a PP-preference noun might be anaphoric but not necessarily a coreferent mention. Thus, grouping PP-preference nouns offers an empirical way for capturing those nouns that are *bridging* anaphors when they appear in a simple definite. For instance, it is not rare that, once a specific company has been introduced into the text, reference is made for the first time to its director simply as *el director* 'the director'.

8. **Neuter definites.** Unlike English, the Spanish definite article is marked for grammatical gender. Nouns might be either masculine or feminine, but a third type of definite article, the neuter one (*lo*), is used to nominalize adjectives and clauses, namely "to create a referential entity" out of a non-nominal

[9]The underscore represents multiword expressions.

[10]When a noun was followed by more than one modifier, only the syntactic type of the first one was taken into account.

Given a definite mention *m*,

1. If *m* is introduced by a neuter definite article, classify as chain starting.
2. If *m* appears in the first sentence of the document, classify as chain starting.
3. If *m* shares the same lexical head with a previous mention or is a storage-unit variant of it, classify as coreferent.
4. If the head of *m* is PP-preference, classify as chain starting.
5. If *m* is a simple definite,
   (a) and the head of *m* appears in the list of storage units, classify as chain starting.
   (b) and the head of *m* is AP-preference, classify as chain starting.
   (c) and *m* is an NE, classify as chain starting.
   (d) Otherwise, classify as coreferent.
6. Otherwise (i.e. *m* is a complex definite), classify as chain starting.

Figure 1: Rule-based algorithm.

item. Since such neuters have a low coreferential capacity, the classification of these NPs as chain starting can favour recall.

## 4 Chain-starting Classifier

In order to test the linguistic cues outlined above, we build two different chain-starting classifiers: a rule-based model and a learning-based one. Both aim to detect those definite NPs for which there is no need to look for a previous reference.

### 4.1 Rule-based approach

The first way in which the linguistic findings in Section 3.2 are tested is by building a rule-based classifier. The heuristics are combined and ordered in the most efficient way, yielding the handcrafted algorithm shown in Figure 1. Two main principles underlie the algorithm: (i) simple definites tend to be coreferent mentions, and (ii) complex definites tend to be chain starting (if their head has not previously appeared). Accordingly, Step 5 in Figure 1 finishes by classifying simple definites as coreferent, and Step 6 complex definites as chain starting. Before these last steps, however, a series of filters are applied corresponding to the different heuristics. The performance is presented in Table 2.

### 4.2 Machine-learning approach

The second way in which the suggested linguistic cues are tested is by constructing a learning-based classifier. The Weka machine learning toolkit (Witten and Frank, 2005) is used to train a J48 decision tree on a 10-fold cross-validation. A total of eight learning features are considered: (i) head match, (ii) storage-unit variant, (iii) is a neuter definite, (iv) is first sentence, (v) is a PP-preference noun, (vi) is a storage unit, (vii) is an AP-preference noun, (viii) is an NE. All features are binary (either "yes" or "no"). We experiment with different feature vectors, incrementally adding one feature at a time. The performance is presented in Table 3.

## 5 Evaluation

A subset of AnCora-CO-Es consisting of 60 Spanish newspaper articles (23 335 tokens, 5 747 full NPs) is kept apart for the test corpus. AnCora-CO-Es is the coreferentially annotated AnCora-Es corpus, following the guidelines described in (Recasens et al., 2007). Coreference relations were annotated manually with the aid of the PALinkA (Orasan, 2003) and AnCoraPipe (Bertran et al., 2008) tools. Interestingly enough, the test corpus contains 2 575 definite NPs, out of which 1 889 are chain-starting (1401 chain-starting definite NPs are actually isolated entities), namely 73% definites head a coreference chain, which implies that a successful classifier has the potential to rule out almost three quarters of all definite mentions.

Given that chain starting is the majority class and following (Ng and Cardie, 2002), we took the "one class" classification as a naive baseline: all instances were classified as chain starting, giving a precision of 71.95% (first row in Tables 2 and 3).

### 5.1 Performance

Tables 2 and 3 show the results in terms of precision (P), recall (R), and $F_{0.5}$-measure ($F_{0.5}$). $F_{0.5}$-measure,[11] which weights P twice as much as R, is chosen since this classifier is designed as a filter for a coreference resolution module and hence we want to make sure that the discarded cases can be really discarded. P matters more than R.

Each row incrementally adds a new heuristic to the previous ones. The score is cumulative. Notice that the order of the features in Table 2 does

[11] $F_{0.5}$ is computed as $\frac{1.5PR}{0.5P+R}$.

| Cumulative Features | P (%) | R (%) | $F_{0.5}$ (%) |
|---|---|---|---|
| Baseline | 71.95 | 100.0 | 79.37 |
| +Head match | 84.95 | 89.68 | 86.47 |
| +Storage-unit variant | 85.02 | 89.58 | 86.49 |
| +Neuter definite | 85.08 | 90.05 | 86.68 |
| +First sentence | 85.12 | **90.32** | **86.79** |
| +PP preference | 85.12 | 90.32 | 86.79 |
| +Storage unit | 89.65** | 71.54** | 82.67 |
| +AP preference | **89.70**** | 71.96** | 82.89 |
| +Named entity | 89.20* | 78.22** | 85.21 |

Table 2: Performance of the rule-based classifier.

| Cumulative Features | P (%) | R (%) | $F_{0.5}$ (%) |
|---|---|---|---|
| Baseline | 71.95 | 100.0 | 79.37 |
| +Head match | **85.00** | 89.70 | 86.51 |
| +Storage-unit variant | 85.00 | 89.70 | 86.51 |
| +Neuter definite | 85.00 | 90.20 | 86.67 |
| +First sentence | 85.10 | 90.40 | 86.80 |
| +PP preference | 85.10 | 90.40 | 86.80 |
| +Storage unit | 83.80 | 93.50** | 86.80 |
| +AP preference | 83.90 | **93.60**** | **86.90** |
| +Named entity | 83.90 | 93.60** | 86.90 |

Table 3: Performance of the learning-based classifier (J48 decision tree).

not directly map the order as presented in the algorithm (Figure 1): the head_match heuristic and the storage-unit_variant need to be applied first, since the other heuristics function as filters that are effective only if head match between the mentions has been first checked. Table 3 presents the incremental performance of the learning-based classifier for the different sets of features.

Diacritics ** ($p<.01$) and * ($p<.05$) indicate whether differences in P and R between the reduced classifier (head_ match) and the extended ones are significant (using a one-way ANOVA followed by Tukey's post-hoc test).

### 5.2 Discussion

Although the central role played by the head_match feature has been emphasized by prior work, it is striking that such a simple heuristic achieves results over 85%, raising P by 13 percentage points. All in all, these figures can only be slightly improved by some of the additional features. These features have a different effect on each approach: whereas they improve P (and decrease R) in the hand-crafted algorithm, they improve R (and decrease P) in the decision tree. In the first case, the highest R is achieved with the first four features, and the last three features obtain an increase in P statistically significant yet accompanied by a decrease in R also statistically significant. We expected that the second block of features would favour P without such a significant drop in R.

The drop in P in the decision tree is not statistically significant as it is in the rule-based classifier. Our goal, however, was to increase P as much as possible, since false positive errors harm the performance of the subsequent coreference resolution system much more than false negative errors, which can still be detected at a later stage. The very same attributes might prove more efficient if used as additional learning features within the vector of a coreference resolution system rather than as an independent pre-classifier.

From a linguistic perspective, the fact that the linguistic heuristics increase P provides support for the hypotheses about the grammaticized definite article and the existence of storage units. We carried out an error analysis to consider those cases in which the features are misleading in terms of precision errors. The first_sentence feature, for instance, results in an error in (4), where the first sentence includes a coreferent NP.

(4) La expansión de la piratería en *el Sudeste de Asia* puede destruir las economías de *la región*.
'The expansion of piracy in *South-East Asia* can destroy the economies of *the region*.'

Classifying PP-preference nouns as chain starting fails when a noun like *el protagonista* 'the protagonist', which could appear as the first mention in a film critique, happens to be previously mentioned with a different head. Likewise, not using the same head in cases such as *la competición* 'the competition' and *la Liga* 'the League' accounts for the failure of the storage_unit or named_entity feature, which classify the second mention as chain starting. On the other hand, some recall errors are due to head_match, which might link two NPs that despite sharing the same head point to a different entity (e.g. *el grupo Agnelli* 'the Agnelli group' and *el grupo industrial Montedison* 'the industrial group Montedison').

## 6 Conclusions and Future Work

The paper presented a corpus-driven chain-starting classifier of definite NPs for Spanish, pointing out and empirically supporting a series of linguistic features to be taken into account. Given that definiteness is very much language dependent, the AnCora-Es corpus was mined to infer some linguistic hypotheses that could help in the automatic identification of chain-starting definites. The information from different linguistic levels (lexical, semantic, morphological, syntactic, and pragmatic) in a computationally not expensive way casts light on potential features helpful for resolving coreference links. Each resulting heuristic managed to improve precision although at the cost of a drop in recall. The highest improvement in precision (89.20%) with the lowest loss in recall (78.22%) translates into an $F_{0.5}$-measure of 85.21%. Hence, the incorporation of linguistic knowledge manages to outperform the baseline by 17 percentage points in precision.

Priority is given to precision, since we want to assure that the filter prior to coreference resolution module does not label as chain starting definite NPs that are coreferent. The classifier was thus designed to minimize false positives. No less than 73% of definite NPs in the data set are chain starting, so detecting 78% of these definites with almost 90% precision could have substantial savings. From a linguistic perspective, the improvement in precision supports the linguistic hypotheses, even if at the expense of recall. However, as this classifier is not a final but a prior module, either a filter within a rule-based system or one additional feature within a larger learning-based system, the shortage of recall can be compensated at the coreference resolution stage by considering other more sophisticated features.

The results here presented are not comparable with other existing classifiers of this type for several reasons. Our approach would perform differently for English, which has a lower number of definite NPs. Secondly, our classifier has been evaluated on a corpus much larger than prior ones such as Uryupina's (2003). Thirdly, some classifiers aim at detecting non-anaphoric NPs, which are not the same as chain-starting. Fourthly, we have empirically explored the contribution of the set of heuristics with respect to the head_match feature. None of the existing approaches compares its final performance in relation with this simple but extremely powerful feature. Some of our heuristics do draw on previous work, but we have tuned them for Spanish and we have also contributed with new ideas, such as the use of storage units and the preference of some nouns for a specific syntactic type of modifier.

As future work, we will adapt this chain-starting classifier for Catalan, fine-tune the set of heuristics, and explore to what extent the inclusion of such a classifier improves the overall performance of a coreference resolution system for Spanish. Alternatively, we will consider using the suggested attributes as part of a larger set of learning features for coreference resolution.

## Acknowledgments

We would like to thank the three anonymous reviewers for their suggestions for improvement. This paper has been supported by the FPU Grant (AP2006-00994) from the Spanish Ministry of Education and Science, and the Lang2World (TIN2006-15265-C06-06) and Ancora-Nom (FFI2008-02691-E/FILO) projects.

## References

Chinatsu Aone and Scott W. Bennett. 1996. Applying machine learning to anaphora resolution. In S. Wermter, E. Riloff and G. Scheler (eds.), *Connectionist, Statistical and Symbolic Approaches to Learning for Natural Language Processing*. Springer Verlag, Berlin, 302-314.

David L. Bean and Ellen Riloff. 1999. Corpus-based identification of non-anaphoric noun phrases. In *Proceedings of the ACL 1999*, 373-380.

Manuel Bertran, Oriol Borrega, Marta Recasens, and Bàrbara Soriano. 2008. AnCoraPipe: A tool for multilevel annotation. *Procesamiento del Lenguaje Natural*, 41:291-292.

Joan Bybee and Paul Hopper. 2001. Introduction to frequency and the emergence of linguistic structure. In J. Bybee and P. Hopper (eds.), *Frequency and the Emergence of Linguistic Structure*. John Benjamins, Amsterdam, 1-24.

Kari Fraurud. 1990. Definiteness and the processing of NPs in natural discourse. *Journal of Semantics*, 7:395-433.

Xiaoqiang Luo, Abe Ittycheriah, Hongyan Jing, Nanda Kambhatla, and Salim Roukos. 2004. A mention-synchronous coreference resolution algorithm based on the Bell tree. In *Proceedings of ACL 2004*.

Christopher Lyons. 1999. *Definiteness*. Cambridge University Press, Cambridge.

Vincent Ng and Claire Cardie. 2002. Identifying anaphoric and non-anaphoric noun phrases to improve coreference resolution. In *Proceedings of COLING 2002*.

NIST. 2003. ACE Entity detection and tracking. V.2.5.1.

Constantin Orasan. 2003. PALinkA: A highly customisable tool for discourse annotation. In *Proceedings of the 4th SIGdial Workshop on Discourse and Dialogue*.

Massimo Poesio and Renata Vieira. 1998. A corpus-based investigation of definite description use. *Computational Linguistics*, 24(2):183-216.

Massimo Poesio, Mijail Alexandrov-Kabadjov, Renata Vieira, Rodrigo Goulart, and Olga Uryupina. 2005. Does discourse-new detection help definite description resolution? In *Proceedings of IWCS 2005*.

Marta Recasens, M. Antònia Martí, and Mariona Taulé. 2007. Where anaphora and coreference meet. Annotation in the Spanish CESS-ECE corpus. In *Proceedings of RANLP 2007*. Borovets, Bulgaria.

Marta Recasens, M. Antònia Martí, and Mariona Taulé. 2009. First-mention definites: more than exceptional cases. In S. Featherston and S. Winkler (eds.), *The Fruits of Empirical Linguistics*. Volume 2. De Gruyter, Berlin.

Wee M. Soon, Hwee T. Ng, and Daniel C. Y. Lim. 2001. A machine learning approach to coreference resolution of noun phrases. *Computational Linguistics*, 27(4):521-544.

Mariona Taulé, M. Antònia Martí, and Marta Recasens. 2008. AnCora: Multilevel Annotated Corpora for Catalan and Spanish. In *Proceedings of the 6th International Conference on Language Resources and Evaluation (LREC 2008)*,

Olga Uryupina. 2003. High-precision identification of discourse-new and unique noun phrases. In *Proceedings of the ACL 2003 Student Workshop*, 80-86.

Kees van Deemter and Rodger Kibble. 2000. Squibs and Discussions: On coreferring: coreference in MUC and related annotation schemes. *Computational Linguistics*, 26(4):629-637.

Renata Vieira and Massimo Poesio. 2000. An empirically based system for processing definite descriptions. *Computational Linguistics*, 26(4):539-593.

Ian Witten and Eibe Frank. 2005. Data Mining: Practical machine learning tools and techniques. Morgan Kaufmann.

Xiaofeng Yang, Guodong Zhou, Jian Su, and Chew L. Tan. 2003. Coreference resolution using competition learning approach. In *Proceedings of ACL 2003*. 176-183.

# Speech emotion recognition with TGI+.2 classifier

**Julia Sidorova**
Universitat Pompeu Fabra
Barcelona, Spain
julia.sidorova@upf.edu

## Abstract

We have adapted a classification approach coming from optical character recognition research to the task of speech emotion recognition. The classification approach enjoys the representational power of a syntactic method and efficiency of statistical classification. The syntactic part implements a tree grammar inference algorithm. We have extended this part of the algorithm with various edit costs to penalise more important features with higher edit costs for being outside the interval, which tree automata learned at the inference stage. The statistical part implements an entropy based decision tree (C4.5). We did the testing on the Berlin database of emotional speech. Our classifier outperforms the state of the art classifier (Multilayer Perceptron) by 4.68% and a baseline (C4.5) by 26.58%, which proves validity of the approach.

## 1 Introduction

In a number of applications such as human-computer interfaces, smart call centres, etc. it is important to be able to recognise people's emotional state. An aim of a speech emotion recognition (SER) engine is to produce an estimate of the emotional state of the speaker given a speech fragment as an input. The standard way to do SER is through a supervised machine learning procedure (Sidorova et al., 2008). It also should be noted that a number of alternative classification strategies has been offered recently, such as unsupervised learning (Liu et al., 2007) and numeric regression (Grimm et al., 2007) etc, and which are preferable under certain conditions.

Our contribution is a new algorithm of a mixed design with syntactic and statistical learning, which we borrowed from optical character recognition (Sempere, Lopez, 2003), extended, and adapted for SER. The syntactic part implements tree grammar inference (Sakakibara, 1997), and the statistical part implements C4.5 (Quinlan, 1993). The intuitive reasons underlying this solution are as follows. We would like to have a classification approach that enjoys the representational power of a syntactic method and efficiency of statistical classification. First we model the objects by means of a syntactic method, i.e. we map samples into their representations. A representation of a sample is a set of seven numeric values, signifying to which degree a given sample resembles the averaged pattern of each of seven classes. Second, we learn to classify the mappings of samples, rather than feature vectors of samples, with a powerful statistical method. We called the classifier *TGI+*, which stands for Tree Grammar Inference and the plus is for the statistical learning enhancement. In this paper we present the second version of TGI+, which extends TGI+.1 (Sidorova et al., 2008) and the difference is that we have added various edit costs to penalise more important features with higher edit costs for being outside the interval, which tree automata learned at the inference stage. We evaluated TGI+ against a state of the art classifier. To obtain a state of the art performance, we constructed a speech emotion recogniser, following the classical supervised learning approach with a top performer out of more than 20 classifiers from the weka package, which turned out to be multilayer perceptron (MLP) (Witten, Frank, 2005). Experimental results showed that TGI+ outperforms MLP by 4.68%.

The structure of this paper is as follows: in this section below we explain construction of a classical speech emotion recognizer, in Section 2 we explain TGI+; Section 3 reports testing results for both, the state of the art recogniser and TGI+. Section 4 and 5 is discussion and conclusions.

*Proceedings of the EACL 2009 Student Research Workshop*, pages 54–60,
Athens, Greece, 2 April 2009. 

### 1.1 Classical Speech Emotion Recogniser

A classical speech emotion recognizer is comprised of three modules: Feature Extraction, Feature Selection, and Classification. Their performance will serve as a baseline for TGI+ recognizer.

#### 1.1.1 Feature Extraction and Selection

In the literature there is a consensus that global statistics features lead to higher accuracies compared to the dynamic classification of multivariate time-series (Schuller et al., 2003). The feature extraction module extracts 116 global statistical features, both prosodic and segmental, a full list and explanations for which can be found in (Sidorova, 2007).

The feature selection module implements a wrapper approach with forward selection (Witten, Frank, 2005) in order to automatically select the most relevant features extracted by the previous module.

#### 1.1.2 Classification

The classification module takes an input as a feature vector created by the feature selector, and applies the Multilayer Perceptron classifier (MLP) (Witten, Frank, 2005), in order to assign a class label to it. The labels are the emotional states to discriminate among. For our data, MLP turned out to be the top performer among more than 20 other different classifiers; details of this comparative testing can be found in (Sidorova, 2007).

## 2 TGI+ classifier

The organisation of this section is as follows. In paragraph 2.1 we explain the TGI+.1 classifier and show how its parts work together. TGI+.2 is an extension of TGI+.1 and we explain it right afterwards. In paragraph 2.2 we briefly remind the C4.5 algorithm. Further in the paper in paragraph 4.1 we show that our TGI+ algorithm was correctly constructed and that we arrived to a meaningful combination of methods from different pattern recognition paradigms.

### 2.1 TGI+

TGI+.1 is comprised of four major steps we explain below. Fig 1 graphically depicts the procedure.

*Step 1: In order to perform tree grammar inference we represent samples by tree structures.* Divide the training set into two subsets $T_1$ (39% of training data) and $T_2$ (the rest of training data). Utterances from $T_1$ are converted into tree structures, the skeleton of which is defined by the grammar below. $S$ denotes a start symbol of the formal grammar (in the sense of a term-rewriting system):

$\{S \longrightarrow$ ProsodicFeatures SegmentalFeatures;
ProsodicFeatures $\longrightarrow$ Pitch Intensity Jitter Shimer;
SegmentalFeatures $\longrightarrow$ Energy Formants;
Pitch $\longrightarrow$ Min Max Quantile Mean Std MeanAbsoluteSlope;
etc. $\}$

The *etc.* stands for further terminating productions, i.e. the productions which have low level features on their right hand side. All trees have 116 leaves, each corresponding to one of the 116 features from the sample feature vector. We put trees from one class into one set. In our dataset we have the following seven classes to recognise among: fear, disgust, happiness, boredom, neutral, sadness and anger. Therefore, we have seven sets of trees. We put trees from one class into one set.

*Step 2: Apply tree grammar inference to learn seven automata accepting a different type of emotional utterance each.* Grammar inference is a method to learn a grammar from examples. In our case, it is *tree* grammar inference, because we deal with trees representing utterances. The result of this step is seven automata, one for each of seven emotions to be recognised.

*Step 3: Calculate edit distances between obtained tree automata and trees in the training set.* Edit distances are then calculated between each automaton obtained at step two and each tree representing utterances from the training set ($T_1 \cup T_2$). The calculated edit distances are put into a matrix of size: (cardinality of the training set) $\times$ 7 (the number of classes).

*Step 4: Run C4.5 over the matrix to obtain a decision tree.* The C4.5 algorithm is run over this matrix in order to obtain a decision tree, classifying each utterance into one of the seven emotions, according to edit distances between a given utterance and the seven tree automata. The accuracies obtained from testing this decision tree are the accuracies of TGI+.1.

TGI+.2 Our extension of the algorithm as proposed in (Sempere, Lopez, 2003) has to do with Step 3. In TGI+.1 all edit costs equated to 1. In

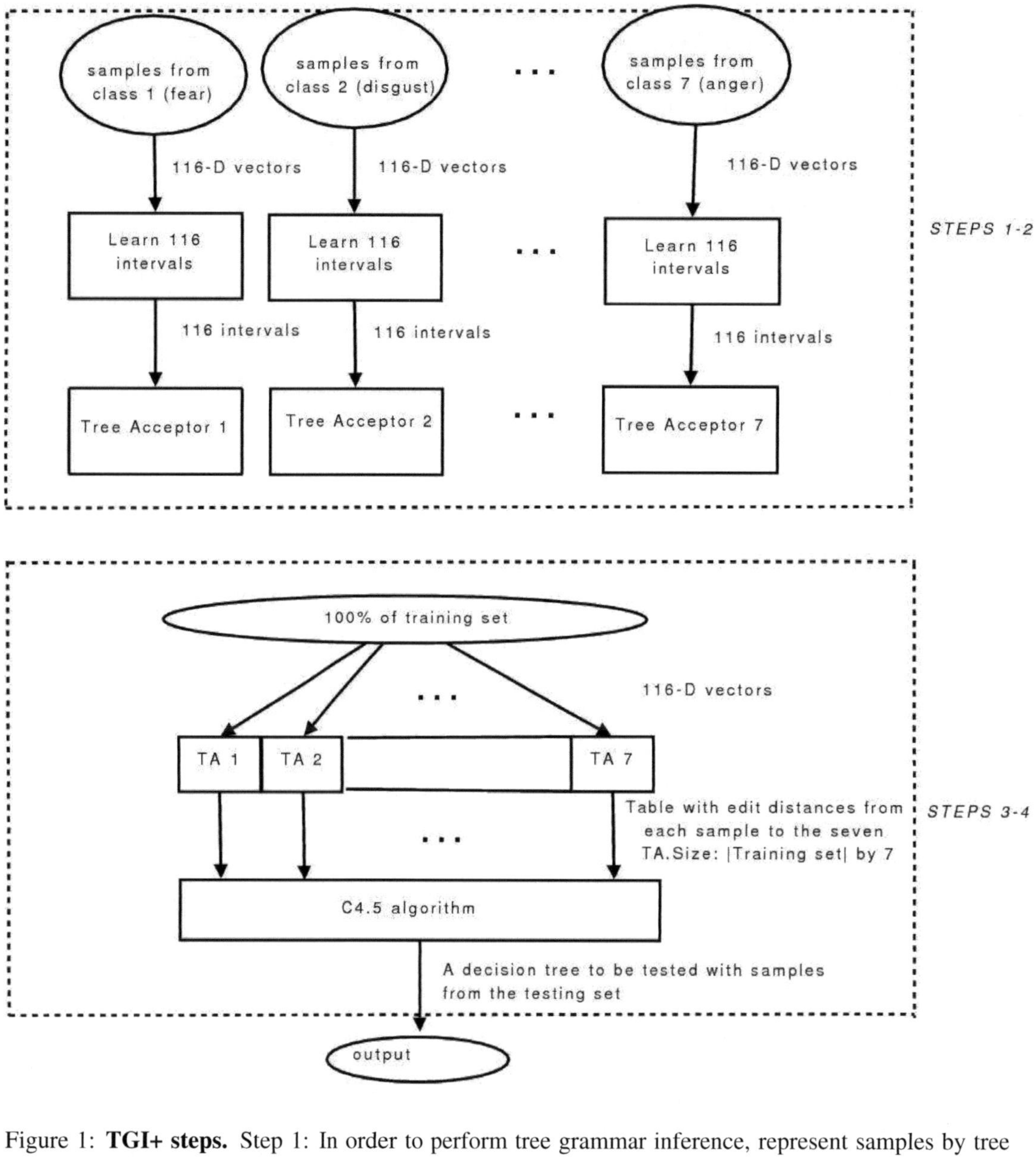


Figure 1: **TGI+ steps.** Step 1: In order to perform tree grammar inference, represent samples by tree structures. Step 2: Apply tree grammar inference to learn seven automata accepting a different type of emotional utterance each. Step 3: Calculate edit distances between obtained tree automata and trees in the training set. While calculating edit distances, penalise more important features with higher costs for being outside its interval. The set of such features is determined exclusively for every class through a feature selection procedure. Step 4: Run C4.5 over the matrix to obtain a decision tree.

other words, if a feature value fits the interval a tree automaton has learned for it, the acceptance cost of the sample is not altered. If a feature value is outside the interval the automaton has learnt for it, the acceptance cost of the sample processed is incremented by one. In TGI+.2 some edit costs have a coefficient greater than 1 (1.5 in the current version). In other words, more important features are penalised with higher costs for being outside its interval. The set of these more important features is determined exclusively for every class (anger, neutral, etc.) through a feature selection procedure. The feature selection procedure implements a wrapper approach with forward selection.

Concluding the algorithm description, let us explain how TGI+ classifiers an input sample, which is fed to the automata in the form a 116 dimensional feature vector. Firstly TGI+ calculates distances from the sample to seven tree automata (the automata learnt 116 feature intervals at the inference step). Secondly TGI+ uses the C 4.5 decision tree to classify the sample (the decision tree was learnt from the table, where distances to seven automata to all the training samples had been put).

### 2.2 C4.5 Learning algorithm

C4.5 belongs to the family of algorithms that employ a topdown greedy search through the space of possible decision trees. A decision tree is a representation of a finite set of if-then-else rules. The main characteristics of decision trees are the following:

1. The examples can be defined as a set of numerical and symbolic attributes.
2. The examples can be incomplete or contain noisy data.
3. The main learning algorithms work under Minimum Description Length approaches.

The main learning algorithms for decision trees were proposed by Quinlan (Quinlan, 1993). First, he defined ID3 algorithm based on the information gain principle. This criterion is performed by calculating the entropy that produces every attribute of the examples and by selecting the attributes that save more decisions in information terms. C4.5 algorithm is an evolution of ID3 algorithm. The main characteristics of C4.5 are the following:

1. The algorithm can work with continuous attributes.
2. Information gain is not the only learning criterion.
3. The trees can be post-pruned in order to refine the desired output.

## 3 Experimental work

We did the testing on acted emotional speech from the Berlin database (Burkhardt el al., 2005). Although acted material has a number of well known drawbacks, it was used to establish a proof of concept for the methodology proposed and is a benchmark database for SER. In the future work we plan to do the testing on real emotions. The Berlin Emotional Database (EMO-DB) contains the set of emotions from the MPEG-4 standard (anger, joy, disgust, fear, sadness, surprise and neutral). Ten German sentences of emotionally undefined content have been acted in these emotions by ten professional actors, five of them female. Throughout perception tests by twenty human listeners 488 phrases have been chosen that were classified as more than 60% natural and more than 80% clearly assignable. The database is recorded in 16 bit, 16 kHz under studio noise conditions.

As for the testing protocol, 10-fold cross-validation was used. Recall, precision and F measure per class are given in Tables 3, 4.1 and 4.2 for C4.5, MLP and TGI+, respectively. The overall accuracy of MLP, the state of the art recogniser, is 73.9% and the overall accuracy of the TGI+ based recogniser is 78.58%, which is a 4.68% $\pm$ 3.45% in favour of TGI+. The confidence interval was calculated as follows: $Z\sqrt{\frac{p(1-p)}{n}}$, where $p$ is accuracy, $n$ is cardinality of the data set, and $Z$ is a constant for the confidence level of 95%, i.e. $Z = 1.96$. The proposed TGI+ has also been evaluated against C4.5 to find out which is the contribution of moving from the feature vector representation of samples to the distance to automata one. C4.5 performs with 52.9% of acuracy, which is 25.68% less than TGI+. The positive outcome of such contrastive testing in favour of TGI+ was expected, because TGI+ was designed to enjoy strengths of two paradigms: syntactic and statistical, while MLP (or C4.5) is a powerful single paradigm statistical method.

| class | precision | recall | F measure |
|---|---|---|---|
| fear | 0.49 | 0.44 | 0.46 |
| disgust | 0.26 | 0.24 | 0.26 |
| happiness | 0.35 | 0.36 | 0.35 |
| boredom | 0.49 | 0.55 | 0.52 |
| neutral | 0.51 | 0.46 | 0.49 |
| sadness | 0.71 | 0.82 | 0.76 |
| anger | 0.69 | 0.7 | 0.7 |

Table 1: Baseline recognition with C4.5 on the Berlin emotional database. The overall accuracy is 52.9%, which is 25.68% less accurate than TGI+.

| class | precision | recall | F measure |
|---|---|---|---|
| fear | 0.82 | 0.74 | 0.77 |
| disgust | 0.72 | 0.74 | 0.73 |
| happiness | 0.52 | 0.49 | 0.51 |
| boredom | 0.73 | 0.75 | 0.74 |
| neutral | 0.71 | 0.78 | 0.75 |
| sadness | 0.88 | 0.94 | 0.91 |
| anger | 0.75 | 0.76 | 0.75 |

Table 2: State of the art recognition with MLP on the Berlin emotional database. The overall accuracy is 73.9%, which is 4.68% less accurate than TGI+.

## 4 Discussion

### 4.1 Correctness of algorithm construction

While constructing TGI+, it is of critical importance that the following condition holds: *The accuracy of TGI+ is better than that of tree acceptors and C4.5.* If this condition holds, then TGI+ is well constructed. We tested TGI+, tree automata as acceptors and C4.5 on the same Berlin database under the same experimental settings. The tree automata and C4.5 perform with 43% and 52.9% of accuracy respectively, which is 35.58% and 25.68% worse than the accuracy of TGI+. Therefore the condition is met and we can state that we arrived to a meaningful combination of methods from different pattern recognition paradigms.

### 4.2 A combination of statistical and syntactic recognition

Syntactic recognition is a form of pattern recognition, where items are presented as pattern structures, which take account of more complex interrelationships between features than simple numeric feature vectors used in statistical classification. One way to represent such structure is strings (or trees) of a formal language. In this case differences in the structures of the classes are encoded as different grammars. In our case, we have numeric data in place of a finite alphabet, which is more traditional for syntactic learning. The syntactic method does the mapping of objects into their models, which can be classified more accurately than objects themselves.

| class | precision | recall | F measure |
|---|---|---|---|
| fear | 0.66 | 0.66 | 0.66 |
| disgust | 0.6 | 0.6 | 0.6 |
| happiness | 0.86 | 0.73 | 0.81 |
| boredom | 0.81 | 0.72 | 0.77 |
| neutral | 0.64 | 0.79 | 0.71 |
| sadness | 0.83 | 0.83 | 0.83 |
| anger | 0.89 | 0.93 | 0.91 |

Table 3: Performance of the TGI+ based emotion recognizer on the Berlin emotional database. The overall accuracy is 78.58%.

### 4.3 Why tree structures?

Looking at the algorithm, it might seem redundant to have tree acceptors, when the same would be possible to handle with a finite state automaton (that accepts the class of regular string languages). Yet tree structures will serve well to add different weights to tree branches. The motivation behind is that acoustically some emotions are transmitted with segmental features and others with prosodic, e.g. prosody can be prioritised over segmental features or vice versa (see also Section 4.5).

### 4.4 Selection of C4.5 as a base classifier in TGI+

A natural question is: given that MLP outperforms C4.5, which are the reasons for having C4.5 as a base classifier in TGI+ and not the top statistical classifier? We followed the idea of (Sempere, Lopez, 2003), where C4.5 was the base classifier. We also considered the possibility of having MLP in place of C4.5. The accuracies dramatically went down and we abandoned this alternative.

### 4.5 Future work

*I. Tuning parameters.* There are two tuning parameters. To exclude the possibility of overfitting, the testing settings should be changed to the protocol with disjoint training, validation and testing sets. We have not done the experiments under the new training/testing settings, yet we can use the old 10-f cross validation mode to see the trends. Tuning parameter 1 is the point of division of the training set into the two subsets $T_1$ and $T_2$, i.e. a division of the training data to train the statistical and syntactic classifier. The division point should be shifted from 5% for syntactic and 100% for statistical to 100% to train both syntactic and statistical models. The point of division of the training data is an accuracy sensitive parameter. Our rough analysis showed that the resulting function (point of division for abscissa and accuracy for ordinate) has a hill shape with one absolute maximum, and we made a division roughly at this point: 39% of the training data for the syntactic model. Finding the best division in fair experimental settings remains for future work.

Tuning parameter 2 is a set of edit costs assigned to different branches of the tree acceptors. A linguistic approach is an alternative to the feature selection we followed so far. This is the point at which finite state automata cease to be an alternative modelling device. The motivation behind is that acoustically some emotions are transmitted with segmental features and others with prosodic (Barra, et al., 1993). A coefficient of 1.5 on the prosodic branches brought 2% of improvement of recognition for boredom, neutral and sadness.

*II. Testing TGI+ on authentic emotions.* It has been shown that authentic corpora have very different distributions compared to acted speech emotions (Vogt, Andre, 2005). We must check whether TGI+ is also a top performer, when confronted with authentic corpora.

*III. Complexity and computational time.* A number of classifiers, like MLP (but not C4.5) require a prior feature selection step, while TGI+ always uses a complete set of features, therefore better accuracies come at the cost of higher computational complexity. We must analyse such advantages and disadvantages of TGI+ compared to other popular classifiers.

## 5 Conclusions

We have adapted a classification approach coming from optical character recognition research to the task of speech emotion recognition. The general idea was that we would like a classification approach to enjoy the representational power of a syntactic method and the efficiency of statistical classification. The syntactic part implements a tree grammar inference algorithm. The statistical part implements an entropy based decision tree (C4.5). We did the testing on the Berlin database of emotional speech. Our classifier outperforms state of the art classifier (Multilayer Perceptron) by 4.68% and a baseline (C4.5) by 26.58%, which proves validity of the approach.

## 6 Acknowledgements

This research was supported by AGAUR, the Research Agency of Catalonia, under the BE-DRG 2007 mobility grant. We would like to thank Lab of Spoken Language Systems, Saarland University, where much of this work was completed.

## References

Barra R., Montero J.M., Macias-Guarasa, DHaro, L.F., San-Segundo R., Cordoba R. 2005. *Prosodic and segmental rubrics in emotion identification.* Proc. ICASSP 2005, Philadelphia, PA, March 2005.

Burkhardt, F., Paeschke, A., Rolfes, M., Sendlmeier, W., Weiss, B. 2002. *A database of German Emotional Speech.* Proc. Interspeech 2005, ISCA, pp 1517-1520, Lisbon, Portugal, 2005.

Grimm M., Kroschel K., Narayanan S. 2007. *Support vector regression for automatic recognition of spontaneous emotions in speech*, Proc. of ICASSP, Honolulu, Hawaii, April 2007.

Liu, J., Chen, C., Bu, J., You, M, Tao, J. 2007. *Speech emotion recognition using an enhanced co-training algorithm*, in Proc. of ICME, Bejing, China, July, 2007.

Lopez D., Espana, S. 2002. *Error-correcting tree-language inference.* Pattern Recognition Letters 23, pp. 1-12. 2002

Sakakibara, Y. 1997. *Recent advances of grammatical inference.* Theoretical Computer Science 185, pp. 15-45. Elsevier. 1997.

Schuller B., Rigoll G. Lang M. 2003. *Hidden Markov Model-Based Speech Emotion Recognition*, Proc. of ICASSP 2003, Vol. II, pp. 1-4, Hong Kong, China, 2003.

Sempere J. M., Lopez D. 2003. *Learning decision trees and tree automata for a syntactic pattern recognition task.* Pattern Recognition and Image Analysis. Lecture notes in CS. Berlin. Volume 2652. pp. 943-950, 2003.

Sidorova J. 2007. *DEA report: Speech Emotion Recognition.* Appendix 1 (for the feature list) and Section 3.3. (for a comparative testing of various weka classifiers) . http://www.glicom.upf.edu/tesis/sidorova.pdf Universitat Pompeu Fabra

Sidorova J., McDonough J., Badia T. 2008. *Automatic Recognition of Emotive Voice and Speech*, in (Eds.) K. Izdebski. Emotions in The Human Voice, Vol. 3, Chap. 12, Plural Publishing, San Diego, CA, 2008.

Quinlan, J.R. 1993. *C4.5: Programs For Machine Learning*. Morgan Kaufmann, Los Altos. 1993.

Vogt, T. Andre, E. 2005. *Comparing feature sets for acted and spontaneous speech in view of automatic emotion recognition.* Proc. ICME 2005, Amsterdam, Netherlands, 2005.

Witten I.H., Frank E. 2005. Sec. 7.1 (for feature selection) and Sec. 10.4 (for multilayer perceptron) in *Data Mining. Practical Machine Learning Tools and Techniques.* Elsevier. 2005.

# A Comparison of Merging Strategies for Translation of German Compounds

**Sara Stymne**
Department of Computer and Information Science
Linköping University, Sweden
sarst@ida.liu.se

## Abstract

In this article, compound processing for translation into German in a factored statistical MT system is investigated. Compounds are handled by splitting them prior to training, and merging the parts after translation. I have explored eight merging strategies using different combinations of external knowledge sources, such as word lists, and internal sources that are carried through the translation process, such as symbols or parts-of-speech. I show that for merging to be successful, some internal knowledge source is needed. I also show that an extra sequence model for part-of-speech is useful in order to improve the order of compound parts in the output. The best merging results are achieved by a matching scheme for part-of-speech tags.

## 1 Introduction

In German, as in many other languages, compounds are normally written as single words without spaces or other word boundaries. Compounds can be binary, i.e., made up of two parts (1a), or have more parts (1b). There are also coordinated compound constructions (1c). In a few cases compounds are written with a hyphen (1d), often when one of the parts is a proper name or an abbreviation.

(1) a. Regierungskonferenz
*intergovernmental conference*

b. Fremdsprachenkenntnisse
*knowledge of foreign languages*

c. See- und Binnenhäfen
*sea and inland ports*

d. Kosovo-Konflikt
*Kosovo conflict*

e. Völkermord
*genocide*

German compounds can have English translations that are compounds, written as separate words (1a), other constructions, possibly with inserted function words and reordering (1b), or single words (1e). Compound parts sometimes have special compound forms, formed by addition or truncations of letters, by *umlaut* or by a combination of these, as in (1a), where the letter *-s* is added to the first part, *Regierung*. For an overview of German compound forms, see Langer (1998).

Compounds are productive and common in German and other Germanic languages, which makes them problematic for many applications including statistical machine translation. For translation into a compounding language, fewer compounds than in normal texts are often produced, which can be due to the fact that the desired compounds are missing in the training data, or that they have not been aligned correctly. Where a compound is the idiomatic word choice in the translation, a MT system can instead produce separate words, genitive or other alternative constructions, or only translate one part of the compound.

The most common way to integrate compound processing into statistical machine translation is to split compounds prior to training and translation. Splitting of compounds has received a lot of focus in the literature, both for machine translation, and targeted at other applications such as information retrieval or speech recognition.

When translating into a compounding language there is a need to merge the split compounds after translation. In order to do this we have to identify which words that should be merged into compounds, which is complicated by the fact that the translation process is not guaranteed to produce translations where compound parts are kept together.

*Proceedings of the EACL 2009 Student Research Workshop*, pages 61–69,
Athens, Greece, 2 April 2009. ©2009 Association for Computational Linguistics

In this article I explore the effects of merging in a factored phrase-based statistical machine translation system. The system uses part-of-speech as an output factor. This factor is used as a knowledge source for merging and to improve word order by using a part-of-speech (POS) sequence model.

There are different knowledge sources for merging. Some are external, such as frequency lists of words, compounds, and compound parts, that could be compiled at split-time. It is also possible to have internal knowledge sources, that are carried through the translation process, such as symbols on compound parts, or part-of-speech tags. Choices made at split-time influence which internal knowledge sources are available at merge-time. I will explore and compare three markup schemes for compound parts, and eight merging algorithms that use different combinations of knowledge sources.

## 2 Related Work

Splitting German compounds into their parts prior to translation has been suggested by many researchers. Koehn and Knight (2003) presented an empirical splitting algorithm that is used to improve translation from German to English. They split all words in all possible places, and considered a splitting option valid if all the parts are existing words in a monolingual corpus. They allowed the addition of *-s* or *-es* at all splitting points. If there were several valid splitting options they chose one based on the number of splits, the geometric mean of part frequencies or based on alignment data. Stymne (2008) extended this algorithm in a number of ways, for instance by allowing more compound forms. She found that for translation into German, it was better to use the arithmetic mean of part frequencies than the geometric mean. Using the mean of frequencies can result in no split, if the compound is more frequent than its parts.

Merging has been much less explored than splitting since it is common only to discuss translation from compounding languages. However, Popović et al. (2006) used merging for translation into German. They did not mark compound parts in any way, so the merging is based on two word lists, with compound parts and full compounds found at split-time. All words in the translation output that were possible compound parts were merged with the next word if it resulted in a known compound. They only discussed merging of binary compounds. The drawback of this method is that novel compounds cannot be merged. Nevertheless, this strategy led to improved translation measured by three automatic metrics.

In a study of translation between English and Swedish, Stymne and Holmqvist (2008) suggested a merging algorithm based on part-of-speech, which can be used in a factored translation system with part-of-speech as an output factor. Compound parts had special part-of-speech tags based on the head of the compound, and merging was performed if that part-of-speech tag matched that of the following word. When compound forms had been normalized the correct compound form was found by using frequency lists of parts and words compiled at split-time. This method can merge unseen compounds, and the tendency to merge too much is reduced by the restriction that POS-tags need to match. In addition coordinated compounds were handled by the algorithm. This strategy resulted in improved scores on automatic metrics, which were confirmed by an error analysis.

Koehn et al. (2008) discussed treatment of hyphened compounds in translation into German by splitting at hyphens and treat the hyphen as a separate token, marked by a symbol. The impact on translation results was small.

There are also other ways of using compound processing to improve SMT into German. Popović et al. (2006) suggested using compound splitting to improve alignment, or to merge English compounds prior to training.

Some work has discussed merging of not only compounds, but of all morphs. Virpioja et al. (2007) merged translation output that was split into morphs for Finnish, Swedish and Danish. They marked split parts with a symbol, and merged every word in the output which had this symbol with the next word. If morphs were misplaced in the translation output, they were merged anyway, possibly creating non-existent words. This system was worse than the baseline on Bleu (Papineni et al., 2002), but an error analysis showed some improvements.

El-Kahlout and Oflazer (2006), discuss merging of morphs in Turkish. They also mark morphs with a symbol, and in addition normalize affixes to standard form. In the merging phase, surface forms were generated following morphographemic rules. They found that morphs were often translated out of order, and that merging based purely on symbols gave bad results. To reduce this risk, they constrained splitting to allow only morphologically correct splits, and by grouping some morphemes. This lead to less ordering problems in the translation output and gave improvements over the baseline.

Compound recombination have also been applied to German speech recognition, e.g. by (Berton et al., 1996), who performed a lexical search to extend the word graph that is output by the speech recogniser.

## 3 Compound Processing

German compounds are split in the training data and prior to translation. After translation, the parts are merged to form full compounds. The knowledge sources available to the merging process depend on which information is carried through the translation process.

The splitting algorithm of Stymne (2008) will be used throughout this study. It is slightly modified such that only the 10 most common compound forms from a corpus study of Langer (1998) are allowed, and the hyphen in hyphened compounds is treated as a compound form, analogous to adding for instance the letter *s* to a part.

The annotation of compound parts influences the merging process. Choices have to be made concerning the form, markup and part-of-speech of compound parts. For the form two options have been considered, keeping the original compound form, or normalizing it so that it coincides with a normal word. Three types of marking have been investigated, no marking at all (*unmarked*), a marking symbol that is concatenated to all parts but the last (*marked*), or using a separate symbol between parts (*sepmarked*). The sepmarked scheme has different symbols for parts of coordinated compounds than for other compounds. Parts are normalized in the unmarked and sepmarked schemes, but left in their compound form in the marked scheme, since the symbol separates them from ordinary words in any case.

There is also the issue of which part-of-speech tag to use for compound parts. The last part of the compound, the head, always has the same part-of-speech tag as the full compound. Two schemes are explored for the other parts. For the marked and unmarked system, a part-of-speech tag that is derived from that of the last part of the word is used. For the sepmarked scheme the most common part-of-speech tag of the part from the tagged monolingual corpus is used.

In summary, the three markup schemes use the following combinations, exemplified by the result of splitting the word *begrüßenswert* (*welcome*, literally *worth to welcome*)

- **Unmarked:** no symbol, normalization, special POS-tags
  *begrüßen* ADJ-PART *wert* ADJ
- **Marked:** symbol on parts, no normalization, special POS-tags
  *begrüßens#* ADJ-PART *wert* ADJ
- **Sepmarked:** symbol as separate token, normalization, ordinary POS-tags
  *begrüßen* VV @#@ COMP *wert* ADJ

### 3.1 Merging

There is no guarantee that compound parts appear in a correct context in the translation output. This fact complicates merging, since there is a general choice between only merging those words that we know are compounds, and merging all occurrences of compound parts, which will merge unseen compounds, but probably also merge parts that do not form well-formed compounds. There is also the issue of parts possibly being part of coordinated compounds.

The internal knowledge sources that can be used for merging depends on the markup scheme used. The available internal sources are markup symbols, part-of-speech tags, and the special tags for compound parts. The external resources are frequency lists of words, compounds and parts, possibly with normalization, compiled at split-time.

For the unmarked and sepmarked scheme, reverse normalization, i.e., mapping normalized compound parts into correct compound forms, has to be applied in connection with merging. As in Stymne and Holmqvist (2008), all combinations of compound forms that are known for each part are looked up in the word frequency list, and the most frequent combination is chosen. If there are no known combinations, the parts are combined from left to right, at each step choosing the most frequent combination.

Three main types of merging algorithms are investigated in this study. The first group, inspired

| Name | Description |
| --- | --- |
| word-list | Merges all tokens that have been seen as compound parts with the next part if it results in a known word, from the training corpus |
| word-list + head-pos | As word-list, but only merges words where the last part is a noun, adjective or verb |
| compound-list | As word-list, but for known compounds from split-time, not for all known words |
| symbol | Merges all tokens that are marked with the next token |
| symbol + head-pos | As symbol, but only merges words where the last part is a noun, adjective or verb |
| symbol + word-list | A mix of symbol and word-list, where marked compounds are merged, if it results in a known word |
| POS-match | Merges all tokens with a compound part-of-speech tag, if the tag match the tag of the next token |
| POS-match + coord | As POS-match, but also adds a hyphen to parts that are followed by the conjunction *und* (*and*) |

Table 1: Merging algorithms

by Popović et al. (2006), is based only on external knowledge sources, frequency lists of words or compounds, and of parts, compiled at split-time. Novel compounds cannot be merged by these algorithms. The second group uses symbols to guide merging, inspired by work on morphology merging (Virpioja et al., 2007). In the unmarked scheme where compound parts are not marked with symbols, the special POS-tags are used to identify parts instead[1]. The third group is based on special part-of-speech tags for compounds (Stymne and Holmqvist, 2008), and merging is performed if the part-of-speech tags match. This group of algorithms cannot be applied to the sepmarked scheme.

In addition a restriction that the head of the compound should have a compounding part-of-speech, that is, a noun, adjective, or verb, and a rule to handle coordinated compounds are used. By using these additions and combinations of the main algorithms, a total of eight algorithms are explored, as summarized in Table 1. For all algorithms, compounds can have an arbitrary number of parts.

If there is a marked compound part that cannot be combined with the next word, in any of the algorithms, the markup is removed, and the part is left as a single word. For the sepmarked system, coordinated compounds are handled as part of the symbol algorithms, by using the special markup symbol that indicates them.

### 3.2 Merging Performance

To give an idea of the potential of the merging algorithms, they are evaluated on the split test reference corpus, using the unmarked scheme. The corpus has 55580 words, of which 4472 are identified as compounds by the splitting algorithm. Of these 4160 are known from the corpus, 245 are novel, and 67 are coordinated. For the methods based on symbols or part-of-speech, this merging task is trivial, except for reverse normalization, since all parts are correctly ordered.

Table 2 shows the number of errors. The POS-match algorithm with treatment of coordination makes 55 errors, 4 of which are due to coordinated compounds that does not use *und* as the conjunction. The other errors are due to errors in the reverse normalization of novel compounds, which has an accuracy of 79% on this text. The POS-match and symbol algorithms make additional errors on coordinated compounds. The head-pos restriction blocks compounds with an adverb as head, which gave better results on translation data, but increased the errors on this evaluation. The word list method both merges many words that are not compounds, and do not merge any novel compounds. Using a list of compounds instead of words reduces the errors slightly.

## 4 System Description

The translation system used is a factored phrase-based translation system. In a factored translation model other factors than surface form can be used, such as lemma or part-of-speech (Koehn and Hoang, 2007). In the current system part-of-speech is used only as an output factor in the target language. Besides the standard language model a sequence model on part-of-speech is used, which can be expected to lead to better word order in the translation output. There are no input factors, so no tagging has to be performed prior to translation, only the training corpus needs to be tagged. In addition, the computational overhead is small. One possible benefit gained by using part-of-speech as an output factor is that ordering, both in general, and of compound parts, can be improved. This hypothesis is tested by trying two system setups, with and without the part-of-speech sequence model. In addition part-of-speech is used for postprocess-

[1]For the marked scheme using POS-tags to identify compound parts is equivalent to using symbols.

| wlist | wlist+head-pos | clist | symbol | symbol+head-pos | symbol+wlist | POS-match | POS-match+coord |
|---|---|---|---|---|---|---|---|
| 2393 | 1656 | 2257 | 118 | 205 | 330 | 118 | 55 |

Table 2: Number of merging errors on the split reference corpus

| | | Tokens | Types |
|---|---|---|---|
| English | baseline | 15158429 | 63692 |
| German | baseline | 14356051 | 184215 |
| | marked | 15674728 | 93746 |
| | unmarked | 15674728 | 81806 |
| | sepmarked | 17007929 | 81808 |

Table 3: Type and token counts for the 701157 sentence training corpus

ing, both for uppercasing German nouns and as a knowledge source for compound merging.

The tools used are the Moses toolkit (Koehn et al., 2007) for decoding and training, GIZA++ for word alignment (Och and Ney, 2003), and SRILM (Stolcke, 2002) for language models. A 5-gram model is used for surface form, and a 7-gram model is used for part-of-speech. To tune feature weights minimum error rate training is used (Och, 2003), optimized against the Neva metric (Forsbom, 2003). Compound splitting is performed on the training corpus, prior to training. Merging is performed after translation, both for test, and incorporated into the tuning step.

### 4.1 Corpus

The system is trained and tested on the Europarl corpus (Koehn, 2005). The training corpus is filtered to remove sentences longer than 40 words and with a length ratio of more than 1 to 7. The filtered training corpus contains 701157 sentences. 500 sentences are used for tuning and 2000 sentences for testing[2]. The German side of the training corpus is part-of-speech tagged using TreeTagger (Schmid, 1994).

The German corpus has nearly three times as many types, i.e., unique tokens, as the English corpus despite having a somewhat lower token count, as shown for the training corpus in Table 3. Compound splitting drastically reduces the number of types, to around half or less, even though it is still larger than for English. Marking on parts gives 15% more types than no marking.

[2]The test set is *test2007* from the ACL 2008 Workshop on Statistical Machine Translation, `http://www.statmt.org/wmt08/shared-task.html`

## 5 Evaluation

Two types of evaluation are performed. The influence of the different merging algorithms on the overall translation quality is evaluated, using two automatic metrics. In addition the performance of the merging algorithms are analysed in some more detail. In both cases the effect of the POS sequence model is also discussed. Even when the POS sequence model is not used, part-of-speech is carried through the translation process, so that it can be used in the merging step.

### 5.1 Evaluation of Translation

Translations are evaluated on two automatic metrics: Bleu (Papineni et al., 2002) and PER, position independent error-rate (Tillmann et al., 1997). Case-sensitive versions of the metrics are used. PER does not consider word order, it evaluates the translation as a bag-of-word, and thus the systems without part-of-speech sequence models can be expected to do well on PER. Note that PER is an error-rate, so lower scores are better, whereas higher scores are better for Bleu.

These metrics have disadvantages, for instance because the same weight is given to all tokens, both to complex compounds, and to function words such as *und* (*and*). Bleu has been criticized, see e.g. (Callison-Burch et al., 2006; Chiang et al., 2008).

Table 4 and 5 shows the translation results using the different merging algorithms. For the systems with POS sequence models the baseline performs slightly better on Bleu, than the best systems with merging. Without the POS sequence model, however, merging often leads to improvements, by up to 0.48 Bleu points. For all systems it is advantageous to use the POS sequence model.

For the baseline, the PER scores are higher for the system without a POS sequence model, which, compared to the Bleu scores, confirms the fact that word order is improved by the sequence model. The systems with merging are better than the baseline with the POS sequence model. In all cases, however, the systems with merging performs worse when not using a POS sequence model, indicating that the part-of-speech

| | with POS-model | | | without POS-model | | |
|---|---|---|---|---|---|---|
| | unmarked | sepmarked | marked | unmarked | sepmarked | marked |
| word-list | 17.93 | 17.66 | 18.92 | 17.70 | 17.29 | 18.69 |
| word-list + head-pos | 19.34 | 19.07 | 19.60 | 19.13 | 18.63 | 19.38 |
| compound-list | 18.94 | 17.77 | 18.13 | 18.56 | 17.40 | 17.86 |
| symbol | 20.02 | 19.57 | 20.03 | **19.66** | 19.14 | **19.79** |
| symbol + head-pos | 20.02 | 19.55 | 20.01 | **19.75** | 19.12 | **19.78** |
| symbol + word-list | 20.03 | 19.72 | 20.02 | **19.76** | 19.29 | **19.79** |
| POS-match | 20.12 | – | 20.03 | **19.84** | – | **19.80** |
| POS-match + coord | 20.10 | – | 19.97 | **19.85** | – | **19.80** |

Table 4: Translation results for Bleu. Baseline with POS: 20.19, without POS: 19.66. Results that are better than the baseline are marked with bold face.

| | with POS-model | | | without POS-model | | |
|---|---|---|---|---|---|---|
| | unmarked | sepmarked | marked | unmarked | sepmarked | marked |
| word-list | 29.88 | 28.64 | 28.19 | 30.27 | 29.94 | 28.71 |
| word-list + head-pos | 27.49 | **26.07** | 27.26 | 27.78 | 27.22 | 27.84 |
| compound-list | **26.92** | 27.99 | 29.25 | 27.46 | 29.07 | 29.74 |
| symbol | **27.21** | **26.13** | **26.95** | 27.70 | 27.40 | 27.61 |
| symbol + head-pos | **27.11** | **26.10** | **26.92** | 27.34 | 27.35 | 27.54 |
| symbol + word-list | **26.86** | **25.54** | **26.80** | 27.15 | 26.72 | 27.39 |
| POS-match | **26.99** | – | **26.93** | 27.17 | – | 27.53 |
| POS-match + coord | **27.10** | – | **26.93** | 27.28 | – | 27.53 |

Table 5: Translation results for PER. Baseline with POS: 27.22, without POS: 26.49. Results that are better than the baseline are marked with bold face.

sequence model improves the order of compound parts.

When measured by PER, the best results when using merging are achieved by combining symbols and word lists, but when measured by Bleu, the POS-based algorithms are best. The simpler symbol-based methods, often have similar scores, and in a few cases even better. Adding treatment of coordinated compounds to the POS-match algorithm changes scores marginally in both directions. The word list based methods, however, generally give bad results. Using the head-pos restriction improves it somewhat and using a compound list instead of a word list gives different results in the different markup schemes, but is still worse than the best systems. This shows that some kind of internal knowledge source, either symbols or part-of-speech, is needed in order for merging to be successful.

On both metrics, the marked and unmarked system perform similarly. They are better than the sepmarked system on Bleu, but the sepmarked system is a lot better on PER, which is an indication of that word order is problematic in the sepmarked system, with its separate tokens to indicate compounds.

### 5.2 Evaluation of Merging

The results of the different merging algorithms are analysed to find the number of merges and the type and quality of the merges. In addition I investigate the effect of using a part-of-speech model on the merging process.

Table 6 shows the reduction of words[3] achieved by applying the different algorithms. The word list based method produces the highest number of merges in all cases, performing many merges where the parts are not recognized as such by the system. The number of merges is greatly reduced by the head-pos restriction. An investigation of the output of the word list based method shows that it often merges common words that incidentally form a new word, such as *bei* (*at*) and *der* (*the*) to *beider* (*both*). Another type of error is due to errors in the corpus, such as the merge of *umwelt* (*environment*) and *und* (*and*), which occurs in the corpus, but is not a correct German word. These two error types are often prohibited by the head-pos restrictions. The compound list method avoids these errors, but it does not merge compounds that were not split by the splitting algorithm, due to a high frequency, giving a very low number of splits in some cases. There are small differences between the POS-match and symbol algorithms. Not using the POS sequence model results in a higher number of merges for all systems.

A more detailed analysis was performed of the

[3]The reduction of words is higher than the number of produced compounds, since each compound can have more than two parts.

| | with POS-model | | | without POS-model | | |
|---|---|---|---|---|---|---|
| | unmarked | sepmarked | marked | unmarked | sepmarked | marked |
| word-list | 5275 | 5422 | 4866 | 5897 | 5589 | 5231 |
| word-list + head-pos | 4161 | 4412 | 4338 | 4752 | 4601 | 4661 |
| compound-list | 4460 | 4669 | 3253 | 5116 | 4850 | 3534 |
| symbol | 4431 | 4712 | 4332 | 5144 | 4968 | 4702 |
| symbol + head-pos | 4323 | 4671 | 4279 | 4832 | 4899 | 4594 |
| symbol + word-list | 4178 | 4436 | 4198 | 4753 | 4656 | 4530 |
| POS-match | 4363 | – | 4310 | 4867 | – | 4618 |
| POS-match + coord | 4361 | – | 4310 | 4865 | – | 4618 |

Table 6: Reduction of number of words by using different merging algorithms

| | | with POS-model | | | without POS-model | | |
|---|---|---|---|---|---|---|---|
| | | unmarked | sepmarked | marked | unmarked | sepmarked | marked |
| Known | | 3339 | 3594 | 3375 | 3747 | 3762 | 3587 |
| Novel | Good | 168 | 176 | 105 | 104 | 245 | 93 |
| | Bad | 20 | 97 | 8 | 10 | 64 | 7 |
| Coordinated | Good | 43 | 43 | 42 | 42 | 37 | 44 |
| | Bad | 9 | 9 | 3 | 22 | 7 | 5 |
| Single part | Good | 6 | – | 5 | 136 | – | 33 |
| | Bad | 11 | – | 16 | 52 | – | 46 |
| Total | | 3596 | 3919 | 3554 | 4113 | 4115 | 3815 |

Table 7: Analysis of merged compounds

compounds parts in the output. The result of merging them are classified into four groups: merged compounds that are known from the training corpus (2a) or that are novel (2b), parts that were not merged (2c), and parts of coordinated compounds (2d). They are classified as bad if the compound/part should have been merged with the next word, does not fit into its context, or has the wrong form.

(2) a. Naturschutzpolitik
*nature protection policy*

b. UN-Friedensplan
*UN peace plan*

c. * West- zulassen
*west allow*

d. Mittel- und Osteuropa
*Central and Eastern Europe*

For the unmarked and sepmarked systems, the classification was based on the POS-match constraint, where parts are not merged if the POS-tags do not match. POS-match cannot be used for the sepmarked scheme, which has standard POS-tags.

Table 7 shows the results of this analysis. The majority of the merged compounds are known from the training corpus for all systems. There is a marked difference between the two systems that use POS-match, and the sepmarked system that does not. The sepmarked system found the highest number of novel compounds, but also have the highest error rate for these, which shows that it is useful to match POS-tags. The other two systems find fewer novel compounds, but also make fewer mistakes. The marked system has more errors for single parts than the other systems, mainly beacuse the form of compound parts were not normalized. Very few errors are due to reverse normalization. In the unmarked system with a POS sequence model, there were only three such errors, which is better than the results on split data in Section 3.2.

Generally the percentage of bad parts or compounds is lower for the systems with a POS sequence model, which shows that the sequence model is useful for the ordering of compound parts. The number of single compound parts is also much higher for the systems without a POS sequence model. 80% of the merged compounds in the unmarked system are binary, i.e., have two parts, and the highest number of parts in a compound is 5. The pattern for the other systems is similar.

All systems produce fewer compounds than the 4472 in the German reference text. However, there might also be compounds in the output, that were not split and merged. These numbers are not directly comparable to the baseline system, and applying the POS-based splitting algorithm to translation output would not give a fair comparison.

An indication of the number of compounds in a text is the number of long words. In the reference text there are 351 words with at least 20 characters, which will be used as the limit for long words. A manual analysis showed that all these words are compounds. The baseline system produces 209 long words. The systems with merging, discussed above, all produce more long words than the baseline, but less than the reference, between 263 and 307, with the highest number in the marked system. The trend is the same for the systems without a POS sequence model, but with slightly fewer long words than for the systems with merging.

## 6 Discussion

The choice of merging method has a large impact on the final translation result. For merging to be successful some internal knowledge source, such as part-of-speech or symbols is needed. The pure word list based method performed the worst of all systems on both metrics in most cases, which was not surprising, considering the evaluation of the merging algorithms on split data, where it was shown that the word-list based methods merged many parts that were not compounds.

The combination of symbols and word lists gave good results on the automatic metrics. An advantage of this method is that it is applicable for translation systems that do not use factors. However, it has the drawback that it does not merge novel compounds, and finds fewer compounds than most other algorithms. The error analysis shows that many valid compounds are discarded by this algorithm. A method that both find novel compounds, and that works well is that based on POS-match. In its current form it needs a decoder that can handle factored translation models. It would, however, be possible to use more elaborate symbols with part-of-speech information, which would allow a POS-matching scheme, without the need of factors.

The error analysis of merging performance showed that merging works well, especially for the two schemes where POS-matching is possible, where the proportion of errors is low. It also showed that using a part-of-speech sequence model was useful in order to get good results, specifically since it increased the number of compound parts that were placed correctly in the translation output.

The sepmarked scheme is best on the PER metric it is worse on Bleu, and the error analysis shows that it performs worse on merging than the other systems. This could probably be improved by the use of special POS-tags and POS-matching for this scheme as well. It is hard to judge which is best of the unmarked and marked scheme. They perform similarly on the metrics, and there is no clear difference in the error analysis. The unmarked scheme does produce a somewhat higher number of novel compounds, though. A disadvantage of the marked scheme is that the compound form is kept for single parts. A solution for this could be to normalize parts in this scheme as well, which could improve performance, since reverse normalization performance is good on translation data.

The systems with splitting and merging have more long words than the baseline, which indicates that they are more successful in creating compounds. However, they still have fewer long words than the reference text, indicating the need of more work on producing compounds.

## 7 Conclusion and Future Work

In this study I have shown that the strategy used for merging German compound parts in translation output influences translation results to a large extent. For merging to be successful, it needs some internal knowledge source, carried through the translation process, such as symbols or part-of- speech. The overall best results were achieved by using matching for part-of-speech.

One factor that affects merging, which was not explored in this work, is the quality of splitting. If splitting produces less erroneously split compounds than the current method, it is possible that merging also can produce better results, even though it was not clear from the error analysis that bad splits were a problem. A number of more accurate splitting strategies have been suggested for different tasks, see e.g. Alfonseca et al. (2008), that could be explored in combination with merging for machine translation.

I have compared the performance of different merging strategies in one language, German. It would be interesting to investigate these methods for other compounding languages as well. I also want to explore translation between two compounding languages, where splitting and merging would be performed on both languages, not only on one language as in this study.

## References


Enrique Alfonseca, Slaven Bilac, and Stefan Pharies. 2008. Decompounding query keywords from compounding languages. In *Proceedings of ACL-08: HLT, Short Papers*, pages 253–256, Columbus, Ohio.

André Berton, Pablo Fetter, and Peter Regel-Brietzmann. 1996. Compound words in large-vocabulary German speech recognition systems. In *Proceedings of the Fourth International Conference on Spoken Language Processing (ICSLP)*, pages 1165–1168, Philadelphia, Pennsylvania, USA.

Chris Callison-Burch, Miles Osborne, and Philipp Koehn. 2006. Re-evaluating the role of BLEU in machine translation research. In *Proceedings of the 11th Conference of EACL*, pages 249–256, Trento, Italy.

David Chiang, Steve DeNeefe, Yee Seng Chan, and Hwee Tou Ng. 2008. Decomposability of translation metrics for improved evaluation and efficient algorithms. In *Proceedings of the 2008 Conference on Empirical Methods in Natural Language Processing*, pages 610–619, Honolulu, Hawaii.

İlknur Durgar El-Kahlout and Kemal Oflazer. 2006. Initial explorations in English to Turkish statistical machine translation. In *HLT-NAACL 2006: Proceedings of the Workshop on Statistical Machine Translation*, pages 7–14, New York, NY.

Eva Forsbom. 2003. Training a super model look-alike: featuring edit distance, n-gram occurrence, and one reference translation. In *Proceedings of the Workshop on Machine Translation Evaluation: Towards Systemizing MT Evaluation*, pages 29–36, New Orleans, Louisiana.

Philipp Koehn and Hieu Hoang. 2007. Factored translation models. In *Proceedings of the Joint Conference on Empirical Methods in Natural language Processing and Computational Natural Language Learning*, pages 868–876, Prague, Czech Republic.

Philipp Koehn and Kevin Knight. 2003. Empirical methods for compound splitting. In *Proceedings of the 10th Conference of EACL*, pages 187–193, Budapest, Hungary.

Philipp Koehn, Hieu Hoang, Alexandra Birch, Chris Callison-Burch, Marcello Federico, Nicola Bertoldi, Brooke Cowan, Wade Shen, Christine Moran, Richard Zens, Chris Dyer, Ondrej Bojar, Alexandra Constantin, and Evan Herbst. 2007. Moses: open source toolkit for statistical machine translation. In *Proceedings of the 45th Annual Meeting of the ACL, demonstration session*, Prague, Czech Republic.

Philipp Koehn, Abhishek Arun, and Hieu Hoang. 2008. Towards better machine translation quality for the German-English language pairs. In *Proceedings of the Third Workshop on Statistical Machine Translation*, pages 139–142, Columbus, Ohio.

Philipp Koehn. 2005. Europarl: a parallel corpus for statistical machine translation. In *Proceedings of MT Summit X*, Phuket, Thailand.

Stefan Langer. 1998. Zur Morphologie und Semantik von Nominalkomposita. In *Tagungsband der 4. Konferenz zur Verarbeitung natürlicher Sprache (KONVENS)*, pages 83–97, Bonn, Germany.

Franz Josef Och and Hermann Ney. 2003. A systematic comparison of various statistical alignment models. *Computational Linguistics*, 29(1):19–51.

Franz Josef Och. 2003. Minimum error rate training in statistical machine translation. In *Proceedings of the 41st Annual Meeting of ACL*, pages 160–167, Sapporo, Japan.

Kishore Papineni, Salim Roukos, Todd Ward, and Wei-Jing Zhu. 2002. BLEU: a method for automatic evaluation of machine translation. In *Proceedings of the 40th Annual Meeting of the ACL*, pages 311–318, Philadelphia, Pennsylvania.

Maja Popović, Daniel Stein, and Hermann Ney. 2006. Statistical machine translation of German compound words. In *Proceedings of FinTAL – 5th International Conference on Natural Language Processing*, pages 616–624, Turku, Finland. Springer Verlag, LNCS.

Helmut Schmid. 1994. Probabilistic part-of-speech tagging using decision trees. In *Proceedings of the International Conference on New Methods in Language Processing*, Manchester, UK.

Andreas Stolcke. 2002. SRILM - an extensible language modeling toolkit. In *Proceedings of the Seventh International Conference on Spoken Language Processing (ICSLP)*, pages 901–904, Denver, Colorado.

Sara Stymne and Maria Holmqvist. 2008. Processing of Swedish compounds for phrase-based statistical machine translation. In *Proceedings of the European Machine Translation Conference (EAMT08)*, pages 180–189, Hamburg, Germany.

Sara Stymne. 2008. German compounds in factored statistical machine translation. In Aarne Ranta and Bengt Nordström, editors, *Proceedings of GoTAL – 6th International Conference on Natural Language Processing*, pages 464–475, Gothenburg, Sweden. Springer Verlag, LNCS/LNAI.

C. Tillmann, S. Vogel, H. Ney, A. Zubiaga, and H. Sawaf. 1997. Accelerated DP based search for statistical translation. In *Proceedings of the 5 th European Conference on Speech Communication and Technology*, pages 2667–2670, Rhodes, Greece.

Sami Virpioja, Jaako J.Väyrynen, Mathias Creutz, and Markus Sadeniemi. 2007. Morphology-aware statistical machine translation based on morphs induced in an unsupervised manner. In *Proceedings of MT Summit XI*, pages 491–498, Copenhagen, Denmark.

# A Generalized Vector Space Model for Text Retrieval Based on Semantic Relatedness

**George Tsatsaronis** and **Vicky Panagiotopoulou**
Department of Informatics
Athens University of Economics and Business,
76, Patision Str., Athens, Greece
gbt@aueb.gr, vpanagiotopoulou@gmail.com

## Abstract

Generalized Vector Space Models (GVSM) extend the standard Vector Space Model (VSM) by embedding additional types of information, besides terms, in the representation of documents. An interesting type of information that can be used in such models is semantic information from word thesauri like WordNet. Previous attempts to construct GVSM reported contradicting results. The most challenging problem is to incorporate the semantic information in a theoretically sound and rigorous manner and to modify the standard interpretation of the VSM. In this paper we present a new GVSM model that exploits WordNet's semantic information. The model is based on a new measure of semantic relatedness between terms. Experimental study conducted in three TREC collections reveals that semantic information can boost text retrieval performance with the use of the proposed GVSM.

## 1 Introduction

The use of semantic information into text retrieval or text classification has been controversial. For example in Mavroeidis et al. (2005) it was shown that a GVSM using WordNet (Fellbaum, 1998) senses and their hypernyms, improves text classification performance, especially for small training sets. In contrast, Sanderson (1994) reported that even 90% accurate WSD cannot guarantee retrieval improvement, though their experimental methodology was based only on randomly generated pseudowords of varying sizes. Similarly, Voorhees (1993) reported a drop in retrieval performance when the retrieval model was based on WSD information. On the contrary, the construction of a sense-based retrieval model by Stokoe et al. (2003) improved performance, while several years before, Krovetz and Croft (1992) had already pointed out that resolving word senses can improve searches requiring high levels of recall.

In this work, we argue that the incorporation of semantic information into a GVSM retrieval model can improve performance by considering the semantic relatedness between the query and document terms. The proposed model extends the traditional VSM with term to term relatedness measured with the use of WordNet. The success of the method lies in three important factors, which also constitute the points of our contribution: 1) a new measure for computing semantic relatedness between terms which takes into account relation weights, and senses' depth; 2) a new GVSM retrieval model, which incorporates the aforementioned semantic relatedness measure; 3) exploitation of all the semantic information a thesaurus can offer, including semantic relations crossing parts of speech (POS). Experimental evaluation in three TREC collections shows that the proposed model can improve in certain cases the performance of the standard TF-IDF VSM. The rest of the paper is organized as follows: Section 2 presents preliminary concepts, regarding VSM and GVSM. Section 3 presents the term semantic relatedness measure and the proposed GVSM. Section 4 analyzes the experimental results, and Section 5 concludes and gives pointers to future work.

## 2 Background

### 2.1 Vector Space Model

The VSM has been a standard model of representing documents in information retrieval for almost three decades (Salton and McGill, 1983; Baeza-Yates and Ribeiro-Neto, 1999). Let $D$ be a document collection and $Q$ the set of queries representing users' information needs. Let also $t_i$ symbol-

*Proceedings of the EACL 2009 Student Research Workshop*, pages 70–78,
Athens, Greece, 2 April 2009. 

ize term $i$ used to index the documents in the collection, with $i = 1, .., n$. The VSM assumes that for each term $t_i$ there exists a vector $\vec{t_i}$ in the vector space that represents it. It then considers the set of all term vectors $\{\vec{t_i}\}$ to be the generating set of the vector space, thus the space basis. If each $d_k$,(for $k = 1, .., p$) denotes a document of the collection, then there exists a linear combination of the term vectors $\{\vec{t_i}\}$ which represents each $d_k$ in the vector space. Similarly, any query $q$ can be modelled as a vector $\vec{q}$ that is a linear combination of the term vectors.

In the standard VSM, the term vectors are considered pairwise orthogonal, meaning that they are linearly independent. But this assumption is unrealistic, since it enforces lack of relatedness between any pair of terms, whereas the terms in a language often relate to each other. Provided that the orthogonality assumption holds, the similarity between a document vector $\vec{d_k}$ and a query vector $\vec{q}$ in the VSM can be expressed by the cosine measure given in equation 1.

$$cos(\vec{d_k}, \vec{q}) = \frac{\sum_{j=1}^{n} a_{kj} q_j}{\sqrt{\sum_{i=1}^{n} a_{ki}^2 \sum_{j=1}^{n} q_j^2}} \quad (1)$$

where $a_{kj}, q_j$ are real numbers standing for the weights of term $j$ in the document $d_k$ and the query $q$ respectively. A standard baseline retrieval strategy is to rank the documents according to their cosine similarity to the query.

## 2.2 Generalized Vector Space Model

Wong et al. (1987) presented an analysis of the problems that the pairwise orthogonality assumption of the VSM creates. They were the first to address these problems by expanding the VSM. They introduced term to term correlations, which deprecated the pairwise orthogonality assumption, but they kept the assumption that the term vectors are linearly independent[1], creating the first GVSM model. More specifically, they considered a new space, where each term vector $\vec{t_i}$ was expressed as a linear combination of $2^n$ vectors $\vec{m_r}$, $r = 1..2^n$. The similarity measure between a document and a query then became as shown in equation 2, where $\vec{t_i}$ and $\vec{t_j}$ are now term vectors in a $2^n$ dimensional vector space, $\vec{d_k}$, $\vec{q}$ are the document and the query vectors, respectively, as before, $\acute{a}_{ki}, \acute{q}_j$ are the new weights, and $\acute{n}$ the new space dimensions.

$$cos(\vec{d_k}, \vec{q}) = \frac{\sum_{j=1}^{\acute{n}} \sum_{i=1}^{\acute{n}} \acute{a}_{ki} \acute{q}_j \vec{t_i} \vec{t_j}}{\sqrt{\sum_{i=1}^{\acute{n}} \acute{a}_{ki}^{2} \sum_{j=1}^{\acute{n}} \acute{q}_j^{2}}} \quad (2)$$

From equation 2 it follows that the term vectors $\vec{t_i}$ and $\vec{t_j}$ need not be known, as long as the correlations between terms $t_i$ and $t_j$ are known. If one assumes pairwise orthogonality, the similarity measure is reduced to that of equation 1.

## 2.3 Semantic Information and GVSM

Since the introduction of the first GVSM model, there are at least two basic directions for embedding term to term relatedness, other than exact keyword matching, into a retrieval model: (a) compute semantic correlations between terms, or (b) compute frequency co-occurrence statistics from large corpora. In this paper we focus on the first direction. In the past, the effect of WSD information in text retrieval was studied (Krovetz and Croft, 1992; Sanderson, 1994), with the results revealing that under circumstances, senses information may improve IR. More specifically, Krovetz and Croft (1992) performed a series of three experiments in two document collections, CACM and TIMES. The results of their experiments showed that word senses provide a clear distinction between relevant and nonrelevant documents, rejecting the null hypothesis that the meaning of a word is not related to judgments of relevance. Also, they reached the conclusion that words being worth of disambiguation are either the words with uniform distribution of senses, or the words that in the query have a different sense from the most popular one. Sanderson (1994) studied the influence of disambiguation in IR with the use of pseudowords and he concluded that sense ambiguity is problematic for IR only in the cases of retrieving from short queries. Furthermore, his findings regarding the WSD used were that such a WSD system would help IR if it could perform with very high accuracy, although his experiments were conducted in the Reuters collection, where standard queries with corresponding relevant documents (qrels) are not provided.

Since then, several recent approaches have incorporated semantic information in VSM. Mavroeidis et al. (2005) created a GVSM kernel based on the use of noun senses, and their hypernyms from WordNet. They experimentally

[1]It is known from Linear Algebra that if every pair of vectors in a set of vectors is orthogonal, then this set of vectors is linearly independent, but not the inverse.

showed that this can improve text categorization. Stokoe et al. (Stokoe et al., 2003) reported an improvement in retrieval performance using a fully sense-based system. Our approach differs from the aforementioned ones in that it expands the VSM model using the semantic information of a word thesaurus to interpret the orthogonality of terms and to measure semantic relatedness, instead of directly replacing terms with senses, or adding senses to the model.

## 3 A GVSM Model based on Semantic Relatedness of Terms

Synonymy (many words per sense) and polysemy (many senses per word) are two fundamental problems in text retrieval. Synonymy is related with recall, while polysemy with precision. One standard method to tackle synonymy is the expansion of the query terms with their synonyms. This increases recall, but it can reduce precision dramatically. Both polysemy and synonymy can be captured on the GVSM model in the computation of the inner product between $\vec{t_i}$ and $\vec{t_j}$ in equation 2, as will be explained below.

### 3.1 Semantic Relatedness

In our model, we measure semantic relatedness using WordNet. It considers the path length, captured by *compactness* (SCM), and the path depth, captured by *semantic path elaboration* (SPE), which are defined in the following. The two measures are combined to for *semantic relatedness* (SR) beetween two terms. SR, presented in definition 3, is the basic module of the proposed GVSM model. The adopted method of building semantic networks and measuring semantic relatedness from a word thesaurus is explained in the next subsection.

**Definition 1** *Given a word thesaurus O, a weighting scheme for the edges that assigns a weight* $e \in (0,1)$ *for each edge, a pair of senses* $S = (s_1, s_2)$, *and a path of length l connecting the two senses, the semantic compactness of S* ($SCM(S,O)$) *is defined as* $\prod_{i=1}^{l} e_i$, *where* $e_1, e_2, ..., e_l$ *are the path's edges. If* $s_1 = s_2$ $SCM(S,O) = 1$. *If there is no path between* $s_1$ *and* $s_2$ $SCM(S,O) = 0$.

Note that *compactness* considers the path length and has values in the set [0, 1]. Higher *compactness* between senses declares higher semantic relatedness and larger weight are assigned to stronger edge types. The intuition behind the assumption of edges' weighting is the fact that some edges provide stronger semantic connections than others. In the next subsection we propose a candidate method of computing weights. The *compactness* of two senses $s_1$ and $s_2$, can take different values for all the different paths that connect the two senses. All these paths are examined, as explained later, and the path with the maximum weight is eventually selected (definition 3). Another parameter that affects term relatedness is the depth of the sense nodes comprising the path. A standard means of measuring depth in a word thesaurus is the hypernym/hyponym hierarchical relation for the noun and adjective POS and hypernym/troponym for the verb POS. A path with shallow sense nodes is more general compared to a path with deep nodes. This parameter of semantic relatedness between terms is captured by the measure of *semantic path elaboration* introduced in the following definition.

**Definition 2** *Given a word thesaurus O and a pair of senses* $S = (s_1, s_2)$, *where* $s_1, s_2 \in O$ *and* $s1 \neq s2$, *and a path between the two senses of length l, the semantic path elaboration of the path (SPE(S,O)) is defined as* $\prod_{i=1}^{l} \frac{2d_i d_{i+1}}{d_i + d_{i+1}} \cdot \frac{1}{d_{max}}$, *where* $d_i$ *is the depth of sense* $s_i$ *according to O, and* $d_{max}$ *the maximum depth of O. If* $s_1 = s_2$, *and* $d = d_1 = d_2$, $SPE(S,O) = \frac{d}{d_{max}}$. *If there is no path from* $s_1$ *to* $s_2$, $SPE(S,O) = 0$.

Essentially, SPE is the harmonic mean of the two depths normalized to the maximum thesaurus depth. The harmonic mean offers a lower upper bound than the average of depths and we think is a more realistic estimation of the path's depth. SCM and SPE capture the two most important parameters of measuring semantic relatedness between terms (Budanitsky and Hirst, 2006), namely path length and senses depth in the used thesaurus. We combine these two measures naturally towards defining the *Semantic Relatedness* between two terms.

**Definition 3** *Given a word thesaurus O, a pair of terms* $T = (t_1, t_2)$, *and all pairs of senses* $S = (s_{1i}, s_{2j})$, *where* $s_{1i}$, $s_{2j}$ *senses of* $t_1$,$t_2$ *respectively. The semantic relatedness of T (SR(T,S,O)) is defined as* $max\{SCM(S,O) \cdot SPE(S,O)\}$. *SR between two terms* $t_i, t_j$ *where* $t_i \equiv t_j \equiv t$ *and* $t \notin O$ *is defined as* 1. *If* $t_i \in O$ *but* $t_j \notin O$, *or* $t_i \notin O$ *but* $t_j \in O$, *SR is defined as* 0.

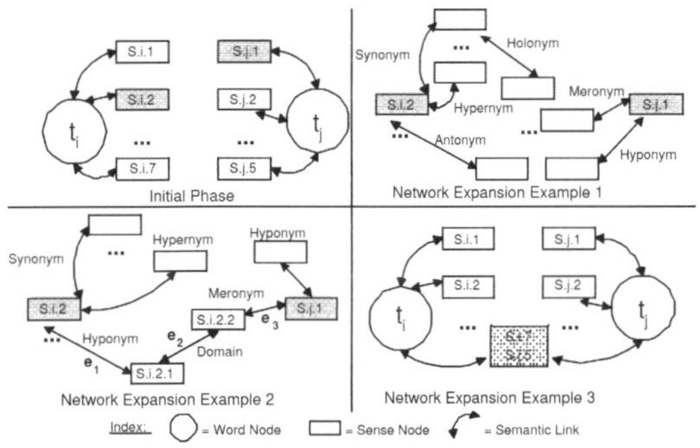


Figure 1: Computation of semantic relatedness.

### 3.2 Semantic Networks from Word Thesauri

In order to construct a semantic network for a pair of terms $t_1$ and $t_2$ and a combination of their respective senses, i.e., $s_1$ and $s_2$, we adopted the network construction method that we introduced in (Tsatsaronis et al., 2007). This method was preferred against other related methods, like the one introduced in (Mihalcea et al., 2004), since it embeds all the available semantic information existing in WordNet, even edges that cross POS, thus offering a richer semantic representation. According to the adopted semantic network construction model, each semantic edge type is given a different weight. The intuition behind edge types' weighting is that certain types provide stronger semantic connections than others. The frequency of occurrence of the different edge types in Wordnet 2.0, is used to define the edge types' weights (e.g. $0.57$ for hypernym/hyponym edges, $0.14$ for nominalization edges etc.).

Figure 1 shows the construction of a semantic network for two terms $t_i$ and $t_j$. Let the highlighted senses $S.i.2$ and $S.j.1$ be a pair of senses of $t_i$ and $t_j$ respectively. All the semantic links of the highlighted senses, as found in WordNet, are added as shown in example 1 of figure 1. The process is repeated recursively until at least one path between $S.i.2$ and $S.j.1$ is found. It might be the case that there is no path from $S.i.2$ to $S.j.1$. In that case $SR((t_i, t_j), (S.i.2, S.j.1), O) = 0$. Suppose that a path is that of example 2, where $e_1, e_2, e_3$ are the respective edge weights, $d_1$ is the depth of $S.i.2$, $d_2$ the depth of $S.i.2.1$, $d_3$ the depth of $S.i.2.2$ and $d_4$ the depth of $S.j.1$, and $d_{max}$ the maximum thesaurus depth. For reasons of simplicity, let $e_1 = e_2 = e_3 = 0.5$, and $d_1 = 3$. Naturally, $d_2 = 4$, and let $d_3 = d_4 = d_2 = 4$. Finally, let $d_{max} = 14$, which is the case for WordNet 2.0. Then, $SR((t_i, t_j), (S.i.2, S.j.1), O) = 0.5^3 \cdot 0.4615 \cdot 0.5^2 = 0.01442$. Example 3 of figure 2 illustrates another possibility where $S.i.7$ and $S.j.5$ is another examined pair of senses for $t_i$ and $t_j$ respectively. In this case, the two senses coincide, and $SR((t_i, t_j), (S.i.7, S.j.5), O) = 1 \cdot \frac{d}{14}$, where $d$ the depth of the sense. When two senses coincide, $SCM = 1$, as mentioned in definition 1, a secondary criterion must be levied to distinguish the relatedness of senses that match. This criterion in $SR$ is $SPE$, which assumes that a sense is more specific as we traverse WordNet graph downwards. In the specified example, $SCM = 1$, but $SPE = \frac{d}{14}$. This will give a final value to $SR$ that will be less than 1. This constitutes an intrinsic property of $SR$, which is expressed by $SPE$. The rationale behind the computation of $SPE$ stems from the fact that word senses in WordNet are organized into synonym sets, named *synsets*. Moreover, synsets belong to hierarchies (i.e., noun hierarchies developed by the hypernym/hyponym relations). Thus, in case two words map into the same synset (i.e., their senses belong to the same synset), the computation of their semantic relatedness must additionally take into account the depth of that synset in WordNet.

### 3.3 Computing Maximum Semantic Relatedness

In the expansion of the VSM model we need to weigh the inner product between any two term vectors with their semantic relatedness. It is obvious that given a word thesaurus, there can be more than one semantic paths that link two senses. In these cases, we decide to use the path that maximizes the semantic relatedness (the product of SCM and SPE). This computation can be done according to the following algorithm, which is a modification of Dijkstra's algorithm for finding the shortest path between two nodes in a weighted directed graph. The proof of the algorithm's correctness follows with theorem 1.

**Theorem 1** *Given a word thesaurus $O$, a weighting function $w : E \rightarrow (0, 1)$, where a higher value declares a stronger edge, and a pair of senses $S(s_s, s_f)$ declaring source ($s_s$) and destination ($s_f$) vertices, then the $SCM(S, O) \cdot SPE(S, O)$ is maximized for the path returned by Algorithm 1, by using the weighting scheme $e_{ij} = w_{ij} \cdot \frac{2 \cdot d_i \cdot d_j}{d_{max} \cdot (d_i + d_j)}$, where $e_{ij}$ the new weight of the edge connecting senses $s_i$ and $s_j$, and $w_{ij}$ the initial*

**Algorithm 1** MaxSR(G,u,v,w)

```
Require: A directed weighted graph G, two
    nodes u, v and a weighting scheme w : E → (0..1).
Ensure: The path from u to v with the maximum
    product of the edges weights.
    Initialize-Single-Source(G,u)
  for all vertices v ∈ V[G] do
      d[v] = −∞
      π[v] = NULL
  end for
  d[u] = 1
    Relax(u, v, w)
  if d[v] < d[u] · w(u, v) then
      d[v] = d[u] · w(u, v)
      π[v] = u
  end if
    Maximum-Relatedness(G,u,v,w)
  Initialize-Single-Source(G,u)
  S = ∅
  Q = V[G]
  while v ∈ Q do
      s = Extract from Q the vertex with max d
      S = S ∪ s
      for all vertices k ∈ Adjacency List of s do
          Relax(s,k,w)
      end for
  end while
  return the path following all the ancestors π of
    v back to u
```

*weight assigned by weighting function $w$.*

**Proof 1** *For the proof of this theorem we follow the course of thinking of the proof of theorem* 25.10 *in (Cormen et al., 1990). We shall show that for each vertex $s_f \in V$, $d[s_f]$ is the maximum product of edges' weight through the selected path, starting from $s_s$, at the time when $s_f$ is inserted into $S$. From now on, the notation $\delta(s_s, s_f)$ will represent this product. Path $p$ connects a vertex in $S$, namely $s_s$, to a vertex in $V - S$, namely $s_f$. Consider the first vertex $s_y$ along $p$ such that $s_y \in V - S$ and let $s_x$ be y's predecessor. Now, path $p$ can be decomposed as $s_s \to s_x \to s_y \to s_f$. We claim that $d[s_y] = \delta(s_s, s_y)$ when $s_f$ is inserted into $S$. Observe that $s_x \in S$. Then, because $s_f$ is chosen as the first vertex for which $d[s_f] \neq \delta(s_s, s_f)$ when it is inserted into $S$, we had $d[s_x] = \delta(s_s, s_x)$ when $s_x$ was inserted into $S$.*

*We can now obtain a contradiction to the above to prove the theorem. Because $s_y$ occurs before $s_f$ on the path from $s_s$ to $s_f$ and all edge weights are nonnegative*[2] *and in $(0, 1)$ we have $\delta(s_s, s_y) \geq \delta(s_s, s_f)$, and thus $d[s_y] = \delta(s_s, s_y) \geq \delta(s_s, s_f) \geq d[s_f]$. But both $s_y$ and $s_f$ were in $V - S$ when $s_f$ was chosen, so we have $d[s_f] \geq d[s_y]$. Thus, $d[s_y] = \delta(s_s, s_y) = \delta(s_s, s_f) = d[s_f]$. Consequently, $d[s_f] = \delta(s_s, s_f)$ which contradicts our choice of $s_f$. We conclude that at the time each vertex $s_f$ is inserted into $S$, $d[s_f] = \delta(s_s, s_f)$.*

*Next, to prove that the returned maximum product is the $SCM(S,O) \cdot SPE(S,O)$, let the path between $s_s$ and $s_f$ with the maximum edge weight product have $k$ edges. Then, Algorithm 1 returns the maximum $\prod_{i=1}^{k} e_{i(i+1)} = w_{s2} \cdot \frac{2 \cdot d_s \cdot d_2}{d_{max} \cdot (d_s + d_2)} \cdot w_{23} \cdot \frac{2 \cdot d_2 \cdot d_3}{d_{max} \cdot (d_2 + d_3)} \cdot \ldots \cdot w_{kf} \cdot \frac{2 \cdot d_k \cdot d_f}{d_{max} \cdot (d_k + d_f)} = \prod_{i=1}^{k} w_{i(i+1)} \cdot \prod_{i=1}^{k} \frac{2 d_i d_{i+1}}{d_i + d_{i+1}} \cdot \frac{1}{d_{max}} = SCM(S,O) \cdot SPE(S,O)$.*

### 3.4 Word Sense Disambiguation

The reader will have noticed that our model computes the SR between two terms $t_i$,$t_j$, based on the pair of senses $s_i$,$s_j$ of the two terms respectively, which maximizes the product $SCM \cdot SPE$. Alternatively, a WSD algorithm could have disambiguated the two terms, given the text fragments where the two terms occurred. Though interesting, this prospect is neither addressed, nor examined in this work. Still, it is in our next plans and part of our future work to embed in our model some of the interesting WSD approaches, like knowledge-based (Sinha and Mihalcea, 2007; Brody et al., 2006), corpus-based (Mihalcea and Csomai, 2005; McCarthy et al., 2004), or combinations with very high accuracy (Montoyo et al., 2005).

### 3.5 The GVSM Model

In equation 2, which captures the document-query similarity in the GVSM model, the orthogonality between terms $t_i$ and $t_j$ is expressed by the inner product of the respective term vectors $\vec{t_i}\vec{t_j}$. Recall that $\vec{t_i}$ and $\vec{t_j}$ are in reality unknown. We estimate their inner product by equation 3, where $s_i$ and $s_j$ are the senses of terms $t_i$ and $t_j$ respectively, maximizing $SCM \cdot SPE$.

$$\vec{t_i}\vec{t_j} = SR((t_i, t_j), (s_i, s_j), O) \qquad (3)$$

Since in our model we assume that each term can be semantically related with any other term, and

[2]The sign of the algorithm is not considered at this step.

$SR((t_i,t_j),O) = SR((t_j,t_i),O)$, the new space is of $\frac{n \cdot (n-1)}{2}$ dimensions. In this space, each dimension stands for a distinct pair of terms. Given a document vector $\vec{d_k}$ in the VSM TF-IDF space, we define the value in the $(i,j)$ dimension of the new document vector space as $d_k(t_i,t_j) = (TF-IDF(t_i,d_k) + TF-IDF(t_j,d_k)) \cdot \vec{t_i}\vec{t_j}$. We add the TF-IDF values because any product-based value results to zero, unless both terms are present in the document. The dimensions $q(t_i,t_j)$ of the query, are computed similarly. A GVSM model aims at being able to retrieve documents that not necessarily contain exact matches of the query terms, and this is its great advantage. This new space leads to a new GVSM model, which is a natural extension of the standard VSM. The cosine similarity between a document $d_k$ and a query $q$ now becomes:

$$cos(\vec{d_k},\vec{q}) = \frac{\sum_{i=1}^{n}\sum_{j=i}^{n} d_k(t_i,t_j) \cdot q(t_i,t_j)}{\sqrt{\sum_{i=1}^{n}\sum_{j=i}^{n} d_k(t_i,t_j)^2} \cdot \sqrt{\sum_{i=1}^{n}\sum_{j=i}^{n} q(t_i,t_j)^2}} \quad (4)$$

where $n$ is the dimension of the VSM TF-IDF space.

## 4 Experimental Evaluation

The experimental evaluation in this work is two-fold. First, we test the performance of the semantic relatedness measure (SR) for a pair of words in three benchmark data sets, namely the Rubenstein and Goodenough 65 word pairs (Rubenstein and Goodenough, 1965)(R&G), the Miller and Charles 30 word pairs (Miller and Charles, 1991)(M&C), and the 353 similarity data set (Finkelstein et al., 2002). Second, we evaluate the performance of the proposed GVSM in three TREC collections (TREC 1, 4 and 6).

### 4.1 Evaluation of the Semantic Relatedness Measure

For the evaluation of the proposed semantic relatedness measure between two terms we experimented in three widely used data sets in which human subjects have provided scores of relatedness for each pair. A kind of "gold standard" ranking of related word pairs (i.e., from the most related words to the most irrelevant) has thus been created, against which computer programs can test their ability on measuring semantic relatedness between words. We compared our measure against ten known measures of semantic relatedness: (HS) Hirst and St-Onge (1998), (JC) Jiang and Conrath (1997), (LC) Leacock et al. (1998), (L) Lin (1998), (R) Resnik (1995), (JS) Jarmasz and Szpakowicz (2003), (GM) Gabrilovich and Markovitch (2007), (F) Finkelstein et al. (2002), (HR) ) and (SP) Strube and Ponzetto (2006). In Table 1 the results of SR and the ten compared measures are shown. The reported numbers are the Spearman correlation of the measures' rankings with the gold standard (human judgements).

The correlations for the three data sets show that SR performs better than any other measure of semantic relatedness, besides the case of (HR) in the M&C data set. It surpasses HR though in the R&G and the 353-C data set. The latter contains the word pairs of the M&C data set. To visualize the performance of our measure in a more comprehensible manner, Figure 2 presents for all pairs in the R&G data set, and with increasing order of relatedness values based on human judgements, the respective values of these pairs that SR produces. A closer look on Figure 2 reveals that the values produced by SR (right figure) follow a pattern similar to that of the human ratings (left figure). Note that the x-axis in both charts begins from the least related pair of terms, according to humans, and goes up to the most related pair of terms. The y-axis in the left chart is the respective humans' rating for each pair of terms. The right figure shows SR for each pair. The reader can consult Budanitsky and Hirst (2006) to confirm that all the other measures of semantic relatedness we compare to, do not follow the same pattern as the human ratings, as closely as our measure of relatedness does (low y values for small x values and high y values for high x). The same pattern applies in the M&C and 353-C data sets.

### 4.2 Evaluation of the GVSM

For the evaluation of the proposed GVSM model, we have experimented with three TREC collections [3], namely TREC 1 (TIPSTER disks 1 and 2), TREC 4 (TIPSTER disks 2 and 3) and TREC 6 (TIPSTER disks 4 and 5). We selected those TREC collections in order to cover as many different thematic subjects as possible. For example, TREC 1 contains documents from the Wall Street Journal, Associated Press, Federal Register, and abstracts of U.S. department of energy. TREC 6 differs from TREC 1, since it has documents from Financial Times, Los Angeles Times and the Foreign Broadcast Information Service.

For each TREC, we executed the standard base-

[3] http://trec.nist.gov/

| | HS | JC | LC | L | R | JS | GM | F | HR | SP | SR |
|---|---|---|---|---|---|---|---|---|---|---|---|
| **R&G** | 0.745 | 0.709 | 0.785 | 0.77 | 0.748 | 0.842 | 0.816 | $N/A$ | 0.817 | 0.56 | **0.861** |
| **M&C** | 0.653 | 0.805 | 0.748 | 0.767 | 0.737 | 0.832 | 0.723 | $N/A$ | 0.904 | 0.49 | **0.855** |
| **353-C** | $N/A$ | $N/A$ | 0.34 | $N/A$ | 0.35 | 0.55 | 0.75 | 0.56 | 0.552 | 0.48 | **0.61** |

Table 1: Correlations of semantic relatedness measures with human judgements.

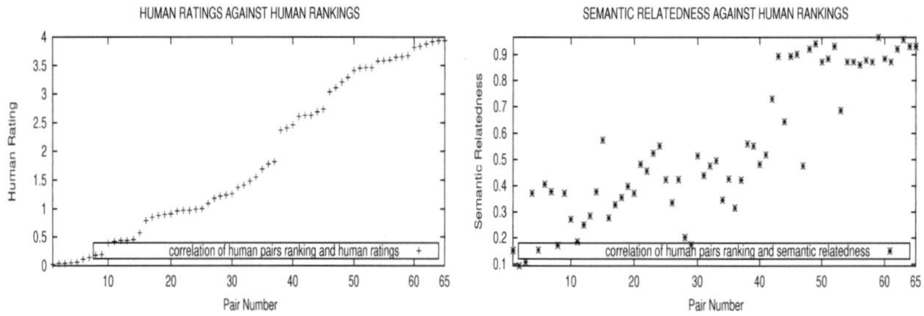


Figure 2: Correlation between human ratings and SR in the R&G data set.

line TF-IDF VSM model for the first 20 topics of each collection. Limited resources prohibited us from executing experiments in the top 1000 documents. To minimize the execution time, we have indexed all the pairwise semantic relatedness values according to the SR measure, in a database, whose size reached 300GB. Thus, the execution of the SR itself is really fast, as all pairwise SR values between WordNet synsets are indexed. For TREC 1, we used topics $51-70$, for TREC 4 topics $201-220$ and for TREC 6 topics $301-320$. From the results of the VSM model, we kept the top-50 retrieved documents. In order to evaluate whether the proposed GVSM can aid the VSM performance, we executed the GVSM in the same retrieved documents. The interpolated precision-recall values in the 11-standard recall points for these executions are shown in figure 3 (left graphs), for both VSM and GVSM. In the right graphs of figure 3, the differences in interpolated precision for the same recall levels are depicted. For reasons of simplicity, we have excluded the recall values in the right graphs, above which, both systems had zero precision. Thus, for TREC 1 in the y-axis we have depicted the difference in the interpolated precision values (%) of the GVSM from the VSM, for the first 4 recall points. For TRECs 4 and 6 we have done the same for the first 9 and 8 recall points respectively.

As shown in figure 3, the proposed GVSM may improve the performance of the TFIDF VSM up to 1.93% in TREC 4, 0.99% in TREC 6 and 0.42% in TREC 1. This small boost in performance proves that the proposed GVSM model is promising. There are many aspects though in the GVSM that we think require further investigation, like for example the fact that we have not conducted WSD so as to map each document and query term occurrence into its correct sense, or the fact that the weighting scheme of the edges used in SR generates from the distribution of each edge type in WordNet, while there might be other more sophisticated ways to compute edge weights. We believe that if these, but also more aspects discussed in the next section, are tackled, the proposed GVSM may improve more the retrieval performance.

## 5 Future Work

From the experimental evaluation we infer that SR performs very well, and in fact better than all the tested related measures. With regards to the GVSM model, experimental evaluation in three TREC collections has shown that the model is promising and may boost retrieval performance more if several details are further investigated and further enhancements are made. Primarily, the computation of the maximum semantic relatedness between two terms includes the selection of the semantic path between two senses that maximizes SR. This can be partially unrealistic since we are not sure whether these senses are the correct senses of the terms. To tackle this issue, WSD techniques may be used. In addition, the role of phrase detection is yet to be explored and

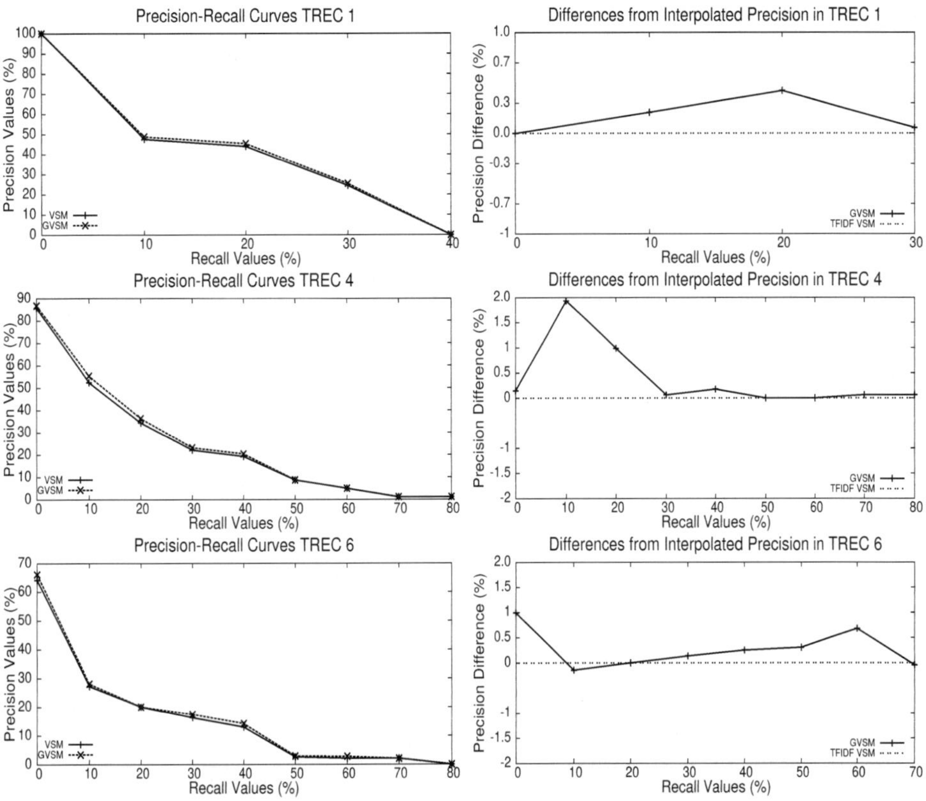


Figure 3: Differences (%) from the baseline in interpolated precision.

added into the model. Since we are using a large knowledge-base (WordNet), we can add a simple method to look-up term occurrences in a specified window and check whether they form a phrase. This would also decrease the ambiguity of the respective text fragment, since in WordNet a phrase is usually monosemous.

Moreover, there are additional aspects that deserve further research. In previously proposed GVSM, like the one proposed by Voorhees (1993), or by Mavroeidis et al. (2005), it is suggested that semantic information can create an individual space, leading to a dual representation of each document, namely, a vector with document's terms and another with semantic information. Rationally, the proposed GVSM could act complementary to the standard VSM representation. Thus, the similarity between a query and a document may be computed by weighting the similarity in the terms space and the senses' space. Finally, we should also examine the perspective of applying the proposed measure of semantic relatedness in a query expansion technique, similarly to the work of Fang (2008).

## 6 Conclusions

In this paper we presented a new measure of semantic relatedness and expanded the standard VSM to embed the semantic relatedness between pairs of terms into a new GVSM model. The semantic relatedness measure takes into account all of the semantic links offered by WordNet. It considers WordNet as a graph, weighs edges depending on their type and depth and computes the maximum relatedness between any two nodes, connected via one or more paths. The comparison to well known measures gives promising results. The application of our measure in the suggested GVSM demonstrates slightly improved performance in information retrieval tasks. It is on our next plans to study the influence of WSD performance on the proposed model. Furthermore, a comparative analysis between the proposed GVSM and other semantic network based models will also shed light towards the conditions, under which, embedding semantic information improves text retrieval.

## References


R. Baeza-Yates and B. Ribeiro-Neto. 1999. *Modern Information Retrieval*. Addison Wesley.

S. Brody, R. Navigli, and M. Lapata. 2006. Ensemble methods for unsupervised wsd. In *Proc. of COLING/ACL 2006*, pages 97–104.

A. Budanitsky and G. Hirst. 2006. Evaluating wordnet-based measures of lexical semantic relatedness. *Computational Linguistics*, 32(1):13–47.

T.H. Cormen, C.E. Leiserson, and R.L. Rivest. 1990. *Introduction to Algorithms*. The MIT Press.

H. Fang. 2008. A re-examination of query expansion using lexical resources. In *Proc. of ACL 2008*, pages 139–147.

C. Fellbaum. 1998. *WordNet – an electronic lexical database*. MIT Press.

L. Finkelstein, E. Gabrilovich, Y. Matias, E. Rivlin, Z. Solan, G. Wolfman, and E. Ruppin. 2002. Placing search in context: The concept revisited. *ACM TOIS*, 20(1):116–131.

E. Gabrilovich and S. Markovitch. 2007. Computing semantic relatedness using wikipedia-based explicit semantic analysis. In *Proc. of the 20th IJCAI*, pages 1606–1611. Hyderabad, India.

G. Hirst and D. St-Onge. 1998. Lexical chains as representations of context for the detection and correction of malapropisms. In *WordNet: An Electronic Lexical Database, chapter 13*, pages 305–332, Cambridge. The MIT Press.

M. Jarmasz and S. Szpakowicz. 2003. Roget's thesaurus and semantic similarity. In *Proc. of Conference on Recent Advances in Natural Language Processing*, pages 212–219.

J.J. Jiang and D.W. Conrath. 1997. Semantic similarity based on corpus statistics and lexical taxonomy. In *Proc. of ROCLING X*, pages 19–33.

R. Krovetz and W.B. Croft. 1992. Lexical ambiguity and information retrieval. *ACM Transactions on Information Systems*, 10(2):115–141.

C. Leacock, G. Miller, and M. Chodorow. 1998. Using corpus statistics and wordnet relations for sense identification. *Computational Linguistics*, 24(1):147–165, March.

D. Lin. 1998. An information-theoretic definition of similarity. In *Proc. of the 15th International Conference on Machine Learning*, pages 296–304.

D. Mavroeidis, G. Tsatsaronis, M. Vazirgiannis, M. Theobald, and G. Weikum. 2005. Word sense disambiguation for exploiting hierarchical thesauri in text classification. In *Proc. of the 9th PKDD*, pages 181–192.

D. McCarthy, R. Koeling, J. Weeds, and J. Carroll. 2004. Finding predominant word senses in untagged text. In *Proc, of the 42nd ACL*, pages 280–287. Spain.

R. Mihalcea and A. Csomai. 2005. Senselearner: Word sense disambiguation for all words in unrestricted text. In *Proc. of the 43rd ACL*, pages 53–56.

R. Mihalcea, P. Tarau, and E. Figa. 2004. Pagerank on semantic networks with application to word sense disambiguation. In *Proc. of the 20th COLING*.

G.A. Miller and W.G. Charles. 1991. Contextual correlates of semantic similarity. *Language and Cognitive Processes*, 6(1):1–28.

A. Montoyo, A. Suarez, G. Rigau, and M. Palomar. 2005. Combining knowledge- and corpus-based word-sense-disambiguation methods. *Journal of Artificial Intelligence Research*, 23:299–330, March.

P. Resnik. 1995. Using information content to evaluate semantic similarity. In *Proc. of the 14th IJCAI*, pages 448–453, Canada.

H. Rubenstein and J.B. Goodenough. 1965. Contextual correlates of synonymy. *Communications of the ACM*, 8(10):627–633.

G. Salton and M.J. McGill. 1983. *Introduction to Modern Information Retrieval*. McGraw-Hill.

M. Sanderson. 1994. Word sense disambiguation and information retrieval. In *Proc. of the 17th SIGIR*, pages 142–151, Ireland. ACM.

R. Sinha and R. Mihalcea. 2007. Unsupervised graph-based word sense disambiguation using measures of word semantic similarity. In *Proc. of the IEEE International Conference on Semantic Computing*.

C. Stokoe, M.P. Oakes, and J. Tait. 2003. Word sense disambiguation in information retrieval revisited. In *Proc. of the 26th SIGIR*, pages 159–166.

M. Strube and S.P. Ponzetto. 2006. Wikirelate! computing semantic relatedness using wikipedia. In *Proc. of the 21st AAAI*.

G. Tsatsaronis, M. Vazirgiannis, and I. Androutsopoulos. 2007. Word sense disambiguation with spreading activation networks generated from thesauri. In *Proc. of the 20th IJCAI*, pages 1725–1730.

E. Voorhees. 1993. Using wordnet to disambiguate word sense for text retrieval. In *Proc. of the 16th SIGIR*, pages 171–180. ACM.

S.K.M. Wong, W. Ziarko, V.V. Raghavan, and P.C.N. Wong. 1987. On modeling of information retrieval concepts in vector spaces. *ACM Transactions on Database Systems*, 12(2):299–321.

# Aligning Medical Domain Ontologies for Clinical Query Extraction

**Pinar Wennerberg**
Siemens AG, Munich Germany
TU Darmstadt, Darmstadt Germany
pinar.wennerberg.ext@siemens.com

## Abstract

Often, there is a need to use the knowledge from multiple ontologies. This is particularly the case within the context of medical imaging, where a single ontology is not enough to provide the complementary knowledge about anatomy, radiology and diseases that is required by the related applications. Consequently, semantic integration of these different but related types of medical knowledge that is present in disparate domain ontologies becomes necessary. Medical ontology alignment addresses this need by identifying the semantically equivalent concepts across multiple medical ontologies. The resulting alignments can then be used to annotate the medical images and related patient text data. A corresponding semantic search engine that operates on these annotations (i.e. alignments) instead of simple keywords can, in this way, deliver the clinical users a coherent set of medical image and patient text data.

## 1 Introduction

As the content of numerous ontologies in the biomedical domain increases, so does the need for sharing and reusing this body of knowledge. Often, there is a need to use the knowledge from multiple ontologies. This is particularly the case within the context of medical imaging, where a single ontology is not enough to support the necessary heterogeneous tasks that require complementary knowledge about human anatomy, radiology and diseases. Medical imaging constitutes the context of this work, which lies within the Theseus-MEDICO[1] use case.

The Theseus-MEDICO use case has the objective of building the next generation of intelligent, scalable, and robust search engine for the medical imaging domain. MEDICO's proposed solution relies on ontology based semantic annotation of the medical image contents and the related patient data.

Semantic annotation of medical image contents and patient text data allows for a mark-up with meaningful meta-information at a higher level of granularity that goes beyond simple keywords. Therefore, the data which is processed and stored in this way can be efficiently retrieved by a corresponding search engine such as the one envisioned in MEDICO.

The diagnostic analysis of medical images typically concentrates around three questions (a) what is the anatomy here? (b) what is the name of the body part here? (c) is it normal or is it abnormal? Therefore, when a radiologist looks for information, his search queries most likely contain terms from various information sources that provide this kind of knowledge.

To satisfy the radiologist's information need, this scattered knowledge has to be gathered and integrated from disparate ontologies, in particular from those about human anatomy, radiology and diseases. Subsequently, the medical image contents and the related patient data have to be annotated with this information (i.e. ontology concepts and relationships) rather than the single elements from independent ontologies.

Three ontologies that address the three questions above are relevant to gather the necessary knowledge about human anatomy, radiology and diseases. These are the Foundational Model of Anatomy[2] (FMA), Radiology Lexicon[3] (RadLex) and the Thesaurus of the National Cancer Institute[4] (NCI), respectively.

[1] http://theseus-programm.de/scenarios/en/medico

[2] http://sig.biostr.washington.edu/projects/fm/FME/index.html

[3] http://www.rsna.org/radlex

[4] http://nciterms.nci.nih.gov/NCIBrowser/Connect.do?dictionary=NCI_Thesaurus&bookmarktag=1

*Proceedings of the EACL 2009 Student Research Workshop*, pages 79–87,
Athens, Greece, 2 April 2009. 

Given this context, the semantic integration of these ontologies as knowledge sources becomes critical. Ontology alignment addresses this requirement by identifying semantically equivalent concepts in multiple ontologies. These concepts are then made compatible with each other through meaningful relationships. Hence, our goal is to identify the correspondences between the concepts of different medical ontologies that are relevant to the medical image contents.

The rest of this paper is organized as follows. In the next section we explain the motivation behind aligning the medical ontologies. Section 3 discusses related work in ontology alignment in general and in the biomedical domain. In section 4 we introduce our approach and explain why it goes beyond existing methods. Here we also explain the application scenario, which exhibits how aligned medical ontologies can contribute to the identification of relevant clinical search queries. Section 5 introduces the materials and methods that are relevant for this work. Finally 6 and 7 discusses the planned evaluation and presents the roadmap for the remaining work, respectively

## 2 Motivation

The following scenario illustrates how the alignment of medical ontologies facilitates the integration of medical knowledge that is relevant to medical image contents from multiple ontologies. Suppose that we want to help a radiologist, who searches for related information about the manifestations of a certain type of lymphoma on a certain organ, e.g. liver, on medical images. As discussed earlier the three types of knowledge that serves him would be about the human anatomy (liver), the organ's location in the body (e.g. upper limb, lower limb, neighboring organs etc.) and whether what he sees is normal or abnormal (pathological observations, symptoms, and findings about lymphoma).

Once we know what the radiologist is looking for we can support him in his search in that we present him an integrated view of only the liver lymphoma relevant portions of the patient health records (or of *that* patient's record), PubMed abstracts as reference resource, drug databases, experience reports from other colleagues, treatment plans, notes of other radiologists or even discussions from clinical web discussion boards.

From the NCI Thesaurus we can obtain the information that *'liver lymphoma'* is the synonym for *'hepatic lymphoma'*, for which holds:

*'hepatic lymphoma'*
*'disease_has_primary_anatomic_site'*
*'liver'*
*'hematopoietic and lymphatic system'*
*'gastrointestinal system'*

With this information we can now move on to the FMA to find out that *'hepatic artery'* is a *part of* the *'liver'* (such that any finding that indicates lymphoma at the *hepatic artery* would also imply the lymphoma at the *liver*). RadLex on the other hand informs that *'liver surgery'* is a *'treatment' 'procedure'*. Various types of this *'treatment' 'procedure'* are *'hepatectomy'*, *'hepatic lobectomy'*, *'hepatic segmentectomy'*, *'hepatic subsegmentectomy'*, *'hepatic trisegmentectomy'* or *'hepatic wedge excision'*, which can be used for disease treatment.

Consequently, the radiologist who searches for information about liver lymphoma is presented with a set of patient health records, PubMed abstracts, radiology images etc. that are annotated using the terminology above. In this way, the radiologist's search space is reduced to a significantly small portion of the overdose of information available in multiple data stores. Moreover, he receives coherent data, i.e. images and patient text data that are related to each other, from a single access point without having to login to several different data stores at different locations.

## 3 Related Work

Ontology alignment is commonly understood as a special case of semantic integration that concerns the semi-automatic discovery of semantically equivalent concepts (sometimes also relations) across two or more ontologies.

There are two commonly adopted approaches to ontology alignment; schema-based and instance-based, where most systems use both. Accordingly, the input of the former approach is the ontology schema only, whereas the input of the latter is the instance data i.e. the data that have been annotated with the ontology schema. Both approaches take advantage of linguistic and graph-based methods to help identify the correspondences. The most recent and comprehensive overview of work ontology alignment in general is reported by Euzenat and Shvaiko (2007).

Ontology alignment is an increasingly active research field in the biomedical domain, especially in association with the Open Biomedical

Ontologies (OBO)[5] framework. The OBO consortium establishes a set of principles to which the biomedical ontologies shall conform to for purposes of interoperability. The OBO conformant ontologies, such as the FMA, are available at the National Center for Biomedical Ontology (NCBO) BioPortal[6].

Johnson *et al.* (2006) take an information retrieval approach to discover relationships between the Gene Ontology (GO) and three other OBO ontologies (ChEBI[7], Cell Type[8] and BRENDA Tissue[9]). Here, GO ontology concepts are treated as documents, they are indexed using Lucene[10] and are matched against the search queries, which are the concepts from the other three ontologies. Whenever a match is found, it is taken as an evidence of a correspondence. This approach is efficient and easy to implement and can therefore be successful with large medical ontologies. However, it does not account for the complex linguistic structure typically observed at the concept labels of the medical ontologies, which may result in inaccurate matches.

The focus of the work reported by Zhang *et al.* (2004) is to compare two different alignment approaches that are applied to two different ontologies about human anatomy. The subject ontologies are the FMA and the Generalized Architecture for Languages, Encyclopedias and Nomenclatures for Medicine[11] (GALEN). Both approaches use a combination of lexical and structural matching techniques, however one of them additionally employs an external resource (the Unified Medical Lexicon UMLS[12]) to obtain domain knowledge. In this work the authors point to the fact that medical ontologies contain implicit relationships, especially in the multiword concept names that can be exploited to discover more correspondences. This thesis builds on this finding and investigates further methods, e.g. the use of transformation grammars, to discover the implicit information observed at concept labels of the medical ontologies.

On the medical imaging side, there are activities that concentrate around ImageClef[13] campaign, which concerns the cross-language image retrieval and which runs as a part of the Cross-Language Evaluation Forum (CLEF)[14] on multilingual information access. Here, the Medical Annotation and the Medical Retrieval tasks benchmark systems on efficient annotation and retrieval of medical images. However, these activities are organized taking an information retrieval and image parsing perspective and do not focus on semantic information integration. Nevertheless, the campaign releases valuable imaging and text data that can be used.

## 4 Approach and Contributions

Here, we describe our approach for the alignment of medical ontologies and outline the contributions of this thesis. In this respect, we first specify the general requirements for medical ontology alignment, which are then addressed by our approach. These are followed by the statement of the hypotheses of this work. Secondly, the materials that are relevant for this work are introduced. In particular, we describe the semantic resources and our domain corpora. Finally, an application scenario is described that exhibits the benefits of aligning medical ontologies. We describe this scenario as '*Clinical Query Extraction*' and explain the idea behind.

### 4.1 Requirements for medical ontology alignment

Drawing upon our experiences with the medical ontologies along the MEDICO use case we have identified some of their common characteristics that are relevant for the alignment process. These can be summarized as:

1. Generally, they are very large models.
2. They have extensive *is-a* hierarchies up to ten thousands of classes, which are organized according to different views.
3. They have complex relationships, where classes are connected by a number of different relations.
4. Their terminologies are rather stable (especially for anatomy) in that they should not differ much in the different models.
5. The modeling principles for them are well defined and documented.

Based on these characteristics and the general requirements of the MEDICO use case, we de-

[5] http://www.obofoundry.org/
[6] http://www.bioontology.org/ncbo/faces/index.xhtml
[7] www.obofoundry.org/cgi-bin/detail.cgi?id=chebi
[8] www.obofoundry.org/cgi-bin/detail.cgi?id=cell
[9] www.obofoundry.org/cgi-bin/detail.cgi?id=brenda
[10] http://lucene.apache.org/java/docs/
[11] http://www.opengalen.org
[12] http://www.nlm.nih.gov/research/umls/
[13] http://imageclef.org
[14] http://www.clef-campaign.org/

rived the following requirements specifically for aligning medical ontologies:

**Linguistic processing**: Medical ontologies are typically linguistically rich. For example, the FMA contains concept names as long as *'Anastomotic branch of right anterior inferior cerebellar artery with right superior cerebellar artery'*. Such long multi-word terms are usually rich with implicit semantic relations. This characteristic shall be exploited by an intensive use of linguistic alignment methods.

**Use of external resources:** As we are in a specific domain (medicine) and as we are not domain experts, we are in lack of domain knowledge. This missing domain knowledge shall be acquired from external resources, for example UMLS. Synonymy information in this resource and in other terminological resources is of particular interest.

**Non-machine learning approach**: We do not have access to much instance data. This is partly because we are domain dependent. A more important reason, however, is that the special resource, the patient health records, which would provide a large amount of relevant instance data is very difficult to obtain due to legal issues. Therefore, machine learning approaches, which require large portions of training data are not the optimal approach for our purposes.

**Structural matching**: Medical ontologies typically come with rich structures that go beyond the basic *is-a* hierarchy. Most of them include a hierarchical ordering along the *part-of* hierarchies. Ontologies such as FMA additionally have part-of classification with higher granularity that include relations such as *'constitutional part-of', 'systemic part-of' etc.* This rich structure of the medical ontologies shall be used to validate (or improve) the alignments that have been obtained as a result of the linguistic processing and the lexical matching.

**Sequential matching:** Medical ontologies are complex, so that their automatic processing is usually expensive. Therefore, a target concept will be identified (this target concept/term will be in practice the search query of the clinician. More details are explained under section 6.2) First lexical matching techniques shall be applied to identify the search query relevant parts of the ontologies. In other words, those concepts that lexically match the query shall be aligned as first. In this way, the lexical match acts as a filter on the medical ontology and decreases the amount of the computation necessary.

### 4.2 Assumptions

Given this context, we focus on the evaluation of the following hypotheses:

1. Valid relationships (equivalence or other) exist between concepts from FMA, RadLex and from NCI.
2. Relationships between non-identical concept labels from the three ontologies can be discovered if these have common reference in a more general medical ontology.
3. Concept labels in these ontologies are most often in the form of long natural language phrases with regular grammars. Meaningful relationships (e.g. synonymy) across the three ontologies can be derived by processing these labels using transformation grammars.
4. Identification of medical image related query patterns (i.e. a certain combination of concept labels and relations) from corpora is more efficient when it is done based on the alignments.

### 4.3 Approach

The ontology alignment approach proposed in this thesis has three main aspects. It suggests a combinatory strategy that is based on (a) the linguistic analysis of the ontology concept labels (the linguistic aspect), (b) on corpus analysis (context information aspect) and (c) on human-computer interaction e.g. relevance feedback (user interaction aspect).

The linguistic aspect draws on the observation that concept labels in medical ontologies (especially those about human anatomy) often contain implicit semantic relations as discussed by Mungall (2004), e.g. equivalence. By observing common patterns in the multi-word terms that are typical for the concept labels of the medical ontologies these relations can be made explicit.

Transformation grammars can help here to detect the syntactic variants of the ontology concept labels. In other words, with the help of rules, the concept labels can be transformed into semantically equivalent but syntactically different word forms. For example, one concept label from the FMA and its corresponding commonly observed pattern (in brackets) is:

'Blood in aorta' (noun preposition noun)

Using a transformation rule of the form,

noun1 preposition:'in' noun2 => noun2 noun1

we can generate a variant as below with the equivalent semantics:

'aorta blood' (noun noun)

This is profitable for at least two reasons. Firstly, it can help resolve possible semantic ambiguities (if one variant is ambiguous the other one can be preferred). Secondly, identified variants can be used to compare linguistic (textual) contexts of ontology concepts in corpora leading to the second aspect of our approach.

Subsequently, the second aspect, the corpus analysis, builds on comparing linguistic (textual) contexts of ontology concepts in corpora and it assumes that concepts with similar meaning (originating from different ontologies) will appear in similar linguistic contexts. Here, the linguistic context of an ontology class (e.g. *'terminal ileum'* from the FMA as in the example below) can be defined as the document in which it appears, the sentence in which it appears and a window of size N in which it appears. For example, a window size -5, +5 for the FMA concept *"terminal ileum"* would be:

*'Focal lymphoid hyperplasia of the* ***terminal ileum*** *presenting mantle zone hyperplasia with clear cytoplasm'*

can be represented as a vector in form of:

<token -5, token -4, … , token +4, token +5>
<focal, lymphoid, hyperplasia, of, the, presenting, mantle, zone, hyperplasia, with>

These vectors can then be pairwise compared, where most similar vectors indicate similar meaning of corresponding ontology concepts and alignment between ontology concepts follows from this.

Finally, with the user interaction aspect we understand dynamic models of the ontology integration process. Within this dynamic process the ontology alignment happens during an interactive dialogue between the user and the system. In this way, clarifications and questions that elicit user's feedback support the ontology alignment process. An example interactive dialogue can be:

(1) **Radiologist**: Show me the images of Ms. Jane Doe, she has "Amyotrophic Lateral Sclerosis" (*NCI Cancer Thesaurus concept*)

(2) **System**: Ms. Doe doesn't have any images of "Amyotrophic Lateral Sclerosis". Is it equivalent to "Lou Gehrig Disease" (*equivalent NCI Cancer Thesaurus concept*) or to "ALS" (*equivalent RadLex concept*)? That attacks the neurons i.e. the nerve cells (*FMA concept*) Stephan Hawkins has it.

(3) **Radiologist**: Yes, that is true.

(4) **System** Ok. ALS is a kind of "Neuro Degenerative Disorder" (*super-concept from RadLex*) Do you want to see other images on Neuro Degenerative Disorders?

This dialogue illustrates a real life question answering dialogue; where the utterances (2) and (4) contain the system questions, and utterance (3) is the user's interactive mapping feedback. This aspect is based on the approach explained in more detail in (Sonntag, 2008).

## 5 Materials and Methods

### 5.1 Terminological resources

**Foundational Model of Anatomy (FMA)** is the most comprehensive machine processable resource on human anatomy. It covers 71,202 distinct anatomical concepts and more than 1.5 million relations instances from 170 relation types. The FMA can be accessed via the Foundational Model Explorer[15].

FMA also provides synonym information (up to 6 per concept), for example one synonym for *'Neuraxis'* is the *'Central nervous system'*. Because single inheritance is one of the modeling principles used in the FMA, every concept (except for the root) stands in a unique *is-a* relation to other concepts. Additionally, concepts are connected by seven kinds of part-of relationships (e.g., *part of, constitutional part of, regional part of*). The version we currently refer to is the version available in August 2008.

The **Radiology Lexicon (RadLex)** is a controlled vocabulary developed and maintained by the Radiological Society of North America (RSNA) for the purpose of uniform indexing and retrieval of radiology information, including images. RadLex contains 11962 terms related to anatomy pathology, imaging techniques, and diagnostic image qualities. RadLex terms are organized along several relationships hence several hierarchies. Each term will participate in one of the relationships with its parent. Synonym information is given whenever it is present such as

[15] http://fme.biostr.washington.edu:8089/FME/

in *'Schatzki ring'* and *'lower esophageal mucosal ring'*. Examples of radiology specific relationships are *'thickness of projected image'* or *'radiation dose'*.

The **National Cancer Institute Thesaurus (NCI)** provides standard vocabularies for cancer research. It covers around 34.000 concepts from which 10521 are related to Disease, Abnormality, Finding, 5901 are related to Neoplasm, 4320 to Anatomy and the rest are related to various other categories such as Gene, Protein, etc. The ontology model is structured around three components i.e. Concepts, Kinds and Roles. Concepts are represented as nodes in an acyclic graph, Roles are directed edges between the nodes and they represent the relationships between them. Kinds on the other hand are disjoint sets of concepts and they constrain the domain and the range of the relationships. Each concept belongs to only one Kind. Except for the root concept, every other concept has at least one *is-a* relationship to another concept.

Every concept has one preferred name (e.g., *'Hodgkin Lymphoma'*). Additionally, 1,207 concepts have a total of 2,371 synonyms (e.g., *Hodgkin Lymphoma* has synonym *'Hodgkin's Lymphoma', 'Hodgkin's disease'* and *'Hodgkin's Disease'*). The version we currently refer to is the version in June 2008 (08.06d).

### 5.2 Data

The **Wikipedia anatomy, radiology** and **disease corpora** have been constructed based on the Anatomy[16], Radiology[17] and Diseases[18.] sections of the Wikipedia. Patient records would be the first choice, but due to strict anonymization requirements they are difficult to compile. Therefore, as an initial resource we constructed the corpora based on the Wikipedia.

To set up the three corpora the related web pages were downloaded and a specific XML version for them was generated. The text sections of the XML files were run through the TnT part-of-speech parser (Brants, 2000) to extract all nouns in the corpus. Then a relevance score (chi-square) for each noun was computed by comparing anatomy, radiology and disease frequencies respectively with those in the British National Corpus (BNC)[19.] In total there are 1410 such XML files about human anatomy, 526 about disease, and 150 about radiology.

The **PubMed lymphoma corpus** is set up to target the specific domain knowledge about lymphoma, a special type of cancer (one major use case of MEDICO is lymphoma). Thus, the lymphoma relevant subterminology from the NCI Thesaurus was extracted. This subterminology includes information about lymphoma types, their relevant thesaurus codes, synonyms, hyperonyms (or parent terms) and the corresponding thesaurus definitions.

Using the lymphoma terminology, we identified from PubMed an initial set of most frequently reported lymphomas, e.g. the top five is *'Non-Hodgkin's Lymphoma'*, *'Burkitt's Lymphoma'*, *'T-Cell Non-Hodgkin's Lymphoma'*, *'Follicular Lymphoma'*, and *'Hodgkin's Lymphoma'* in that order. The lymphoma corpus currently consists of XML files about two main lymphoma types i.e. *'Mantle Cell Lymphoma'* and for *'Diffuse Large B-Cell Lymphoma'*. The former includes 1721 files and the latter 111.

The **clinical questions corpus** consists of health related questions asked among the medical experts and that were collected during a scientific survey. These questions (without answers) are available through the Clinical Questions Collection[20] online repository. It can either be searched or browsed, for example, by a specific disease category. An example question from the Clinical Questions Collection is *"What drugs are folic acid antagonists?"* For each question, additional information about the expert asking the question, e.g. time, purpose etc. are encoded.

To create the clinical questions corpus we downloaded the categories Neoplasms as well as Menic and Lymphatic Diseases from the Clinical Questions Collection website. For each existing HTML page that reports on a question, we created a corresponding XML file. Currently there are 796 questions our questions corpus.

The **clinical discussions corpus** is ongoing work and it will be a corpus, whose contents will be compiled from the various clinical discussion boards across the Web. These discussion boards usually contain questions and answers between and among the medical experts and patients. We expect the language to be less technical because of the user profile. The purpose of this corpus is to have a resource of clinical questions together

[16]http://en.wikipedia.org/wiki/Category:Anatomy

[17] http://en.wikipedia.org/wiki/Category:Radiology

[18] http://en.wikipedia.org/wiki/Category:Diseases

[19] The BNC (http://www.natcorp.ox.ac.uk/) is a 100 million word collection of samples of written and spoken language from a wide range of sources, designed to represent a wide cross-section of current British English.

[20] http://clinques.nlm.nih.gov/JitSearch.html

with their answers as well as experience reports, links to other useful resources in a less technical language. We have already identified a set of relevant clinical discussion boards and analyzed their contents and structure.

## 6 Evaluation Strategies

We distinguish between two kinds of evaluation techniques that can be applied to assess the quality of the alignments.

*Direct evaluation methods* compare the results relative to human judgments as explained by Pedersen *et al.* (2007), which in our case would be the assessment and the resulting feedback of the clinical experts. This kind of evaluation, however, is not very realistic in our context due to the unavailability of a representative number of clinical experts.

*Indirect evaluation methods,* on the other hand, consider the performance of an application that uses the alignments. Hence, any improvement in the performance of the application when it uses the alignments can be attributed to the quality of the alignments. In the following two subsections we first describe the baseline and then explain the planned application that shall use the alignments. The performance of this application, with and without the alignments, will be taken as a measure on the quality of these alignments.

### 6.1 Baseline and Comparison to Other Systems

Our baseline for comparison is string matching after normalization on the concept labels from the input ontologies. Survey results (van Hage and Aleksovski, 2007) suggest that this method is currently the simplest and the most intuitive method being used for ontology alignment (or similar) tasks. Thus, the results of our matching approach will be in the first place compared with the results of this simple matching strategy.

The Ontology Alignment Evaluation Initiative[21] (OAEI) offers a service evaluate the alignment results for its participant matching systems. The competing systems are evaluated on consensus test cases at four different tracks. The evaluation at the anatomy track, which is the most relevant one for us, has been done either by comparing the systems' resulting alignments to reference alignments (absolute comparison) or to each other (relative comparison).

[21] http://oaei.ontologymatching.org

### 6.2 Clinical Query Extraction

We conceive of the clinical query extraction process as a use case that shows the benefits of semantic integration by means of ontology alignments.

Clinical query extraction, (Oezden Wennerberg *et al.*, 2008; Buitelaar *et al.*, 2008) is the process of predicting patterns for typical clinical queries given domain ontologies and corpora. It is motivated by the fact that when developing search systems for healthcare professionals, it is necessary to know what kind of information they search for in their daily working tasks. As interviews with clinicians are not always possible, alternative solutions become necessary to obtain this information.

Clinical query extraction is a technique to semi-automatically predict possible clinical queries without having to depend on clinical interviews. It requires domain corpora (i.e. disease, anatomy and radiology) and domain ontologies to be able to process statistically most relevant concepts in the ontologies and the relations that hold between them. Consequently, concept-relation-concept triplets are identified, for which the assumption is that the statistically most relevant triplets are more likely to occur in clinical queries.

Clinical query extraction can be viewed as a special case of term/relation extraction. Related approaches from the medical domain are reported by Bourigault and Jacquemin (1999) and Le Moigno *et al.* (2002).

The identification of query patterns (i.e. the concept-relation-concept triplets) starts with the construction of domain corpora from related Web resources such as Wikipedia[22] and PubMed[23]. As next, use case relevant parts from domain ontologies are extracted. The frequency of the concepts from the extracted sub-ontologies in the domain corpora versus the frequencies in a domain independent corpus determines the domain specificity of the concepts.

This statistical term/concept profiling can be viewed as a function that takes the domain (sub)ontologies and the corpora as input and returns the partially weighted domain ontologies as output, where the terms/concepts are ranked according to their weights. An example query pattern can look like:

[22] http://www.wikipedia.org/

[23] http://www.ncbi.nlm.nih.gov/pubmed/

| | | |
|---|---|---|
| [ANATOMICAL STRUCTURE] | located_in AND | [ANATOMICAL STRUCTURE] |
| [[RADIOLOGY IMAGE]Modality] | is_about AND | [ANATOMICAL STRUCTURE] |
| [[RADIOLOGY IMAGE]Modality] | shows_ symptom | [DISEASE SYMPTOM] |

The clinical query extraction approach, as illustrated so far, builds on using domain ontologies, however on using them independently. That is, the entire statistical term profiling is based on processing the use case relevant terms (i.e. concepts) of the ontologies in isolation. In this respect the clinical query pattern extraction is a good potential application that can be used to evaluate the quality of the ontology alignments.

As the current process is based on single concepts, the natural extension will be to perform the extraction based on aligned concepts. Any improvement in the identification of the query patterns from corpora can then be attributed to the quality alignments.

## 7 Future Directions

Regarding the linguistic aspect of the ontology alignment approach, the next step will be to concentrate on the definition of the transformation grammar to generate the semantic equivalent concepts.

A further consideration is to explore whether other relations beyond synonymy such as hyponymy or hyperonymy can also be generated and whether this is profitable. To accord for the second aspect, the most suitable vector model will be determined and tested and applied on the current corpora. As required by the third, user interaction aspect, a dialogue that is most representative of a real life use case will be modeled.

Currently, some of the existing alignment frameworks, e.g. COMA++[24] or PhaseLibs[25] are being tested for their performance with FMA, RadLex and NCI. The observations on the strengths and the weaknesses of these systems will give more insights for the requirements for our system.

Other tasks that are relevant for achieving the goal of this thesis concentrate on two main topics; the collection and the preparation of data and the evaluation of the alignment approach. Subsequently, the clinical questions corpus will be expanded and will be used to evaluate the clinical query patterns. As explained earlier, the efficient identification of the clinical query patterns based on the alignments will be regarded as one means to assess the performance of the alignment approach. Parallels, a complementary corpus compiled from relevant clinical discussion boards will be prepared for the same purpose.

As required by the linguistic aspect of our approach an initial grammar will be set up and be continuously improved to detect the variants of the ontology concepts labels from the three ontologies mentioned earlier. Transformation rules will be used for this purpose.

The open question about whether the ontology relations shall also be aligned will be investigated to determine the trade-offs of including vs. excluding them from the process. We consider using an external resource such as UMLS to obtain background knowledge that can help resolve possible semantic ambiguities. The appropriateness and adoptability of this resource will be assessed. Finally, the evaluation the overall ontology alignment approach will be carried out, whereby a possible participation the OAEI may also be considered.

**Acknowledgments**
This research has been supported in part by the THESEUS Program in the MEDICO Project, which is funded by the German Federal Ministry of Economics and Technology under the grant number 01MQ07016. The responsibility for this publication lies with the authors. Special thanks to Prof. Dr. Iryna Gurevych of TU Darmstadt, to Daniel Sonntag and Paul Buitelaar of DFKI Saarbrücken, and to Sonja Zillner of Siemens AG for fruitful discussions. Additionally, we are thankful to our clinical partner Dr. Alexander Cavallaro of the University Hospital Erlangen.

## References

Bourigault D and Jacquemin C, 1999: *Term extraction + term clustering: An integrated platform for computer-aided terminology*, in Proceedings EACL-99.

Buitelaar P., Oezden Wennerberg P., Zillner S., 2008: *Statistical Term Profiling for Query Pattern Mining*. In:Proc. of ACL 2008 BioNLP Workshop (ACL'2008). Columbus, Ohio, USA, 19 June 2008.

[24] http://dbs.uni-leipzig.de/Research/coma.html
[25] http://phaselibs.opendfki.de/

Euzenat J, Shvaiko P., 2007: *Ontology Matching*. Springer-Verlag; Juni 2007

Johnson H.L, Cohen K.B., Baumgartner W.A. Jr., Lu Z, Bada M, Kester T, Kim H, Hunter L, 2006: *Evaluation of lexical methods for detecting relationships between concepts from multiple ontologies*. Pac. Symp Biocomput, pp. 28-39, 2006 American Psychological Association. 1983. Publications Manual. American Psychological Association, Washington, DC

Le Moigno S., Charlet J., Bourigault D., Degoulet P., and Jaulent M-C, 2002: *Terminology extraction from text to build an ontology in surgical intensive care*. AMIA, Annual Symposium, 2002. 9-13. USA

Mungall C.J, 2004: *Obol: integrating language and meaning in bio-ontologies* Comparative and Functional Genomics, vol.5, no. 6-7, pp. 509+, August 2004

Oezden Wennerberg P, Buitelaar P, Zillner S, 2008: *Towards a Human Anatomy Data Set for Query Pattern Mining based on Wikipedia and Domain Semantic Resources*. In:Proc. of a Workshop on Building and Evaluating Resources for Biomedical Text Mining (LREC'2008). Marrakech, Marocco, 26 May 2008.

Pedersen T, Pakhomov S.V., Patwardhan S and C.G. Chute, (2007): *Measures of semantic similarity and relatedness in the biomedical domain*, Journal of Biomedical Informatics, vol. In Press, Corrected Proof.

Sonntag D, 2008. *Towards dialogue-based interactive semantic mediation in the medical domain* In Third International Workshop on Ontology Matching at ISWC, 2008

van Hage W.R, Isaac A, Aleksovski A (2007): *Sample Evaluation of Ontology-Matching Systems*. EON 2007: 41-50

Zhang S, Mork P, Bodenreider O, 2004: *Lessons learned from aligning two representations of anatomy* In: Hahn U, Schulz S, Cornet R, editors. Proceedings of the First International Workshop on Formal Biomedical Knowledge Representation (KR-MED 2004); 2004. p. 102-108

# Extraction of definitions using grammar-enhanced machine learning

**Eline Westerhout**
Utrecht University
Trans 10, 3512 JK, Utrecht, The Netherlands
E.N.Westerhout@uu.nl

## Abstract

In this paper we compare different approaches to extract definitions of four types using a combination of a rule-based grammar and machine learning. We collected a Dutch text corpus containing 549 definitions and applied a grammar on it. Machine learning was then applied to improve the results obtained with the grammar. Two machine learning experiments were carried out. In the first experiment, a standard classifier and a classifier designed specifically to deal with imbalanced datasets are compared. The algorithm designed specifically to deal with imbalanced datasets for most types outperforms the standard classifier. In the second experiment we show that classification results improve when information on definition structure is included.

## 1 Introduction

Definition extraction can be relevant in different areas. It is most times used in the domain of question answering to answer 'What-is'-questions. The context in which we apply definition extraction is the automatic creation of glossaries within elearning. This is a new area and provides its own requirements to the task. Glossaries can play an important role within this domain since they support the learner in decoding the learning object he is confronted with and in understanding the central concepts which are being conveyed in the learning material.

Different approaches for the detection of definitions can be distinguished. We use a sequential combination of a rule-based approach and machine learning to extract definitions. As a first step a grammar is used and thereafter, machine learning techniques are applied to filter the incorrectly extracted data.

Our approach has different innovative aspects compared to other research in the area of definition extraction. The first aspect is that we address less common definition patterns also. Second, we compared a common classification algorithm with an algorithm designed specifically to deal with imbalanced datasets (experiment 1), which seems to be more appropriate for us because we have some data sets in which the proportion of "yes"-cases is extremely low. A third innovative aspect is that we examined the influence of the type of grammar used in the first step (sophisticated or basic) on the final machine learning results (experiment 1). The sophisticated grammar aims at getting the best balance between precision and recall whereas the basic grammar only focuses at getting a high recall. We investigated to which extent machine learning can improve the low precision obtained with the basic grammar while keeping the recall as high as possible and then compare the results to the performance of the sophisticated grammar in combination with machine learning. As a last point, we investigated the influence of definition structure on the classification results (experiment 2). We expect this information to be especially useful when a basic grammar is used in the first step, because the patterns matched with such a grammar can have very diverse structures.

The paper is organized as follows. Section 2 introduces some relevant work in definition extraction. Section 3 explains the data used in the experiments and the definition categories we distinguish. Section 4 discusses the way in which grammars have been applied to extract definitions and the results obtained with them. Section 5 then talks about the machine learning approach, covering issues such as the classifiers, the features and the experiments. Section 6 and section 7 report and discuss the results obtained in the experiments. Section 8 provides the conclusions and presents some future work.

*Proceedings of the EACL 2009 Student Research Workshop*, pages 88–96,
Athens, Greece, 2 April 2009. 

## 2 Related research

Research on the detection of definitions has been pursued in the context of automatic building of dictionaries from text, question-answering and recently also within ontology learning.

In the area of automatic glossary creation, the DEFINDER system combines shallow natural language processing with deep grammatical analysis to identify and extract definitions and the terms they define from on-line consumer health literature (Muresan and Klavans, 2002). Their approach relies entirely on manually crafted patterns. An important difference with our approach is that they start with the concept and then search for a definition of it, whereas in our approach we search for complete definitions.

A lot of research on definition extraction has been pursued in the area of question-answering, where the answers to 'What is'-questions usually are definitions of concepts. In this area, they most times start with a known concept (extracted from the question) and then search the corpus for snippets or sentences explaining the meaning of this concept. The texts used are often well structured, which is not the case in our approach where any text can be used. Research in this area initially relied almost totally on pattern identification and extraction (cf. (Tjong Kim Sang et al., 2005)) and only later, machine learning techniques have been employed (cf. (Blair-Goldensohn et al., 2004; Fahmi and Bouma, 2006; Miliaraki and Androutsopoulos, 2004)).

Fahmi and Bouma (2006) combine pattern matching and machine learning. First, candidate definitions which consist of a subject, a copular verb and a predicative phrase are extracted from a fully parsed text using syntactic properties. Thereafter, machine learning methods are applied on the set of candidate definitions to distinguish definitions from non-definitions; to this end a combination of attributes has been exploited which refer to text properties, document properties, and syntactic properties of the sentences. They show that the application of standard machine learning methods for classification tasks (Naive Bayes, SVM and RBF) considerably improves the accuracy of definition extraction based only on syntactic patterns. However, they only applied their approach on the most common definition type, that are the definitions with a copular verb. In our approach we also distinguish other, less common definition types. Because the patterns of the other types are more often also observed in non-definitions, the precision with a rule-based approach will be lower. As a consequence, the dataset for machine learning will be less balanced. In our approach we applied – besides a standard classification algorithm (Naive Bayes) – also a classification algorithm designed specifically to deal with imbalanced datasets.

In the domain of automatic glossary creation, Kobylinski and Przepiórkowski (2008) describe an approach in which a machine learning algorithm specifically developed to deal with imbalanced datasets is used to extract definitions from Polish texts. They compared the results obtained with this approach to results obtained on the same data in which hand crafted grammars were used (Przepiórkowski et al., 2007) and to results with standard classifiers (Degórski et al., 2008). The best results were obtained with their new approach. The differences with our approach are that (1) they use either only machine learning or only a grammar and not a combination of the two and (2) they do not distinguish different definition types. The advantage of using a combination of a grammar and machine learning, is that the dataset on which machine learning needs to be applied is much smaller and less imbalanced. A second advantage of applying a grammar first, is that the grammar can be used to add information to the candidate definitions which can be used in the machine learning features. Besides, applying the grammar first, gives us the opportunity to separate the four definition types.

## 3 Definitions

Definitions are expected to contain at least three parts. The definiendum is the element that is defined (Latin: that which is to be defined). The definiens provides the meaning of the definiendum (Latin: that which is doing the defining). Definiendum and definiens are connected by a verb or punctuation mark, the connector, which indicates the relation between definiendum and definiens (Walter and Pinkal, 2006).

To be able to write grammar rules we first extracted 549 definitions manually from 45 Dutch text documents. Those documents consisted of manuals and texts on computing (e.g. Word, Latex) and descriptive documents on academic skills and elearning. All of them could be relevant learn-

| Type | Example sentence |
|---|---|
| to be | Gnuplot is een programma om grafieken te maken<br>*'Gnuplot is a program for drawing graphs'* |
| verb | E-learning omvat hulpmiddelen en toepassingen die via het internet beschikbaar zijn en creatieve mogelijkheden bieden om de leerervaring te verbeteren .<br>*'eLearning comprises resources and application that are available via the Internet and provide creative possibilities to improve the learning experience'* |
| punctuation | Passen: plastic kaarten voorzien van een magnetische strip, die door een gleuf gehaald worden, waardoor de gebruiker zich kan identificeren en toegang krijgt tot bepaalde faciliteiten.<br>*'Passes: plastic cards equipped with a magnetic strip, that can be swiped through a card reader, by means of which the identity of the user can be verified and the user gets access to certain facilities. '* |
| pronoun | Dedicated readers. Dit zijn speciale apparaten, ontwikkeld met het exclusieve doel e-boeken te kunnen lezen.<br>*'Dedicated readers. These are special devices, developed with the exclusive goal to make it possible to read e-books.'* |

Table 1: Examples for each of the definition types.

ing objects in an elearning enivronment and are thus representative for the glossary creation context in which we will use definition extraction.

Based on the connectors used in the found patterns, four common definition types were distinguished. The first type are the definitions in which a form of the verb *to be* is used as connector. The second group consists of definitions in which a verb (or verbal phrase) other than *to be* is used as connector (e.g. *to mean*, *to comprise*). It also happens that a punctuation character is used as connector (mainly *:*), such patterns are contained in the third type. The fourth category contains the definitory contexts in which relative or demonstrative pronouns are used to point back to a defined term that is mentioned in a preceding sentence. The definition of the term then follows after the pronoun. Table 1 shows an example for each of the four types. To be able to test the grammar on unseen data, the definition corpus was split in a development and a test part. Table 2 shows some general statistics of the corpus.

| | Development | Test | Total |
|---|---|---|---|
| # documents | 33 | 12 | 45 |
| # words | 286091 | 95722 | 381813 |
| # definitions | 409 | 140 | 549 |

Table 2: General statistics of the definition corpus.

## 4 Using a grammar

To extract definition patterns two grammars have been written on the basis of 409 manually selected definitions from the development corpus. The XML transducer *lxtransduce* developed by Tobin (2005) is used to match the grammars against files in XML format. Lxtransduce is an XML transducer that supplies a format for the development of grammars which are matched against either pure text or XML documents. The grammars are XML documents which conform to a DTD (lxtransduce.dtd, which is part of the software).

The grammars consist of four parts. In the first part, part-of-speech information is used to make rules for matching separate words. The second part consists of rules to match chunks (e.g. noun phrases, prepositional phrases). We did not use a chunker, because we want to be able to put restrictions on the chunks. For example, to match the definiendum, we only want to select relatively simple NPs (mainly of the pattern (Article) - (Adjective) - Noun(s)). The third part contains rules for matching and marking definiendums and connectors. In the last part the pieces are put together and the complete definition patterns are matched. The rules were made as general as possible to prevent overfitting to the corpus.

Two types of grammars have been used: a basic grammar and a sophisticated grammar. With the basic grammar, the goal is to obtain a high recall without bothering too much about precision. The number of rules for detecting the patterns is 26 of which 6 fall in the first category (matching words), 15 fall in the third part (matching parts of definitions) and 5 fall in the fourth category (matching complete definitions). There are no rules of the second category in this grammar (matching chunks), because the focus is on the connector patterns only and not on the pattern of the definiendum and definiens. In the sophisticated grammar the aim is to design rules in such a way that a high recall is obtained while at the same time the precision does not become very low. This grammar contains 40 rules, which is 14 more than contained in the basic grammar. There are 12 rules in part 1,

5 in part 2, 11 rules in the third part and 12 rules in the last part.

The first difference between the basic and the sophisticated grammar is thus the number of rules. However, the main difference is that the basic grammar puts fewer restrictions on the patterns. Restrictions on phrases present in the sophisticated grammar such as 'the definiendum should be an NP of a certain structure' are not present in the basic grammar. For example, to detect *is* patterns, the basic grammar simply marks all words before a form of *to be* as definiendum and the complete sentence containing a form of *to be* as definition. (Westerhout and Monachesi, 2007) describes the design of the sophisticated grammar and the results obtained with it in more detail.

Table 3 shows that the recall is always higher with the basic grammar is considerably, which is what you would expect because fewer restrictions are used. The consequence of using a less strict grammar is that the precision decreases. The gain of recall is much smaller than the loss in precision, and therefore the f-score is also lower when the basic grammar is used.

| type | corpus | precision | recall | f-measure |
|---|---|---|---|---|
| is | SG | 0.25 | 0.82 | 0.38 |
| | BG | 0.03 | 0.98 | 0.06 |
| verb | SG | 0.29 | 0.71 | 0.41 |
| | BG | 0.08 | 0.81 | 0.15 |
| punct | SG | 0.04 | 0.67 | 0.08 |
| | BG | 0.01 | 0.97 | 0.02 |
| pron | SG | 0.05 | 0.47 | 0.10 |
| | BG | 0.03 | 0.66 | 0.06 |
| all | SG | 0.13 | 0.70 | 0.22 |
| | BG | 0.03 | 0.86 | 0.06 |

Table 3: Results with sophisticated grammar (SG) and basic grammar (BG) on the complete corpus.

## 5 Machine learning

The second step is aimed at improving the precision obtained with the grammars, while trying to keep the recall as high as possible. The sentences extracted with the grammars are input for this step (table 3). We thus have two datasets: the first dataset contains sentences extracted with the basic grammar and the second dataset contains sentences extracted with the sophisticated grammar. Because the datasets are relatively small, both development and test results have been included to get as much training data as possible. As a consequence of using the output of the grammars as dataset, the definitions not detected by the grammar are lost already and cannot be retrieved anymore. So, for example, the overall recall for the *is* type where the sophisticated grammar is used as a first step can not become more than 0.82.

The first classifier used is the Naive Bayes classifier, a common algorithm for text classification tasks. However, because some of our datasets are quite imbalanced and have an extremely low percentage of correct definitions, the Naive Bayes classifier did not always perform very well. Therefore, a balanced classifier has been used also for classifying the data. After describing the classifiers, the experiments and the features used within the experiments are discussed.

### 5.1 Classifiers

#### 5.1.1 Naive Bayes classifier

The Naive Bayes classifier has often been used in text classification tasks (Lewis, 1998; Mitchell, 1997; Fahmi and Bouma, 2006). Because of the relatively small size of our dataset and sparseness of the feature vector, the calculated numbers of occurrences were very small and we expected them to provide no additional information to the classifier. For this reason, we used supervised discretization (instead of normal distribution), in which numeric attributes are converted to nominal ones, and in this way removed the information on the number of times $n$-grams occurred in a particular sentence.

#### 5.1.2 Balanced Random Forest classifier

The Naive Bayes (NB) classifier is aimed at getting the best possible overall accuracy and is therefore not the best method when dealing with imbalanced data sets. In our experiments, all datasets are more or less imbalanced and consist of a minority part with definitions and a majority part with non-definitions. The extent to which the dataset is imbalanced differs depending on the type and the grammar that has been applied. Table 4 shows for each type the proportion that constitutes the minority class with definitions. As can be seen from this table, the sets for *is* and *verb* definitions obtained with the sophisticated grammar are the most balanced sets, whereas the others are heavily imbalanced.

The problem of heavily imbalanced data can be addressed in different ways. The approach we adopted consists in a modification of the Random

| | SG (%) | BG (%) |
|---|---|---|
| is | 24.6 | 3.0 |
| verb | 28.9 | 8.1 |
| punct | 4.8 | 1.0 |
| pron | 5.4 | 2.9 |

Table 4: Percentage of correct definitions in sentences extracted with sophisticated (SG) and basic (BG) grammar.

Forest classifier (RF; (Breiman, 2001)). In Balanced Random Forest (BRF; (Chen et al., 2004)), for each decision tree two bootstrapped sets of the same size, equal to the size of the minority class, are constructed: one for the minority class, the other for the majority class. Jointly, these two sets constitute the training set. In our experiments we made 100 trees in which at each node from 20 randomly selected features out of the total set of features the best feature was selected. The final classifier is the ensemble of the 100 trees and decisions are reached by simple voting. We expect the BRF classifier to outperform the NB classifier, especially on the less balanced types.

### 5.2 Experiments

Two experiments have been conducted. Because the datasets are relatively small 10-fold cross validation has been used in all experiments for better reliability of the classifier results.

#### 5.2.1 Comparing classifier types

In the first experiment, the Naive Bayes and the Balanced Random Forest classifiers are compared, both on the data obtained with the sophisticated and basic grammar. As features $n$-grams of the part-of-speech tags were used with $n$ being 1, 2 and 3. The main purpose of this experiment is to compare the performance of the two classifiers to see which method performs best on our data. We expect the advantage of using the BRF method to be bigger when the datasets are more imbalanced, since the BRF classifier has been designed specifically to deal with imbalanced datasets. The second purpose of the experiment is to investigate whether combining a basic grammar with machine learning can give better results than a sophisticated grammar combined with machine learning. Because the datasets will be more imbalanced for each type when the basic grammar is used, we expect the BRF method to perform better than the NB classifier on the definition class. However, the counter effect of using the balanced method will be that the scores on the non-definition class will be worse.

#### 5.2.2 Influence of definition structure

In the second experiment, we investigated whether the structure of a definition provides information that helps when classifying instances for the datasets created with the basic grammar. As features the part-of-speech tag $n$-grams of the definiendum, the first part-of-speech tag $n$-gram of the definiens and the part-of-speech tag $n$-grams of the complete sentence. Because we have seen when developing the sophisticated grammar that the structure of the definiendum is very important for distinguishing definitions from non-definitions, we decided to add information on the structure of this part in the features of the data obtained with the basic grammar. Also the first part of the definiens often seemed to have a comparable structure, therefore we included this part as well in our features. We expect that including this information will result in a better classification result.

## 6 Results

### 6.1 Comparing classifier types

Table 5 shows the results of the different classifiers. When we look at the results for the sophisticated grammar, we see that for the less balanced datasets (i.e. the *punct* and *pron* types) the BRF classifier outperforms the NB classifier. For these two types there were no definitions classified correctly and as a consequence both the precision and the recall are 0. For the other two types the results of the different classifiers are comparable. When the classifiers are used after the basic grammar has been applied, the recall is substantially better for all four types when the BRF method is used. However, the precision is quite low with this approach, mainly due to the low scores for the *punct* and *pron* types. The accuracy of the results, that is, the over all proportion of correctly classified instances, is in all cases higher when the Naive Bayes classifier is used. This is due to the fact that the number of misclassified non-definition sentences is higher when the BRF classifier is used.

Table 6 shows a comparison of the final results obtained with the sophisticated grammar and the basic grammar in combination with the two machine learning algorithms. The performance varies largely per type and the overall score is highly influenced by the *is* and *verb* type, which together

| | Naive Bayes | | | | | | | |
|---|---|---|---|---|---|---|---|---|
| | Sophisticated grammar | | | | Basic grammar | | | |
| | precision | recall | f-measure | accuracy | precision | recall | f-measure | accuracy |
| is | 0.82 | 0.76 | 0.79 | 0.90 | 0.26 | 0.66 | 0.38 | 0.93 |
| verb | 0.77 | 0.75 | 0.76 | 0.86 | 0.67 | 0.17 | 0.27 | 0.93 |
| punct | 0 | 0 | 0 | 0.95 | 0 | 0 | 0 | 0.98 |
| pron | 0.36 | 0.30 | 0.33 | 0.93 | 0 | 0 | 0 | 0.97 |
| all | 0.72 | 0.61 | 0.66 | 0.92 | 0.29 | 0.32 | 0.31 | 0.95 |
| | **Balanced Random Forest** | | | | | | | |
| | Sophisticated grammar | | | | Basic grammar | | | |
| | precision | recall | f-measure | accuracy | precision | recall | f-measure | accuracy |
| is | 0.77 | 0.79 | 0.78 | 0.89 | 0.18 | 0.82 | 0.30 | 0.88 |
| verb | 0.76 | 0.78 | 0.77 | 0.87 | 0.29 | 0.65 | 0.40 | 0.84 |
| punct | 0.13 | 0.61 | 0.22 | 0.79 | 0.06 | 0.61 | 0.10 | 0.79 |
| pron | 0.18 | 0.62 | 0.28 | 0.83 | 0.08 | 0.41 | 0.13 | 0.83 |
| all | 0.43 | 0.74 | 0.55 | 0.84 | 0.15 | 0.68 | 0.24 | 0.85 |

Table 5: Performance of Naive Bayes classifier and Balanced Random Forest classifier on the results obtained with the grammars.

contain 69.8 % of the definitions. For the other two types, the BRF classifier performs considerably better, independent of which grammar has been used in the first step. The overall f-measure is best when the sophisticated grammar is used, where the recall is higher with the BRF classifier and the precision is better with the NB classifier.

| | Naive Bayes | | | |
|---|---|---|---|---|
| | grammar | precision | recall | f-measure |
| is | SG | 0.82 | 0.62 | 0.70 |
| | BG | 0.26 | 0.65 | 0.37 |
| verb | SG | 0.77 | 0.53 | 0.63 |
| | BG | 0.67 | 0.14 | 0.23 |
| punct | SG | 0 | 0 | 0 |
| | BG | 0 | 0 | 0 |
| pron | SG | 0.36 | 0.14 | 0.20 |
| | BG | 0 | 0 | 0 |
| all | SG | 0.72 | 0.43 | 0.54 |
| | BG | 0.29 | 0.27 | 0.28 |
| | Balanced Random Forest | | | |
| | grammar | precision | recall | f-measure |
| is | SG | 0.77 | 0.65 | 0.70 |
| | BG | 0.18 | 0.80 | 0.30 |
| verb | SG | 0.76 | 0.55 | 0.64 |
| | BG | 0.29 | 0.53 | 0.37 |
| punct | SG | 0.13 | 0.42 | 0.20 |
| | BG | 0.06 | 0.52 | 0.10 |
| pron | SG | 0.18 | 0.29 | 0.22 |
| | BG | 0.08 | 0.27 | 0.12 |
| all | SG | 0.43 | 0.52 | 0.47 |
| | BG | 0.15 | 0.57 | 0.24 |

Table 6: Final results of sophisticated grammar (SG) and basic grammar (BG) in combination with Naive Bayes classifier and Balanced Random Forest classifier.

### 6.2 Influence of definition structure

Table 7 shows the results obtained with the BRF classifier on the sentences extracted with the basic grammar when sentence structure is taken into account. When we compare these results to table 5, we see that the overall recall is higher when structural information is provided to the classifier. However, to which extent the structural information contributes to a correct classification of the definitions is different per type and also depends on the amount of structural information provided. When only information on the definiendum and first part of the definiens are included, the precision scores are lower than the results obtained with $n$-grams of the complete sentence. Providing all information, that is, information on definiendum, first part of the definiens and the complete sentence, gives the best results.

| | All information | | | |
|---|---|---|---|---|
| | precision | recall | f-measure | accuracy |
| is | 0.24 | 0.82 | 0.38 | 0.92 |
| verb | 0.29 | 0.81 | 0.43 | 0.82 |
| punct | 0.04 | 0.84 | 0.08 | 0.58 |
| pron | 0.09 | 0.54 | 0.16 | 0.83 |
| all | 0.14 | 0.78 | 0.24 | 0.82 |
| | Definiendum and first $n$-gram of definiens | | | |
| | precision | recall | f-measure | accuracy |
| is | 0.19 | 0.82 | 0.31 | 0.89 |
| verb | 0.25 | 0.78 | 0.38 | 0.80 |
| punct | 0.03 | 0.96 | 0.05 | 0.23 |
| pron | 0.05 | 0.57 | 0.09 | 0.65 |
| all | 0.09 | 0.78 | 0.16 | 0.71 |

Table 7: Performance of Balanced Random Forest classifier with information on sentence structure in features applied on the results obtained with the basic grammar.

For the *is* type, the recall remains the same when structural information is added and the precision increases, especially when all structural information is used. Information on the structure of the definiens and the first $n$-gram of the definiens thus improves the classification results for this type.

The recall of *verb* definitions is higher when structural information is used whereas the precision does not change. The fact that the precision is hardly influenced by adding structural information might be explained by the fact that connectors and connector phrases are quite diverse for this type. As a consequence, different types of first $n$-grams of the definiens might be used and the predicting quality of structural information is smaller.

The classification of the *punct* patterns is quite different depending on the amount of structural information used. The recall increases when structural information is added, whereas the precision decreases. Adding structural information thus results in a low accuracy, especially when only the $n$-grams of the definiendum and the first $n$-gram of the definiens are used. For this type of patterns the structure of the complete definition is thus important for obtaining a reasonable precision.

For the *pronoun* patterns the recall is higher when structural information is included. The precision is slightly higher when all structural information is included, but remarkably lower when only the $n$-grams of the definiendum and the first $n$-gram of the definiens are used. From this we can conclude that for this pattern type information on the structure of the complete definition is crucial to get a reasonable precision.

## 7 Evaluation and discussion

Which classifier performs best depends on the balance of the corpus. For the more balanced datasets the results of the NB and the BRF method are almost the same. The more imbalanced the corpus, the bigger the difference between the two methods, where BRF outperforms the NB classifier. The accuracy is in all cases higher when the NB classifier is used, due to the fact that this classifier scores better on the majority part with non-definitions. The inevitable counter effect of using the BRF method is that the scores on this part are lower, because the two classes now get the same weight.

The answer to the question which grammar should be used in the first step can be viewed from different perspectives, by looking either at the goal or the definition type.

When aiming at getting the highest possible recall, the BRF method in combination with the basic grammar gives the best overall results. However, when using these settings, the precision is quite low. When the goal is to obtain the best balance between recall and precision, this might therefore not be the best choice. In this case, the best option would be to use a combination of the sophisticated grammar and the BRF method, in which the recall is slightly lower than when the basic grammar is used, but the precision is much higher.

We can also view the question which grammar should be used from a different perspective, namely by looking at the definition type. To get the best result for each of the separate types, we would need to use different approaches for the different types. When the BRF method is used, for two types the recall is considerably higher when the basic grammar is used, whereas for the other two types the recall scores are comparable for the two grammars. However, again this goes with a lower precision score, and therefore this may not be the favourable solution in a practical application. So, also when looking at a per type basis, using the sophisticated grammar seems to be the best option when the aim is to get the best balance.

We are now able to answer the questions addressed in the first experiment and summarize our conclusions on which classifier and grammar should be used in table 8. The conclusions are based on the final results obtained after both the grammar and machine learning have been applied (table 6). Although the recall is very important, because of the context in which we want to apply definition extraction the precision also cannot be too low. In a practical application a user would not like it to get 5 or 6 incorrect sentences for each correct definition.

| | Best recall | Best balance |
|---|---|---|
| is | BG + BRF | SG + NB / BRF |
| verb | SG + NB / BRF | SG + NB / BRF |
| punct | BG + BRF | SG + BRF |
| pron | SG / BG + BRF | SG + BRF |

Table 8: Best combination of grammar and classifier when aiming at best recall or best balance.

Information on structure in all cases results in a higher number of correctly classified definitions. The recall for the definition class is for all types remarkably higher when only the $n$-grams of the definiendum and the first $n$-gram of the definiens are considered. However, this goes with a much lower precision and f-score and might therefore not be the best option. When using all information, the best results are obtained: the recall goes up while the precision and f-score do not change considerably. However, although the results are improved, they are still lower then the results obtained with the sophisticated grammar.

A question that might rise when looking at the results for the different types, is whether the punctuation and pronoun patterns should be included when building an application for extracting definitions. Although these types are present in texts – they make up 30 % of the total number of definitions – and can be extracted with our methods, the results are poor compared to the results obtained for the other two types. Especially the bad precision for these types gives reasons to have a closer look at these patterns to discover the reason for these low scores. The bad results might be caused by the amount of training data, which might be too low. Another reason might be that the patterns are more diverse than the patterns of the other types, and therefore more difficult to detect.

It is difficult to compare our results to other work on definition extraction, because we are the only who distinguish different types. However, we try to compare research conducted by Fahmi and Bouma (2006) on the first pattern and Kobyliński and Przepiórkowski (2008) on definitions in general. Fahmi and Bouma (2006) combined a rule-based approach and machine learning for the detection of *is* definitions in Wikipedia articles. Although they used more structured texts, the accuracy they obtained is the same as the accuracy we obtained in our experiments. However, they did not report precision, recall, and f-score for the definition class separately, which makes it difficult to compare their result to ours. Kobyliński and Przepiórkowski (2008) applied machine learning on unstructured texts using a balanced classifier and obtained a precision of 0.21, a recall of 0.69 and an f-score of 0.33 with an overall accuracy of 0.85. These scores are comparable to the scores we obtained with the basic grammar in combination with the BRF classifier. Using the sophisticated grammar in combination with BRF outperforms the results they obtained. From this we can conclude that using a sophisticated grammar has advantages over using machine learning only.

## 8 Conclusions and future work

On the basis of the results we can draw some conclusions. First, the type of grammar used in the first step influences the final results. With the features and classifiers used in our approach, the sophisticated grammar gives the best results for all types. The added value of a sophisticated grammar is also confirmed by the fact that the results Kobyliński and Przepiórkowski (2008) obtained without using a grammar are lower then our results with the sophisticated grammar. A second lesson learned is that it is useful to distinguish different definition types. As the results vary depending on which type has to be extracted, adapting the approach to the type to be extracted will result in a better overall performance. Third, the degree to which the dataset is imbalanced influences the choice for a classifier, where the BRF performs better on less balanced datasets. As there are many other NLP problems in which there is an interesting minority class, the BRF method might be applied to those problems also. From the second experiment, we can conclude that taking definition structure into account helps to get better classification results. This information has not been implemented in other approaches yet and other work on definition extraction can thus profit from this new insight.

The results obtained so far clearly indicate that a combination of a rule-based approach and machine learning is a good way to extract definitions from texts. However, there is still room for improvement, and we will work on this in the next months. In near future, we will investigate whether our results improve when more linguistic information is added in the features. Especially for the basic grammar, we expect it to be possible to get a better recall when more information is added. We can make use of the grammar rules implemented in the sophisticated grammar to see there which information might be relevant. To improve the precision scores obtained with the sophisticated grammar, we will also look at linguistic information that might be relevant. However, improving this score using linguistic information will be more difficult, because the grammar already filtered out a lot of incorrect patterns. To improve results obtained with this grammar, we will therefore look at different features, such as features based on document structure, keywordiness of definiendum and similarity measures.

## References


S. Blair-Goldensohn, K. R. McKeown, and A. Hazen Schlaikjer, 2004. *New Directions In Question Answering*, chapter Answering Definitional Questions: A Hybrid Approach. AAAI Press.

L. Breiman. 2001. Random Forests. *Machine Learning*, 46:5–42.

C. Chen, A. Liaw, and L. Breiman. 2004. Using random forest to learn imbalanced data. Technical Report 666, University of California, Berkeley.

Ł. Degórski, M. Marcińczuk, and A. Przepiórkowski. 2008. Definition extraction using a sequential combination of baseline grammars and machine learning classifiers. In *Proceedings of the Sixth International Conference on Language Resources and Evaluation, LREC 2008.*

I. Fahmi and G. Bouma. 2006. Learning to identify definitions using syntactic features. In R. Basili and A. Moschitti, editors, *Proceedings of the EACL workshop on Learning Structured Information in Natural Language Applications.*

Ł. Kobyliński and A. Przepiórkowski. 2008. Definition extraction with balanced random forests. In B. Nordström and A. Ranta, editors, *Advances in Natural Language Processing: Proceedings of the 6th International Conference on Natural Language Processing, GoTAL 2008*, pages 237–247. Springer Verlag, LNAI series 5221.

D. D. Lewis. 1998. Naive (Bayes) at forty: The independence assumption in information retrieval. In Claire Nédellec and Céline Rouveirol, editors, *Proceedings of ECML-98, 10th European Conference on Machine Learning*, number 1398, pages 4–15, Chemnitz, DE. Springer Verlag, Heidelberg, DE.

S. Miliaraki and I. Androutsopoulos. 2004. Learning to identify single-snippet answers to definition questions. In *Proceedings of COLING 2004*, pages 1360–1366.

T. M. Mitchell. 1997. *Machine learning*. McGraw-Hill.

S. Muresan and J. Klavans. 2002. A method for automatically building and evaluating dictionary resources. In *Proceedings of the Language Resources and Evaluation Conference (LREC 2002).*

A. Przepiórkowski, Ł. Degórski, M. Spousta, K. Simov, P. Osenova, L. Lemnitzer, V. Kubon, and B. Wójtowicz. 2007. Towards the automatic extraction of denitions in Slavic. In *Proceedings of BSNLP workshop at ACL.*

E. Tjong Kim Sang, G. Bouma, and M. de Rijke. 2005. Developing offline strategies for answering medical questions. In D. Mollá and J. L. Vicedo, editors, *Proceedings AAAI 2005 Workshop on Question Answering in Restricted Domains.*

R. Tobin. 2005. Lxtransduce, a replacement for fsgmatch. `http://www.ltg.ed.ac.uk/~richard/ltxml2/lxtransduce-manual.html`.

S. Walter and M. Pinkal. 2006. Automatic extraction of definitions from German court decisions. In *Proceedings of the workshop on information extraction beyond the document*, pages 20–28.

E. N. Westerhout and P. Monachesi. 2007. Extraction of Dutch definitory contexts for elearning purposes. In *Proceedings of CLIN 2006.*

# Author Index